A

CENTURIAL HISTORY

OF THE

MENDON ASSOCIATION

OF CONGREGATIONAL MINISTERS, WITH

THE CENTENNIAL ADDRESS,

DELIVERED AT FRANKLIN, MASS., NOV. 19, 1851,

AND

BIOGRAPHICAL SKETCHES OF THE MEMBERS AND LICENTIATES.

BY REV. MORTIMER BLAKE.

BOSTON:
PUBLISHED FOR THE ASSOCIAT
BY SEWALL HARDING,
113 WASHINGTON STREET.
1853.

ANDOVER: JOHN D. FLAGG,
STEREOTYPER AND PRINTER.

INTRODUCTION.

THE history of this volume is as follows. At a meeting of the Mendon Association at Foxboro, April 16, 1850, on motion of Br. M. Blake, it was voted, that there be a Committee chosen to prepare a History of Mendon Association. Brs. M. Blake and T. Thacher were appointed. Mr. Thacher soon after decided to remove to California, and the subject remained untouched until the next year; when, upon examination of the few ancient documents in possession of the scribe, it was found that the Association had nearly reached the close of its *first* century. The fact was informally communicated to some of the members, at the meeting of the State Association at Wrentham, in June, 1851, and at the next regular meeting, at Auburndale, August 12th, it was decided to observe the centennial day, November 19th, with appropriate public services. Franklin was selected as a central and very appropriate place for the meeting, and Rev. M. Blake was appointed to deliver an address. The scribe was instructed to issue special invitations to attend, to all the living former members and licentiates.

An account of the meeting is abridged from the Congregationalist of the following week.

"The first public service was held on Tuesday evening, 18th inst. This was of the nature of a conference, in which a number of the older licentiates and former members of the body, participated. The time was mostly given up to historical reminiscences; and to feeling allusions to the great and good who were once with us, but now are passed away. Rev. Dr. Ide remarked: 'I joined the Association thirty-seven years ago. It was a large and flourishing body, but now all of them but one are dead. I have seen eighteen beloved brethren laid in the grave. At the time of joining, I was not only the youngest, but the feeblest and weakest of them all, and did not expect to live long; but through help obtained of God, I continue unto the present day. I have belonged to the Association fifteen years longer than any other member.' He proceeded to speak of his fellow-laborers in the ministry; said that God had blessed their labors. He had witnessed signal and glorious revivals of religion in every church in the Association.

"Rev. J. O. Barney alluded to Dr. Emmons as the instrument of his conversion, by one sermon, which he heard when he was a very wicked boy.

"Rev. M. Moore spoke of the fathers that approbated him in 1812, — Emmons, Fisk, Howe, Wilder, Holman, Dickinson, Thompson, all now dead but the last-named, who was present.

"Rev. D. Brigham said he should rather go down to the regions of the lost from almost any other place than Franklin, divine truth had been there so plainly exhibited.

"Rev. Messrs. Perkins, Cobb, and Harding, made brief and pertinent allusions to the brethren who used to converse with them at the meetings of this body. Every heart seemed to be full; and the fact was more than once spoken of, that it must be a terrible guilt which continues in impenitence, after having enjoyed the ministry of such able and godly men.

"On Wednesday, at 10 o'clock, A. M., some forty or more of the past members of the Association convened in the meeting-house, to attend the services of the centennial celebration. Prayer was offered by Rev. Alvan Cobb of West Taunton. After the address, the company were invited to partake of a bountiful collation provided in the vestry; after which the brethren separated, feeling that it had been an occasion of deep and peculiar interest, and that it was good to call to mind those champions of the faith, who lived to shape the morals and theology of happy New England, and to behold with exultation and gratitude the fruits of their toil."

The author of the address, given upon the above occasion, was by vote requested to prepare the same for publication, with a list of the members and licentiates from the beginning, and such notes and historical appendix as he deemed appropriate. Hence the following volume, and the long delay of its publication.

A desire to make the biographical sketches as complete as possible, and the delays of an extensive correspondence with reference to this end, have deferred the publication of the address to this date. And after all our researches, some vacancies must be left, which it is hoped may yet be filled, should another edition ever be called for.

The author feels it due to himself to add, that the discourse was prepared during the anxieties of a distressing and doubtful sickness of one of his family, which compelled him to select a general theme, and less appropriate than undisturbed leisure would have permitted.

It is also due to the members of the Association to say, that the compiler is alone responsible for the manner in which their vote to publish its History has been executed,— as but the plan of the work, and not its details, has been submitted for their approval.

The volume, as it is, is offered to the public, as the *first* contribution from the unexplored annals of ministerial associations, towards the yet unwritten ecclesiastical history of New England.

MORTIMER BLAKE.

Mansfield, Mass., Nov. 19, 1852.

CENTENNIAL ADDRESS.

I. SAMUEL, 2, 30, l. c.

"THEM THAT HONOR ME I WILL HONOR, AND THEY THAT DESPISE ME SHALL BE LIGHTLY ESTEEMED."

THESE words express the general reason why God would disinherit the house of Eli from the high priest's office, which had been entailed upon it forever. "His sons had made themselves vile, and he restrained them not." They had brought the services of the sanctuary into contempt with the people by their profligacy, and he had only opposed weak remonstrances instead of the decisive measures which became his office. Wherefore, God, jealous of his worship, determined to transfer the high-priesthood to another branch of the Aaronic family.

God announced this rejection, not only by a vision to young Samuel, but by the mouth of "a man of God" sent to Eli with the particular message,—"The Lord God of Israel saith, I said indeed that thy house, and the house of thy father, should walk before me forever; but now the Lord saith, Be it far from me; for them that honor me I will honor, and they that despise me shall be lightly esteemed."

This doom, I may observe, was afterwards accomplished when Solomon removed Abiathar, — the last high-priest of the line of Ithamar, of which line Eli was the first, — and placed Zadoc, of the house of Eleazer, in the high-priest's office.

The general principle on which this ejection proceeded admits of a great variety of special applications. But the present occasion, as well as the occasion on which God uttered the words of the text, points out the particular application to be selected: viz. *to ministerial labor and ministerial success.*

God honors the ministry which honors him, and that which despises him, he lightly esteems.

This proposition may require some explanatory observations; *first*, in respect to the manner in which ministers as such, may honor or despise God; and, *secondly*, the manner in which God expresses his honor or disesteem of their ministry: —

I. I observe, then, that God possesses certain rights which belong to him, as the Sovereign Ruler of the universe, and he justly claims that these rights shall be cordially yielded unto him by his intelligent creatures. Those who cheerfully render unto God the glory due unto his name, honor him. They who deny or indifferently treat his claims, despise him. Every one who cordially submits to the government of God, and loves his sovereign authority over himself, honors him. He who resists that sovereignty, despises his Maker.

In particular, that ministry of the Gospel honors God, which makes the Divine glory the prime incentive to labor for the salvation of men, — which exhibits the foundations of the Gospel as laid deep in the sovereign grace of God, or his "just liberty" to treat his guilty creatures according to his holy pleasure, — and which draws the motives to repentance from the inherent evil of sinning against the rightful claims of the Almighty.

But that ministry despises God which represents the plan of Redemption to be a device chiefly of God's pity to *men;* as if it were *their* deliverance from misery which *first* and most moved him to the thoughts of their salvation; and which makes the sinner's safety his own prime motive of endeavor.

The former exalts God as a sovereign, and abases transgressors. The latter exalts man, and makes the wisdom and mercy of God mere servants to secure man's endless happiness. One mode of preaching the Gospel makes the glory of God the end of all his doings, and the redemption of sinners a means to illustrate that glory. The other mode of preaching makes human happiness the chief end of all God's works and of man's efforts.

All the various systems of religious doctrine and styles of religious teaching may be put into one or the other of these classes, as their tendency and effect are to exalt God or abase him. And according to this their character, God honors or lightly esteems them.

II. The indications of God's approval or disapproval of our ministry are not difficult of detection, if a sufficiently long period be subjected to examination.

The temporary popularity of any doctrines, measures, or men, is obviously no criterion, for they may be congenial to the natural heart.

The honor which God bestows descends first into the heart, — making that pure and joyful; and then displays itself in the life; as the transfiguration-glory of Christ beamed outwards through his countenance, and caused his raiment to be white and glistering.

God honors the ministry of those who honor him, by giving a success evinced in the purity, stability, and harmony of the church, and its enlargement by genuine revivals of religion. The ministry which he lightly esteems is unacknowledged by the Holy Spirit, and leads men into dangerous errors, or lulls them in security, apathy, and the sleep of eternal death.

The fruits of a ministry honored of God, are the edification of the church and the conversion of sinners. The fruits of a ministry he lightly esteems, are the church's virtual extinction and sinners' ruin.

After this lengthy definition of the terms of the text, I come to its demonstration. And the occasion reminds me, that I may pass by the many logical reasons which confirm its truthfulness, and confine myself to what may be termed its historic illustration.

And I will assert, that the history of religion, from the earliest times, shows that God has honored that ministry which has honored him, and that which has despised him he has lightly esteemed. Especially does the progress of the Redeemer's kingdom in this New England most significantly illustrate this assertion. I say especially, because here the ministry has brought forth its fruits unhelped and unhindered by many causes which have obscured its agency elsewhere. So that the actual results of every species of ministration can be here approximately ascertained. Such a cursory glance as we can now give to this field with reference to this single point, will make the truth of these observations sufficiently obvious.

The beginning of each of the three centuries of our religious history, has been marked by a new and striking phase, whose results have been developed in the remainder of each century.

The first century bore the impress of the pure and devoted ministry of the Puritan preachers.

The second century was marked by the labors of Edwards and his coadjutors and opposers, in the great revival beginning in 1735, and extending onwards to the disturbances of the Revolution.

The third century has witnessed the reanimation of evangelical religion, and its collision with the ripened fruits of Arminianism.

Omitting subordinate causes, *the chief agency in these fluctuations of our Religious History belongs to the character and aim of the pulpit ministrations.*

A hasty review of these three periods of our history will show, that when the ministry has exalted God, by clearly presenting his sovereignty, and by exposing the fallacy of self-righteous hopes, true religion has flourished, and the churches have been strengthened and multiplied. When ministers in their preaching have obscured the sovereignty of God and the essential distinction of saints and sinners, the wise and foolish have slumbered together.

Let us take this review.

I. The first ministers of these colonies were eminently godly and self-denying men. With talents fitted by nature and by study to take possession of the highest places of influence and honor in England, and most of them actually occupying them, they conscientiously resigned lucrative and important situations, because they could not, in them, worship God as he required; and they came here, with the like-minded of their flock, where no civil authority should vie with the claims of God. Such men would not, and did not, dimly apprehend nor obscurely present the truths of God, to obey which they had already sacrificed so much. They were the beloved associates of Bates, and Howe, and Baxter, and Owen ; and like these well-known defenders of the faith, they put foremost in their preaching the great truths of the sovereignty of God, and his electing purposes ; a Divine Redeemer and his vicarious atonement.

Some who love to boast of a Puritanic descent for the sake of their legacies, studiously obliviate the fact of the high Calvinism of those worthies. But if they have not left learned and scientific systems of theology, it in no wise follows that they lightly esteemed the great principles of the doctrines of grace. These doctrines were *not* the points at issue between themselves and the church they left, and they called not for a labored defence when the protestant world were remarkably harmonious on the chief points of doctrine.

In examining the theology of the first ministers of New England, we are not to forget the main object for which they came hither. Says President Oakes in his election sermon of 1673, "It is worthy to be remembered by these churches, that it was not on account of any peculiar sentiments in doctrinal matters, that our wise and good fathers left their native country, and came into this then howling wilderness ; for they agreed to the doctrinal articles of the church of England, as much as the conformists to that parliamentary church, and indeed much more so than most of them. But it was from a pure respect to ecclesiastical discipline and order, and to a more refined worship, that these excellent men, our ancestors, transplanted themselves, with their families, to this land." And to this same purport agrees the preface to the confession of faith adopted by the synod of 1679. "There have been some who have reflected upon these New England churches, for our defect in this matter, as if our principles were not known: whereas it is well known, that as to matters of doctrine, we agree with other Reformed churches. Nor was it that but what concerns worship and discipline, that caused our fathers to come into this wilderness, while it was a land not sown, that so they might have liberty to practise accordingly."

The Theology of the Puritans will therefore not be found drawn up in voluminous systems, scientifically defined and lengthily argued. Yet New England had a Theology from the beginning, and her first ministers were very particular to state the fact to the world.

The historian of Harvard University may gravely wonder that there was not "some form of sound words, some creed, some catechism, some medulla Theologia," yet there was a creed; publicly adopted by the Pastors and messengers of all the churches in the colonies. The synod of 1648 distinctly declare—"Our churches here, as (by the grace of Christ) we believe and profess the same doctrine of the truth of the Gospel, which generally is received in all the Reformed churches in Europe, so especially we desire not to vary from the doctrine of faith and truth held forth by the churches of our native country." The same assertion is substantially repeated by every succeeding synod even to the last.

Now the confession of the Westminster Assembly—

the Savoy confession, and the New England confession of 1680 are known. Let the querist review those exponents of the faith of our fathers, mark the central object of their belief,—the prominence of special grace in Redemption,—and let him ponder, whether the men who ventured their lives for their faith would belie their published creeds in their pulpit ministrations, and dimly exhibit in the desk truths which they laid at the basis of their theological system.

Their works—thanks to the Doctrinal Tract and Book Society—will soon be accessible to moderns, and we can see if Jesus Christ on the throne of his glory was not the end of their preaching, as he was of their conversion!

Say the venerable Higginson and Hubbard, in their testimony to the order of the Gospel in the churches of New England, "We that saw the persons, who from four famous colonies, assembled in the synod, that agreed on our Platform of church discipline (that is, the synod of 1648), cannot forget their excellent character. They were men of great renown in the nation from whence the Laudian persecution exiled them: their learning, their holiness, their gravity, struck all that knew them with admiration. They were Timothies in their houses, Chrysostoms in pulpits, Augustines in their disputations. The prayers, the studies, the humble inquiries, with which they sought after the mind of God, were as likely to prosper as any men's upon earth, and the sufferings wherein they were confessors for the name of the truth of the Lord Jesus Christ, add unto the arguments which would persuade us, that our gracious Lord would reward and honor them, with communicating much of his truth unto them."

Our mathematics may be confounded by their interminable subdivisions of a subject, our rhetorical taste may be offended at their far-fetched illustrations, and our exegetical rules at the application of some of their proof-texts, but we cannot deny that they emphatically exalted God as the just Disposer of all things, and abased man as a sinner deserving endless punishment for his guilty rebellion.

They bowed with silent deference to the word of God, and most devoutly followed what they believed to be its teachings, whether they wished to test a doctrine, found a state, or forestall a vicious practice.

And need I say, God honored the ministry of those worthy men? Dr. Increase Mather tells us, "In a sermon before the houses of Parliament and the Westminster Assembly the preacher exclaimed, 'I have lived in a country seven years, and all that time I never heard one profane oath, and all that time I did never see a man drunk in that land. Where was that country? It was New England.'"

But God bestowed more than these temporal blessings. His Holy Spirit was present in those primitive churches, and under the faithful, energetic aim of his sword of truth, "the slain of the Lord were many."

It is said of Mr. Shepard, of Cambridge, that "he scarce ever preached a sermon, but some or other of his congregation were struck with great distress of soul, and cried out aloud in agony, "What shall I do to be saved." Though his voice was low, yet so searching was his preaching, and so great a power attending as an hypocrite could not easily bear it, and it seemed almost irresistible."

The first forty years of our churches' history was a

period of almost continuous revivals. The influences of God's grace came down, not as in these later times, in occasional showers, but as the gentle dew, continually descending upon the earth. "It was a common question for those who were detained at home, to put to their friends who had attended meeting, whether anybody appeared to be wrought upon to-day."

In consequence of this blessing upon ministeral fidelity, the churches increased and multiplied.

In the Cambridge synod of 1648, twenty-eight years after the first settlement in New England, were represented thirty-nine churches. These were in the colonies of Plymouth and Massachusetts. Add the four churches in the Connecticut colonies, and the three in New Hampshire, and there were, in a population of less than thirty thousand, forty-six churches, each with its sanctuary and most of them with two ministers each; being a place of worship and one or two ministers for every six hundred and fifty souls. The ablest of these churches were *poorer* in this world's goods than many congregations now who think the scanty support of one minister a burden too great to bear. But those godly men prised the faithful ministry of the word, more than bodily luxuries; and God blessed them in soul and estate. In fifty years, the number of churches arose to seventy-six, although the reaction in favor of puritanism in England under Cromwell, had nearly arrested the flow of immigration.

And in all those churches there was one Lord, one faith, one baptism; "and they continued steadfast in the Apostles' doctrine and fellowship, and in breaking of bread, and in prayers," until certain men crept in unawares into the pulpits of New England, and gave to the silver trumpets of the Gospel an unwarranted utterance. Then the days of our Zion's glory for a time passed away. God as a holy Sovereign, before whom the wicked shall not stand, was despised, and in return, his long favored heritage was lightly esteemed.

The causes of a temporary desertion had been for some time at work. What has been termed the half-way covenant was proposed in 1662, and extensively adopted, by which persons of not scandalous lives, yet not pretending to be regenerated men were, on owning the covenant, admitted to the privileges of church-membership.

No prudential reasons could arrest the evils of this radical innovation upon the constitution of the churches, not the least of which evils was the introduction of unconverted men into the ministry. This woful fact was even justified. Even the acute Stoddard, of strong Presbyterial tendencies, and who had been a main cause of making this breach in the walls of Zion,—publicly argued that "unconverted ministers have certain official duties which they may lawfully perform,"—and, consequently, upon which the people may lawfully attend.

The character of their pulpit ministrations speedily revealed the character of such incumbents. The Gospel was clothed in a dress, which fettered its athletic grasp. Unregenerate doings became the key to open the kingdom of Heaven. It was preached and believed, that impenitent men may prepare the way for their own regeneration, and that while they are busy in their self-righteous formalities, they are doing very well. The germ of Arminianism was not only dropped in a prepared soil, it was tilled and watered: and rapidly it struck its roots down wards and shot its branches upwards.

The Holy Spirit, thus deprived of his office-work, returned for a season to heaven. The churches dwindled away, or were filled with ungodly members, and Zion's banners of past victories hung drooping in the dust. There was sorrowful occasion for the pathetic lament of the aged Increase Mather, who at first earnestly stemmed the changing tide, but whose fading eye failed to detect the real inlet of the flood of evils. "Look into our pulpits," says he, "and see if there is such a glory there as once there was. New England has had teachers eminent for learning, and no less eminent for holiness, and all ministerial accomplishments. When will Boston see a Cotton and a Norton again? When will New England see a Hooker, a Shepard, a Mitchell, not to mention others? Look into our civil state. Does Christ reign there as once he did? How many churches, how many towns are there in New England, that we may sigh over them, and say, 'Thy glory is gone.'"

Truly the first period of our religious history teaches that they that despise God shall be lightly esteemed!

II. I pass to the second period.

Though God spake against Ephraim, he earnestly remembered him still. His sustaining promise to ancient Zion deserted was not recalled. "For a small moment have I forsaken thee; but with great mercies will I gather thee. In a little wrath I hid my face from thee for a moment; but with everlasting kindness will I have mercy on thee, saith the Lord thy Redeemer."

God was preparing the way for its fulfilment. He was raising up a youth in an obscure village in the Connecticut colony, and was leading him through the miry depths of his own depravity, that he might, through pain-fully-gained self-knowledge, proclaim the truths of sovereign and special grace to a slumbering generation.

In 1734, Jonathan Edwards preached his sermons on 'Justification by Faith alone.' Multitudes condemned the introduction of such a controversial theme into the pulpit. But God's Spirit owned his truth and came down in marvellous power amongst the faithful shepherd's flock. Above three hundred in Northampton became the hopeful subjects of Divine grace. Other watchmen, waiting in the darkness, saw the light, and they sounded out the Gospel-call with a new energy. Sleeping assemblies were startled, heard, and believed. The great revival of 1740 had begun.

Notwithstanding its bitter opposition and its manifest extravagances towards the close, that revival must be acknowledged to be a work of God, which proved the reanimation of the fainting churches. President Edwards, under whose ministry it was first manifested, and in its purest stage, was no artful, fascinating orator. He stood calm and serene in his pulpit, while he reasoned of righteousness, temperance, and judgment to come. In plain but solemn language he preached on such themes as: 'Men naturally God's enemies;' 'the Justice of God in the Damnation of Sinners;' 'Wicked Men useful in their destruction only;' 'Sinners in the hands of an angry God;' 'God exercises his sovereign Mercy in the salvation of Sinners;' and the people often cried out in such agony of conviction, that he had to request them to be still, that he might be heard.

In that time of refreshing from the presence of the Lord, carried on by the labors of Edwards, Whitefield, the Tennents, and others, it was abundantly evident, that *the most numerous and most decided cases of conversion took place under the clearest exhibitions of the sovereign grace of God in the salvation of men.* The most successful ministers were preëminently marked for the prominence they gave to this aspect of the Gospel. They demolished the curious distinctions that dreaming speculatists had traced over the space which separates the sinner from his God; they stripped him of his filmy guises, put on to hide his inborn deformity, and brought him under the burning gaze of Jehovah's awful holiness. They knocked away the props of his tottering hopes and let him fall, helpless, into the hands of a sovereign God, who can justly destroy or graciously save. They banished the apologies of a natural necessity of sinning, and made their hearers feel that they were voluntary transgressors of a holy law, and deserved eternal death; and that their only hope of deliverance lay in the will of him "who hath mercy on whom he will have mercy, and whom he will he hardeneth." And what wonder if men cried out in agony, "Men and brethren, what shall we do?" And what wonder if, struck with the agreement of such an aspect of the Gospel with their own convictions, multitudes believed?

If in anything Theology as a science then received a New England type, it mainly consisted in making sin to consist in a voluntary selfishness, which could be embraced by the mind as a conscious reality, and to whose charge the heart had to confess, with self-conviction of its truth.

The definitions of depravity which made it to be an inherited physical, intellectual, and moral corruption, antedating the sinner's agency, if not his individual being, were then invaded, and the deadening inference fell with it, that man must wait the operations of the Divine Spirit to restore what he himself cannot reach. Instead thereof, man's ruin was made to stand out as really his own voluntary work, for which God and his own conscience held him responsible. Because his lack of holiness sprang from his own voluntary wilfulness of choosing the fancied happiness of self to the glory of God. Religion was no longer the belief of a nicely-adjusted system of opinions, neither a zeal in unregenerate doings, but a radical change of the affections from selfishness to benevolence.

The actual amount of influence of the deep researches of President Edwards upon the theology of his times, remains to be determined. It cannot be doubted that he exposed many untenable positions, which had been taken by the defenders of truth, and that he did make new and valuable contributions to the treasures of doctrinal knowledge. Few perhaps would adopt literally the encomium of Dr. Dwight, that he,

> "— In one little life, the Gospel more
> Disclosed than all earth's myriads kenned before."

Yet all admit that the pearl of great price, so to speak, sparkled with fresh brilliancy and with a brighter play of colors, under the friction of his powerful hand. He certainly presented its salient points in clear and sharp outline, and he removed much of the incrustation which had accumulated on its faces and dimmed their original brightness. In other words, he carefully defined the terms of Theology and clearly showed the arguments on which its truths really rested, and as clearly showed what arguments weakened the force of truth and exposed it to perversion.

Had he only exhibited Theology as a rational and harmonious system, he would deserve the high honor God bestowed upon his labors. But he did more. Guided by a singular sagacity, always true to the lode-star of Revelation, he searched regions of truth before unexamined, and returned safely, as few others could have done, laden with rich spoils, which he laid at the feet of "Him in whom are hid all the treasures of wisdom and knowledge." The younger Edwards specifies ten particulars wherein his father made improvements in Theology.* The chief of them respect the subjects of liberty and necessity, the nature of true virtue, the origin of moral evil, the atonement, imputation, the nature of experimental religion and regeneration. The substance of these consists in bringing God and man near together, and shortening the chain connecting the moral agency of the Creator and the creature. Many of these points were followed out by Bellamy, Hopkins, Emmons, and others, and made to cast a clearer light upon some of the obscurities of theological science.†

---

* See Edwards's Works, Vol. I, p. 481, Doct. Tract Soc. Edition.

† The history of doctrinal theology in New England is a rich and yet unexplored field, and a volume upon the subject a desideratum which ought to be supplied. Inquiry and research has had unrestricted freedom, and every position has been most rigorously scrutinized, assaulted, and defended, and the progress and results would furnish a captivating and valuable theme. President Edwards has been lauded, but who has traced his actual progress in investigation, and shown what he actually did in theology? Who has fully exhibited the influence of the studies, preaching, and printing of Bellamy and Hopkins upon their contemporaries and successors? Who has analyzed 'New England Theology,' and

Without deciding whether President Edwards is to be considered the father of Hopkinsianism, it is certain that he believed and stated some of its leading peculiarities, however he might have reconciled them with opinions elsewhere uttered in his works.

The influence of such a view of Divine truth as Edwards and his associates and successors presented, so far as it extended, was felt in the preparation of sermons, and in their delivery, and in their reception. It fashioned that metaphysical, argumentative style, — that doctrine, proof and inference method, — of sermonizing, which still characterizes most of the pulpits of Massachusetts, and imparts to them much of their efficiency.

This mode of preaching has been severely criticised. But if such were human depravity, as Edwards, Bellamy, and Hopkins defined it, its defences were not to be demolished by a volley of proof texts from a phalanx of exegetical comments in quaint uniform; but by some one mighty truth from God's word aimed at the gate of the understanding, under cover of which, earnest logic made

---

traced its elements along their respective channels, up to the parental source? Is it not time that this were fully, fairly, thoroughly done? The great quaternions of the last century deserve it. Dr. Hopkins, especially, has been viewed through some such medium as Cromwell has until lately been, — a cold, abstract speculatist, with a meagre retinue of disciples, now diminished to a point. His able memoir, by Prof. Park, has refuted this impression, and shown the leader of the New Divinity to have been one of the mightiest and most influential minds of America, full of benevolent plans, which now bless the world by their practical operation.

repeated charges, through the breach, upon the conscience and heart.

Sinners that had long stood the pattering of divisions and subdivisions, and, like the walls of Jotapata, had only become harder under the concussion, fell now at once before the sword of the Word, when wielded by Him who knows the joints of the soul and spirit. This practical, common-sense theology — if New England may have the glory of it — was a sure earnest of that honor which cometh from God only. The blessed fruits of the ministerial labors of the Edwardses and their contemporaries — of Bellamy, Hopkins, Strong, West of Stockbridge, Spring, Emmons, and others — are still clustering and ripening to refresh the people of God. The honor which God bestowed upon them that thus honored him, still circles the brows and sparkles on the robes of Zion. The churches which sympathized with the spirit of those times of refreshing stand to-day, perhaps without exception, with the light of that gracious visitation lingering about their walls and watch-towers, and clothing them in beauty and radiance. But there were many ministers and churches who looked either suspiciously or hatingly upon the revivals of the last century. Some honestly opposed, regarding only the excesses of their close. But many wickedly maligned a work which so plainly condemned them of having sadly mistaken the spirit of the Gospel.

The results and the cause of this hostile attitude towards vital piety thus revived were not long concealed. The opposing ministers mostly took with rapidity the few remaining steps which separated them from open Arminianism. The leader of the opposition stopped not in his haste, till he reached the middle of the great desert of Universalism. The churches, losing sight of their fleeing shepherds, wandered dreamily on, tithing their mint and anise and cummin on their way, undisturbed by the weightier matters of the law, until they were gradually lost in the misty regions of Unitarianism, where many of them are still stumbling and still dreaming.* In rapid succession after the revival of 1740, followed the exciting scenes of the Indian wars, the oppressions of the English parliament, the stirring times of the Revolutionary war, the formation of the Federal Government. They absorbed the thoughts and energies of the country, and the light of Zion was for a time again obscured.

III. The illustration of the sentiment of this discourse might be continued from the present century, but the want of time and a becoming modesty forbid my entering where many before me have the familiar acquaintance of active participation.

I will just say, however, that the deadening influences of the Revolution, and the blasted path of the infidelity imported with our French allies, are still traceable, and Zion has not yet wholly recovered of her sickness and faintness, from eating the fruits of Arminianism. And on the other hand, the vigorous struggles of a few firm lovers of the Gospel of the grace of God, against these

* The new divinity has been repeatedly accused of opening the door for the admission of Unitarianism into the Congregational churches. No accusation is more unfounded. It was the chief barrier to its entire prevalence. Of the Hopkinsian churches, none are known to have become Unitarian. This error flourished exclusively among the opponents to Hopkinsianism.

antagonistic influences, are fresh in remembrance. I need only allude to the surprising evidences of a once secretly and actively driven effort to undermine the foundations of the Gospel revealed by the disclosures of Belsham's chapter on "American Unitarianism." You saw the width to which many eyes were then opened, and the light then reflected on many movements ambiguous before.

The startling cry of alarm was raised from many a watchman who had not been asleep in his observatory. The "Spirit of the Pilgrims" reappeared amongst their descendants. The well-proved weapons of the Panoply were drawn from the "Christian's Armory," and the encounter was earnest.

Many a church planted by the Puritans — the object of their living labors and their dying prayers — found itself suddenly and magically jostled from the sanctuary of its fathers. The legal tribunals seized many a fund, "devoted to Christ and the Church," and even grasped the sacramental vessels, and handed them over to those who accounted the blood of the covenant an unholy thing.

But God appeared for those who boldly honored him when his Gospel was reviled, and he rained down righteousness upon them. Extensive revivals followed, and many a plundered and exiled church was enriched and strengthened, as it came out of the wilderness of its destitution, leaning upon the arm of the Beloved.

Within twenty-five years after the Unitarian controversy, upwards of two hundred Congregational churches were gathered in this state alone, on "the foundation of the Prophets and Apostles, Jesus Christ himself being the chief corner-stone;" and now in the middle of this century of revivals and of active benevolence for the cause of Christ,

> "Let strangers walk around
> The city where we dwell,
> Compass and view the holy ground,
> And mark the buildings well, —

and let them say if God doth not still observe the principle which he announced to the high-priest of Israel more than three thousand years ago: "Them that honor me I will honor, and they that despise me shall be lightly esteemed."

IV. Illustrations of the truth in the text might be drawn from the history of this Association, and of the churches within its bounds. But I am confined to the brief statements of a few facts of general interest, leaving it to you to trace their connection with the general theme.

As the services of this day show, this Association of ministers was organized on the 8th of November, 1751, old style, or on the 19th according to present computation. It was formed in the second parish of Mendon, now called Milford, at the house of Rev. Amariah Frost, pastor of the church in that parish.

Its name was derived from the place of its organization.

On that day, four pastors of neighboring churches, having met together, and as they say, "Being thotful that it might tend to the advancement of y[e] glory of Christ and of his kingdom and interest in this vicinity, for them to associate, have tho't it duty, and accordingly, first voted themselves associated."

These pastors were,

Rev. Joseph Dorr, pastor of the first church in Mendon,
" Nathan Webb, pastor of the church in Uxbridge,
" Amariah Frost, pastor of the second church in Mendon.
" Elisha Fish, pastor of the church in Upton.

Ministerial associations had existed in England as early as 1576, though they were soon put down by Elizabeth as savoring too much of Puritanism. They have existed *here* substantially from the beginning of the country; but at times watched with great jealousy, lest they should prove a stepping-stone to Presbyterianism and ministerial usurpation.* In 1641, the general court virtually authorized such meetings, with the proviso, "that nothing be concluded or imposed by way of authority from one or more churches upon another, but only by way of brotherly conference and consultation." A proviso which more than two centuries has shown to have had but rare application.

In the three towns just mentioned, churches had but recently been gathered.

The first church of Mendon was indeed formed in 1669,

---

* See Christian Observatory, vol. iii., p. 389. The oldest known regular association there given was formed "at Charlestown, N. E., October 13, 1690," and met at the College in Cambridge on "Monday, at nine or ten o'clock in the morning, once in six weeks, or oftener if need shall be." A semi-monthly meeting of the ministers of Boston and vicinity, at the house of the members in succession, was commenced in 1635.

but was broken up by the Indian wars. The second church was not organized until 1741.

The church in Uxbridge was gathered in 1731, by the labors of Mr. Dorr, and that in Upton in 1735.

At the date of the formation of this body, Rev. Mr. Dorr, the moderator, was sixty-two years old, and in the thirty-eighth year of his ministry; Rev. Mr. Webb was forty-four years old, and in the twentieth year of his ministry; Rev. Mr. Frost was thirty-one, and in the eighth year of his settlement; Rev. Mr. Fish was thirty-one, and had been settled but six months.

Of their ministerial character I have not time to speak. A single fact reveals their sympathy with the revival of 1740. The names of Joseph Dorr and Nathan Webb are appended unconditionally to the testimony of the New England pastors in favor of that revival, signed Boston, July 7, 1743.

The other two members were not then settled.

The length of their period of settlement may perhaps indicate the sympathy of their churches with them in this particular.

Mr. Dorr ministered to his people over fifty-one years; Mr. Webb, forty-one years; Mr. Frost, forty-nine years; and Mr. Fish, forty-four years; and each died among his own people, and was succeeded by a pastor of like faith with himself.

Wars and civil commotions arose soon after the formation of this body, and it shared the general depression of religious interest. But it arose again when those commotions subsided. The accession of Dr. Emmons to its numbers in 1783, and his vigorous activity for more than half a century, put new life into its meetings, and made them a center of earnest deliberation and of powerful influence.

Questions of deep and vital interest were discussed, various sermons, essays, tractates, and periodicals were published by the Association, and other measures, of lasting value to the progress of truth, and whose influence still operates, had their origin in its deliberations.

Since the organization of this Association, it has enrolled seventy-seven members, of whom forty-two are still living, — our respected moderator being the oldest member, — and twenty are still connected.

In the past century, its territorial center, contrary to the commercial law, has travelled *eastward*, to this spot, where for half that period stood firm and evident the pivot of its moral power.

Its territory, once embracing the pastors in three towns, has variously enlarged, till its outward points have extended from Worcester to Dighton, and from Abington to Seekonk, enclosing the pastors of thirty-three different churches, in twenty-nine different towns. This extent has not been from convenience more than from sympathy with the scheme of theology predominant in this Association.

That scheme, I need not say, has been called Edwardean, Hopkinsian, sometimes Emmonsism. Some call it New England Theology, or, as others term it, New Theology; who, if they will have it considered new, may call it New Testament Theology. It is a system which most obviously — as some say, unduly — exalts and honors God as the Sovereign Ruler of His creatures, and abases man.* And God has not left it without an

* The term Hopkintonian, or Hopkinsian, was applied to this

evidence of his blessing, in the purity and stability of the churches where it has been embraced and taught, and in the rich fruits which it has borne to Zion at large.

While we avow our predilection for the system of doctrines in which we were nurtured, we believe that history will show that system to have been productive of far more good than many are even now disposed to allow. It has modified the current theology of all New England, and given to it its harmony, consistency, and beauty, as it now appears in the creeds of the churches and the teaching of the ministry. Hopkins's system of theology has been, from its publication, a classic in the hands of candidates for the sacred office, and has sharpened the intellect and molded the sentiments of nearly every preacher.

When this Association was formed, Dr. Hopkins says he could count but four or five Edwardean preachers. And one of them — Rev. Dr. Hall, of Sutton — was a member of this body. But within forty years afterwards, he knew of more than a hundred who espoused his own sentiments; and these, he declares, "are the most popular preachers."

In those days, when theological seminaries were not, candidates pursued their studies with private teachers.

---

system of theology in 1770, by Rev. William Hart of Saybrook, Ct. It was previously styled Edwardean, and more generally 'New Divinity.' The designation, New England Theology, appropriately belongs to the views current in the beginning of this century, — the result of the discussions of the last, and which now obtain, with few exceptions, in New England. See Memoir of Hopkins, by Prof. Park, p. 183; and Dr. Pond's Sketches of N. E. Theological History, in the Congregationalist, vol. IV.

And the teachers most numerously resorted to were Hopkinsians. The instructors, par excellence, were Bellamy, Hopkins, Strong, Backus, and Emmons. Andover Seminary was endowed by Hopkinsian funds, and Bangor Seminary was founded as well as endowed by Hopkinsian energy. The theological chairs of both institutions have been filled by Hopkinsian professors. Those at Bangor have all been students of Dr. Emmons.

Of the powerful revivals which prevailed in more than a hundred towns in New England, at the beginning of the present century, it has been said, that "they took place in almost all, if not in every instance, under the preaching of those ministers who had embraced Edwardean principles."*

The influence of Hopkinsianism is no less visible in the history of our benevolent organizations. The first efforts in England to send the Gospel to the heathen originated in Carey's contact with Edwardean theology. The Massachusetts Home Missionary Society is the own child of Hopkinsianism. Its first officers, missionaries, and its periodical, were strongly Hopkinsian.† Its resources came from Hopkinsian churches, and they have been acknowledged to be still its most liberal supporters. The Doctrinal Tract Society was formed by Hopkinsian divines, within the then bounds of this Association, and mostly by its members. Some of the first movements, which resulted in the formation of the American Board, were taken by a young man,—an ardent disciple of

---

* See Hopkins's Letter to Rev. A. Fuller, Prof. Park's Memoir, page 237.

† See Historical Appendix, article Home Missions.

Hopkins and Emmons, who in 1809 unsuccessfully essayed to bring the subject of foreign missions before the General Association of Connecticut; and who next turned his efforts to the establishment of a magazine devoted to this object, and visited Mr. Evarts, then at New Haven, with special reference to the editorship. Mr. Evarts replied, "I will think of it." The following spring, Mr. Evarts was at Charlestown, as editor of the united Panoplist and Magazine, now the Missionary Herald. Rev. W. Jackson, D. D., a Hopkinsian pastor and student of Dr. Emmons, suggested the idea of the *first* education society in America, which his exertion carried into successful operation.

These facts are not mentioned to glorify Hopkinsianism, but as a reply to the occasional insinuation, that it is a system delighting only in abstrusities, and cold towards the wants of a perishing world. A system teaching that all sin consists in voluntary selfishness, and all holiness in disinterested benevolence, must, when cordially embraced, produce just such results as have been indicated.

The religious history of this town might be made to testify to the practical workings of Hopkinsian theology. Here Emmonsism, in its undisputed and undiluted purity, was drawn out and borne to the people for more than half a century — saying nothing of the subsequent time, — and though it was, *unlike* the little book of the Evangelist, bitter to the mouth of some that only *tasted* it, yet to them who inwardly digested it, it was sweet as honey; so sweet, that they retain the relish still, — as this single sanctuary may perhaps indicate. No hostile faith has built it a house in this town, nor in its borders. No liberal creed has decoyed any recruits from this church. Cursed by no funds, but blessed with a legacy of sound doctrines, it has offered no attractions to the spoiler, to try his devices.

Other churches and localities bear witness that God bestows some honor upon Hopkinsian preaching. But I will avoid comparisons, and take shelter behind the assertion of Dr. Dwight, who, in his travels over New England, half a century ago, says, "he found that those ministers who preached the doctrines of grace earnestly were generally Hopkinsians."

The writings of Hopkins, Strong, Smalley, and Emmons, have not only provoked the ire of the reviewer, but they have sharpened the logic of the judge on the bench, have guided the researches of the theological student and pastor, and have clarified and strengthened the faith of many a pious layman, even in the depths of the western wilderness.

I must return once more to that primary meeting of this Association. Besides its four original members, there was one other person present, — a young man who had presented himself for approbation to preach the Gospel. This was David Thurston, afterwards first pastor of the church in West Medway, — the first licentiate and first admitted member of this body. He was the antecedent of a goodly line of successors, applicants for the same recommendation.

I count up one hundred and twenty-one persons approbated to preach the Gospel by Mendon Association. Their history could be given, but statistics are barren subjects for declamation. Amongst them are Presidents of colleges, Theological Professors, Pastors, Evangelists, a goodly number of D. D's. already in fruition, some in expectancy.

If the agency of these one hundred and twenty-one ministers of the Gospel could be traced, it would add another illustration to the truth of the text, "Them that honor me I will honor, and they that despise me shall be lightly esteemed."

But I ought to close; yet indulge me in one or two reflections, suggested by this subject and occasion. — If I overstep your patience you may reflect that you will never be wearied with another centennial discourse before the Mendon Association.

The theme of this discourse, as illustrated by our religious history, points out the *Primary Element of a church's real prosperity or decline.*

It is found in the character of its ministry.

As it was "like people like priest" in the days of Isaiah, so has it been in all following ages. When religious teachers have catered to the lusts of the people, and 'taught for doctrines the commandments of men,' or have timorously or slothfully shunned to declare the whole counsel of God, the people have ripened for desertions and divisions,—have served the world and died in indifference. But when the ministers of Christ have fully and boldly preached the doctrines of grace, piety has flourished, sin has diminished, and death has been robbed of his sting. So the past history of our Zion teaches us. Her days of brightness have been when her heralds sounded the distinctive notes of salvation, clear, full, and piercing to the conscience and heart. Then the trumpets gave a certain sound, the hosts of God's Elect rallied for the conflict and Zion was terrible as an army with banners. And so it must ever be.

It is by the clear exhibition of the truths of the Gospel that the carnal heart is developed, and holy affections are exercised. The milk which the Apostle fed to the Corinthian church, was precisely the doctrines now called strong meat—Entire depravity, special grace, electing love. These truths with their adjuncts, are the sincere milk of the word which God has provided for new born souls, whereby they may grow unto the stature of perfect men in Christ Jesus. And the church which understands the philosophy of its own real growth, will seek to be fed with these truths.

The darkest cloud on the horizon of Zion's prospect, is not the multitude of the rejectors of the Gospel,—but the indifference and even repugnance of some of her professed friends to the fundamental doctrines of the Gospel; at least, a cowardly solicitude lest they should be preached so plainly and so often as to offend the world. This is the spot of leprosy, breaking out in the timber and on the wall of God's spiritual temples, and indicating the existence of decay.

Suffer the exhortation, then, brethren of the churches, to cleave to those humbling but precious truths whose faithful presentation has ever been the means of the church's true prosperity. Be fully persuaded of them in your own minds, and love to hear them preached fully and distinctly. Encourage your ministers to fidelity. We sympathize with the reception of our message. And you know not how much it incites us to fidelity when you show a delight in the doctrines of Sovereign and special grace, and how much it disheartens us to have our brethren in the church predict divisions and dismissions if we declare the whole counsel of God.

II. This subject also points out to us the *only way to be successful and finally accepted ministers of Jesus Christ.*

The power of the ministry lies in the power of the truths of God. The exercise of that power consists in the complete and plain enforcement of those truths. Fidelity, we have reason to hope, God will bless to the edification of Christians and conversion of sinners.

To this result, we need a clear and systematic knowledge of the Gospel, wherein every doctrine shall have its own place and importance; then, an unhesitating confidence in the adaptedness of the Gospel to fit men for eternity; and lastly, an unfaltering courage in declaring its every truth, whether men will hear or whether they will forbear. The soldier needs unwavering confidence in the trustiness of his weapons. The soldier of the cross needs an invincible faith in the adaptation of the sword of the Spirit to slay the carnal heart,—a faith that it needs no polishing, no re-fashioning of his to give it edge and effect. He should never substitute weapons of his own invention, nor go down to the Philistines to sharpen God's armor. He is to approach God's enemies, not with feints and stratagems and masked batteries, but openly and fearlessly, straight onwards, and without a misgiving of victory.

True, the laws of the affections are to be regarded in the mode of presenting truth; but those laws do not require that timorous hesitancy about preaching unwelcome truths, that anxious beclouding and hiding offensive doctrines, which appears too often to-day. No. Mighty is the truth. In its own native, majestic beauty, it is "the wisdom of God and the power of God unto salvation, to every one that believeth." And he who wisely seeks the salvation of his hearers, will preach the truth as purely as he can.

This is not, indeed, the present way to be a popular preacher, courted by the world, and coveted by rich parishes, for then is the offense of the cross ceased; but it is the way to be popular with the angels, waiting to carry up the news of sinners' repentance. It is the way to be approved by the great Head of the church, when he shall come the second time without sin unto salvation.

In earnest fidelity, then, my brethren in the ministry, let us preach the Gospel of the grace of God. Others will not let us forget that we are men; let us remember that we are "ministers of Christ and stewards of the mysteries of God, and moreover that it is required in stewards that a man be found faithful." Only by an ardent piety, and vigorous exhibition of the truth, can we stem the tide now strongly setting towards a rejection of the Bible and the unsteady billows of a general skepticism.

Finally. Let this subject encourage ministers to *fidelity in their trying work.*

You know, my brethren, that to preach the Gospel fully and faithfully, to a world who will not have Christ to reign over them, is no self-pleasing work. Its humbling truths do and must awaken the enmity of the carnal mind, till its enmity is slain. But what if, for our unshrinking fidelity, we meet with indications and expressions of disapproval from a sin-loving world? It is not our master. One is our Master, even Christ, and his "Well done, good and faithful servant," will make us more than conquerors, at the last. Every open indignity, every sly contempt, every ambiguous reception, for our faithful witness of Jesus and of the word of God, will be changed into a sparkling gem in the crown of glory, by the strangely transmuting alchemy of the last day.

And then, too, God will measure the prominence we shall have given to the peculiar points of our message. He will compute the value of the gold, silver, and precious stones, wherewith we shall have enriched the foundation of the Gospel; and he will apply the torch to all the hay, wood, and stubble we may have built thereon; and that which shall stand the fiery test shall indicate our reward. My brethren, in view of such a trial, what matter the reception we may personally receive, if so be that we be found faithful in the day of the Lord Jesus! How die away into inaudible murmurs, both the applauses and the hisses of this world! How fade its honors in the bright beamings of that crown which the Lord, the righteous Judge, will then give to him that hath fought a good fight and hath kept the faith!

And, men and brethren, this day and occasion tell us that that final judgment will soon come. A century of our associational history has passed away, yet the founders of this Association seem to have been hardly committed to the earth.— We enter into their labors for a little while, soon to give an account of our ministry to him that commissioned us. When our faces shall have been hardly forgotten, another century will have passed, and another company will be gathered to observe a second centennial epoch. So rapidly, from high summits of observation, does time appear to pass away, and so speedily does the day approach when we all, ministers and people, must be judged, one for our exhibition and other for our reception of the Gospel of salvation.

My brethren, then will the unchangeable principle of Jehovah's government, which I have attempted to set forth, receive its fullest illustration :—Even as the Judge, when on earth, forewarned his ambassadors, " Whosoever shall confess me before men, him shall the Son of Man also confess before the angels of God ; But he that denieth me before men, shall be denied before the angels of God ! "

HISTORICAL APPENDIX.

THE existent records of Mendon Association, for the first thirty years of its existence, consist of only a few loose scraps of paper. These fragments contain little more than the time and place of meeting, and the certificates of approbation to preach the Gospel of candidates now and then examined. Complete records exist from October 7, 1783. The following interesting historical items are added to what is contained in the preceding pages.

A VERBATIM COPY OF THE RECORD OF THE FIRST MEETING OF ASSOCIATION.

A number of Pastors of chhs, viz. of y[e] 1st chh of Christ in Mendon, of y[e] chh of Christ in Uxbridge, of y[e] 2[d] chh of Christ in Mendon, and of y[e] chh of Christ in Upton, being conven[d] at the house of y[e] Rev[d] M[r] Frost, in s[d] Mendon Novemb[r] 8th 1751.

Being thotful that it might tend to the Advancmen[t] of y[e] Glory of Christ and of his Kingdom and Interest in this Vicinity, for them to Associate, have tho't it duty. And Accordingly, 1st Voted themselves Associated, And 2[d] Voted y[e] Rev[d] M[r] Dorr the Moderator of the Association, 3[d] M[r] Webb the Scribe for the pres[t] Meeting. And David Thurston, A. B., having apply[d] himself to us for our advice and countenance with Regard to his purpos[d] Design to Enter into y[e] great and important work of the Evangelical Ministry, after Supplicat[n] to God thro' X[t] the Head of the chh, and careful Enquiry into the Case, offer[d] unto him This Testimonial following — Viz.

These may certify, that we, the Subscribers, Associated Pastors of chhs of Christ, Have, upon the application of M[r] David Thurston, admitted him to examination, in ord[r] to his Regular Introduction to the Preaching of the Gosp[l]. And upon a proper Examination Respecting his Moral Character, his Learning, his Orthodoxy in the Doctrines of the Gosple, and Christian Experience in Religion, are Well Satisfied as to his qualifications for or Entrance upon y[e] Gosple Ministry, and can very freely recommend him to y[e] churches and People of God as a Suitable Person to preach the Gosple, wheresoever he shall by y[e] Providence of God be call[d].

JOSEPH DORR,
NATHAN WEBB,
AMARIAH FROST,
ELISHA FISH.

Mendon, Nov[r]. y[e]8, 1751.

TIME OF MEETINGS.

THE meetings of the Association were held at irregular intervals for several years, gradually settling into some system, until, at the close of the Revolution, June and October became the months of regular meeting. For the first five years the meetings were held at Rev. Mr. Dorr's, the senior member, and standing moderator. During this period Rev. Mr. Webb was scribe. As other members joined, each had the meeting in rotation. But the officers continued unchanged for a long time. The first Tuesday in June and October continued to be the regular time of meeting, until

October, 1821, when the *third* Tuesday of the above months was selected. In 1824, October 19th, the *last* Tuesdays in April and October were adopted. Again in 1831, April 26th, it was voted that an additional meeting be annually held upon the third Tuesday in August. In 1841, August 17th, the *third* Tuesday was reselected for the regular meetings. Finally in 1844, December 17th, voted, that "our future meetings be on the second Tuesday of the month." These frequent changes have been rendered necessary by the increase of other and more general religious meetings.

There are records of two hundred and fourteen regular and occasional meetings of the body.

OFFICERS.

For many years Rev. Mr. Dorr was standing moderator of the Association. After his death, Rev. David Hall, D. D. of Sutton, succeeded him. In 1783, it was determined that the senior member present at each meeting should preside, and that the host of the Association should act as scribe. Under this rule, the following members became virtually standing moderators, namely, Rev. Messrs. Elisha Fish, Amariah Frost, David Sanford, and Nathaniel Emmons, D. D. Dr. Emmons presided over the deliberations of the Association for nearly twenty-five years, and was seldom absent from any of its meetings. In 1841, April 27th, Rev. Elisha Fish was elected as moderator, and continued until January, 1851, the time of his decease. The moderator is now chosen annually in April.

The first arrangement respecting a scribe was found to be defective, and a standing scribe was chosen. The following is a list of the scribes, with the dates of their election.

Rev. John Crane, chosen 12 October, 1802;
" Timothy Dickinson, chosen 9 June, 1812;
" David Long, chosen 12 October, 1813;

Rev. Elam Smalley, chosen 16 August, 1831;
" David Sanford, chosen 30 April, 1839;
" T. D. P. Stone, chosen 11 August, 1846;
" Tyler Thatcher, chosen 17 August, 1847;
" Thomas T. Richmond, chosen 8 October, 1850.

BUSINESS.

The regular exercises at Associational meetings have varied at different dates, according to the number of members and apparent state of religion. The fragmentary scraps of the first quarter of the century give us no information of the business of its meetings, other than the preacher of the public lecture, and the occasional examination of candidates for the Gospel ministry. We naturally infer it to be the discussion of such questions as the times made important and prominent. It is not until 1794, that any of these questions are recorded. Then, "14 October, 1794, it was voted that each member should write upon the following question, and read at the next meeting: 'Whether or not, there be any proof, the Bible being excepted, that there is another state of existence for men?"

Nothing more is said of questions for thirteen years. We may infer that the plan of *written* discussions did not succeed, for the following year it was agreed that each member should read a sermon in rotation for general criticism. Still another change was made in 1797, by substituting a *Concio ad Clerum* by one of the members. This was shortly abandoned, and no substitute adopted until 1807, June 9th; when a committee, chosen for the purpose, proposed a plan, — which was adopted, and has been followed, with slight additions, to the present time, — "That at every meeting, one text of Scripture should be explained, and two questions be discussed, if there be time. And that each member shall present a text of Scripture for explanation, or a question for discussion, from which the Association shall make a selection."

The additions to this plan have been, the reading of a sermon for criticism by the minister at whose house the Association meet, — adopted 18 August, 1835. And the presentation of the skeleton of a sermon by some designated member, — adopted 20 August, 1844. Other additions have been temporarily made.

The following digest of the regulations of this body, now in force, may be here conveniently added: —

STANDING REGULATIONS OF MENDON ASSOCIATION.

1. The meetings shall be held on the second Tuesday in April, August, October, and January, at three o'clock, P. M.

2. The Moderator shall be chosen by ballot annually at the April meeting. The Scribe shall serve until his resignation. He is also Librarian of the Association.*

3. The regular business of each meeting shall be: — Prayer by the Moderator; reading the minutes of the last meeting; sermon for criticism by the host of Association;

* The Library of the Association has consisted of records, documents on file, and a few volumes presented, some by Harvard University, some by members. At the regular meeting in August, 1852, it was unanimously voted to attempt a *complete collection of all the printed works of the past and present Members and Licentiates of the body, and also an autograph sermon of each Member and Licentiate, with an autobiography appended*, as far as they can be obtained. Rev. Charles Simmons, of North Wrentham, was designated to the charge of this collection and authorized to solicit, in behalf of the Association, donations of the publications, and a MS. sermon of Members and Licentiates, from themselves or their surviving friends. It is hoped that the public value of such a collection will secure the complete execution of the plan. Occasional sermons, pamphlets, etc., and the more important bound volumes, upon every subject pertaining to religion, will be gratefully received from their authors and publishers.

written exegesis of a portion of the Scriptures; written essay upon an assigned theme; oral discussion of a previously selected question; a written skeleton of a sermon for criticism; an hour of devotional exercises; and a season of public worship.

4. The examination of candidates for approbation to preach the Gospel will commence with reading a sermon. Their examination takes the precedence of all other business.

5. The place of meeting and the preacher shall be appointed in rotation.

6. The schedules for the General Association of the State shall be forwarded to the delegates before the first of February, and *their* report of the Association shall be presented to this body at the April meeting.

7. When any member of this Association is dismissed from his people, and leaves the ministry for more than one year, we shall not consider him a member of this body.

DOINGS OF THE ASSOCIATION.

THE records of a ministerial association cannot furnish many striking historical facts, formed as it is for professional and private deliberations, whose results appear only in individual benefit. Yet the questions discussed and resolves passed, connected with their dates, may give some light to the past state of religion. We can thus learn what aspects of truth occupied attention, and may sometimes trace important movements to their source in some passing discussion or brief resolution.

The data furnished by our records for conclusions of this sort, are here given for this use, grouped by their affinities, such as they have.

CONSOCIATION OF CHURCHES.

THE first intimation of this subject, found in the few loose documents of the period, is a draft of principles and rules for a consociation, adopted by the Association, and dated Sutton, 17 November, 1756. Some additions were made at the meetings in 1757, and then the subject appears to have been dropped. The churches probably declined to enter into the proposal, as no vote of adoption occurs in the records of the churches which have been examined.

This draft is copied here, as an interesting digest, in the working form, of the principles suggested by the Synod of 1662.

DRAFT FOR A CONSOCIATION, PROPOSED 1756.

To the several Fraternities of the churches of Christ in Mendon, the first church of Sutton, the church of Uxbridge, the church of Upton, the church of Medway Precinct: — The Pastors of said churches send Greeting, Wishing to them Grace, Mercy and Peace, from God our Father and from our Lord Jesus Christ. Dearly Beloved Brethren in Christ:

Whearas, the churches of Christ rightly constituted, according to the Word of God; are to be considered as standing in a Sisterly Relation to each other, (Cant. 8: 8,) being united in the same faith and order, (Eph. 4: 4,) walking by the same Rule, in the use of the same Ordinances, for the same Ends, under one and the same Political Head, the Lord Jesus Christ, Head over all things to the church of God; There must needs, from this their Relation to and Union one with another, be Inferred their Duty of Communion one with another, suitable to that union and relation; Which communion of churches, according to the Definition Given of it, by a Venerable Synod of these churches, Is the Faithful Improvement of the Gifts of Christ, Bestowed upon [them] for his Service and Glory, and their Mutual Good and Edification, according to capacity and opportunity. And further, whereas there hath constantly been in the churches, a Profession of Communion of Churches, one with another, in Giving the right hand of Fellowship at the Gathering of Churches and Ordination of Elders; which import a Consociation, and obligeth to the Practice thereof.

We doe therefore most earnestly call upon the churches under our Pastoral care, and advise them to come into a Mutual and Solemn Agreement, to exercise Communion In and by such acts of Communion as are mentioned in the Result of the Synod, Held by the Elders and Messengers of the churches of the Massachusetts Province, contained in the Platform of Church Discipline, ANNO DOMINI 1648, and in the Result of the Synod of the same Province in 1662, so far as they are agreeable to the Word of God, and more Especially in the following Mentioned acts: —

1. By an hearty careing for one another's wellfare, and by Earnest and fervent Prayer one for another. (Cant. 8: 8. Ps. 122: 6, 7, 8, 9.)

2. By Admitting to occasional communion in Sealing Ordinances, such members of any Particular church in our Consociation, upon satisfying and sufficient Testimonials, of their regular standing in said church, when there shall be no weighty Objection to Barr their Communion.

3. By Admitting to settled and stated Communion in Seals, and Censures, as there shall be Occasion, such Members of any one of our Consociated Churches, as shall be regularly dismissed to our Stated Communion; Provided, there shall be no Sufficient Barr put in against the member or members so Dismissed.

4. When any sufficient Number of the Members of our Consociated Churches having a regular Standing in the

churches, shall be about to Embodie in a church, for the Enjoyment of Gospel Ordinances among themselves, They Procedeing according to Gospel order, and Desireing our Presence, and Assistance in so Good a work: we shall be ready to Assist them, and to hold forth to them the Right hand of Fellowship.

5. For the preserving of Peace and Unity; by giving an account one to another of our Publick Actions, when it is orderly Desired, In order to our Strengthening one another, in our Regular Administrations, Especially by our concurrent Testimony against Persons justly censured.

6. By Seeking and accepting of Help, and Good Advice when Given, and by Affording our Help, best Counsel, and Advice, to each other when the case shall require it. More Especially in the four following cases. 1. In case of Divisions and contentions, when the Peace of any of the Consociated Churches is Disturbed, (Acts 15 : 2.) 2. In cases of more than ordinary Importance; as the Ordination and Deposition of Elders, and the like. 3. In case of Difficult Questions and Controversies that may arise, (Acts 15 : 2.) 4. In case That in any one of our Consociated Churches there should subsist Mall-administrations, Errors, or Offences that remain unhealed, we will be ready to Afford and receive help one from another, for the Healing and removing such Offences, and for the Rectifying such Administrations.

7. By Admonishing One Another when there shall be need and sufficient Reason for it, Especially in such a case as Mall-Administrations, Errors, and Scandals shall continue to subsist in a particular church, after Good Advice given; and if after a first Admonition administered by a Particular church of the Consociation, and a second Admonition Dispensed by a superior Number of the Consociated Churches, the said offending church shall remain, We will then, if the whole Number of the Consociated Churches, or the Majority of them regularly convened, by their Pastors

and Delegates in council, shall Judge necessary, Procede to the Sentence of Non-communion with said church or Peccant Party Therein, agreeable to what is Declared in the 15th chap. of the Platform of Church Dicipline, Sec. 2, Partic. 3d.

POSTSCRIPT.

To Prevent any misunderstanding of the Design of the Consociation of these Churches, or of the true Intent and Meaning of any one of the above-Mentioned acts of communion, we Declare as Followeth.

1st. That Neither the above scheme in General nor any one of the acts of communion in Particular, is so to be understood in the least to Prejudice the Power of Government in any Particular Congregational Church, for we apprehend according to the first Proposition in Answer to the 2nd Question of the General Synod assembled in Boston, 1662, That every church or Particular Congregation of Visible Saints in Gospel order being furnished with a Presbytery, at Least with a Teaching Elder, and walking together in Truth and Peace, hath received from the Lord Jesus, full Power and authority Ecclesiastical, within itself, Regularly to administer all the Ordinanees of Christ, and is not under any other Ecclesiastical Jurisdiction whatsoever, (Mat. 18: 17, 18.) And that the Consociation of Churches is not to hinder the Exercise of this Power, but by counsel from the Word of God, to Direct and strengthen the same, when it may be Done upon Just and Sufficient Reasons.

2nd. It is the Proper work of the Pastors and Delegates of the Consociated churches, when assembled in council, to Debate and Determine controversies of faith, and cases of Conscience, to clear and Hold forth from the Word of God Holy Directions, for the Holy Worship of God, and Good Government of the Church, and to bear witness against mall-administration and corruption in Doctrine or Manners, in a Particular Church; and to give Directions for the Reformation thereof, but not to administer church censures, in a way of Discipline, to the Prejudice of the Power of Government, or Privilege, of any Particular Church.

3d. For the ascertaining the Rights and Powers of the Bretheren in the Ecclesiastical council when convened, it is agreed that the Power of the order of Delegates in voting shall be full equal, to that of the Pastors, And that the Majority of Delegates, as well as the Majority of Pastors or Elders shall be Judged Necessary to constitute a valid act of the Council. [And that the Eldership and Delegates from each church, be they one or more, to have Equal power with oth[r] Churches in Every act of the Consociation.] Added 10 May, 1757.

[1. That this Association in their Proposal to their sev[l] chh[s] of Forming into a Consociation, would be understood as having in View, That y[e] Assemblie's Catechism and N. England Confession of Faith be regarded as Scriptural, and what we are all agreed on in point of orthodoxy.

2. As the mutual Edification of these chhs, (the End of the Consociating,) cannot be Expected but in the way of Xtian Liberty, and to guard ag[st] all Lording it over God's Heritage, We Propose y[t] in case any Particular Consociated chh or chhs shall in Process of Time apprehend their Relation w[t] the Consociation, no longer to their Edification, They may (Regularly or Formally desireing it) be Dismissed, or otherwise, their Desires being thus Signified, Dismiss themselves.] Added 20 Sept. 1757.

N. B. It is Proposed that if the churches manifest their concurrence by vote with the above written Proposal for a Consociation of Churches, That they chuse their Delegates, to stand for one year and no Longer, and so annually, and that they stand ready to Repair to the Place that shall be appointed, when they shall be notified of the time for their convening; and when the said Delegates shall be Elected, that the Pastors of the Several churches notify the Moderator of Mendon Association, in order to their being convened and formed into Council.

JOSEPH DORR,
DAVID HALL,
NATHAN WEBB,
AMARIAH FROST,
ELISHA FISH,
DAVID THURSTON.

Sutton, Nov. the 17, 1756, *at a Meeting of the Mendon Association.*

Nothing occurs in any subsequent records in relation to consociation of churches. The subject of a conference of churches has been often up for consideration, but none was ever formed, because many of the members were so connected elsewhere.

GENERAL ASSOCIATION OF MASSACHUSETTS.

THE action of this body in relation to the General Association of the State, may be next alluded to.

A communication from the Brookfield Association, dated March 22, 1802, was received, proposing the subject of forming a State Association, and inviting correspondence. Whereon it was "voted, 8 June, 1802, to choose a committee to repair to Northampton, to meet the committees of other Associations, agreeably to proposals. Rev. David Sanford and Rev. Samuel Austin were chosen as committee." Both these gentlemen attended the preliminary meeting at Northampton, July 7, 1802. The consideration of their report was deferred from October 1802, until October 1803, when, "the minds of the Association being taken, whether they will accede to the proposal made to them, and send two delegates to the convention next June, the vote passed in the negative." The motion of Rev. Dr. Lyman of Hatfield in the Convention of Congregational Ministers, May 30, 1804, to enlist that body in a general movement to the same end, and which was by vote of convention referred to the district associations, was also rejected by this Association. The subject again came up in 1807, by a letter from the scribe of the General Association, when the same vote of refusal was repeated. So the matter rested until April 1841, when a vote of union was passed. The reason of this long hesitancy may be found mainly in the following sentiment, and in deference to him who uttered it.

"Associationism leads to Consociationism; Consociationism leads to Presbyterianism; Presbyterianism leads to Episcopacy; Episcopacy leads to Roman Catholicism; and Roman Catholicism is an ultimate fact."

BENEVOLENT SOCIETIES.

The attitude of the Association in respect to other public movements, benevolent organizations, etc., will be best shown by the various *resolves* passed at different times. Those on record are given in the order of the dates of their adoption. The more important are copied verbatim.

Nov. 17, 1756. "Upon our information that a donation given to Bellingham Church is alienated to another use, — We the Associated Pastors of Mendon Association, Do Judge, that all such donations for sacred use ought by no means to be in such manner improved as to give just scandal to any; but Rather, considering ye dissolved state of said chh, be reposited in ye hands of ye next Heir of ye Donor to be in Reserve: and for ye use of w^h it was originally Designed w^n y^r shall be occasion.

Oct. 2, 1792. "Voted, as the opinion of this Association, That no man ought to be approbated, as a School-Master, unless he promises to pray in his school every day, and to teach his scholars the Assemblie's Catechise once every week.

Jan. 19, 1795. Association highly approved of and adopted "Prest. Edwards' newly revived plan for a general concert in prayer;" and a lengthy letter, expressive of their cordial union, was addressed to Rev. Walter King.

May 29, 1799. A proposition from the Boston Association for a convention to consider the increase of infidelity and immorality, — approved, and *three* delegates chosen.

June 13, 1809. Association agreed "to catechise the children under their care," and "recommend to heads of families, in their respective congregations to take pains to instruct their children in the use of the Assembly's Shorter Catechism." The same vote was substantially repeated in 1824.

Oct. 31, 1826. "Voted that it be the rule of this Association, that no ardent spirits be presented at their meetings."*

---

* This vote was passed at Seekonk, on the suggestion of the following incident.

The host of the Association, Rev. J. O. Barney, went into Providence on the day previous to the meeting, to procure the due assortment of spirits which immemorial usage had made an important part of his preparation. He accomplished his errand, and at sunset commenced his return, with an extra choice variety of liquors, — as it was his *first* meeting, — densely packed in a large basket in the back of his wagon. As he was abstractly driving, in forgetful haste to reach home, the loud laughter of some men upon the staging of a new house in the outskirts of the city, broke up his reverie, and suggested to him the risk of such unbecoming speed. Instantly thinking of his freight, he looked behind, and lo! fragmentary jugs, demijohns, and bottles, were dancing in and out of the basket, and a ruby stream of wines, brandies, and cordials was allaying the excited dust of the pebbly street! What was to be done? Should he go back and replenish, or take it as a Providential hint, and go on? The late hour decided him to proceed, and state the *calamity* to the venerable body when they assembled. He did so, and they *took the hint*, and promptly banished the side-board

In 1829, votes were passed commending the Massachusetts Missionary Society, and making the Association an auxiliary.

Aug. 16, 1831. "Voted, that this Association, not being an ecclesiastical body, and having no jurisdiction over the churches, cannot consistently give advice to any church or number of churches, as such, in relation to any difficulties under which they may labor."

April 28, 1835. A committee on the conversion of Papists reported, that "as the Romish priesthood have almost unbounded influence over the Catholic population, the first thing to be attempted towards their conversion, is to weaken this powerful influence of the priests."

Aug. 18, 1835. *Resolved,*—"That the members of this Association feel it to be their duty to act as agents for the benevolent societies of the day, in their own congregations; and thus to do what they can to relieve these societies of the necessity of sustaining agents to plead their respective causes within their bounds." A copy was transmitted to the secretaries of the above-intended societies.

Nov. 21, 1837. Voted, "That every member of the Association feels the object of the Seaman's Friends' Society to be important, and will do what he consistently can to aid the friends of said Society."

April 24, 1838. Resolves respecting the American Peace Society.

1. *Resolved,*—That this Association view with deep concern the prevalence of the war spirit in this and in other lands, and deem it highly important to pursue all judicious measures to check and eradicate that spirit.

2. *Resolved,*—That, although we are not prepared to

---

from their meetings. This was the year in which Dr. Beecher preached his six sermons on intemperance, and the American Temperance Society was organized.

deny the right of self-defence, we highly approve the great object of the American Peace Society, to discourage war, and promote the cause of Peace.

3. *Resolved,* — That we recommend it to every brother in this Association, to preach, at least once in each year, on this important subject.

Oct. 18, 1842. Similar resolves were passed respecting the Sabbath, and the American and Foreign Sabbath Union.

Dec. 19, 1843. Was passed a resolve of sympathy and aid for the Western Reserve College.

March 18, 1845. On an unfinished report of a committee on Congregationalism, appointed at Boston, May, 1844, the Association adopted the following result of their deliberations: —

—— "We are agreed that a reassertion of the principles of the Cambridge Platform, with such alterations as shall adapt them to the churches of the present age, is a very desirable object. But there is, as it seems to us, a real discrepancy between the Report and the Platform in respect to several very important principles. For instance, in proposing to make the decision of ecclesiastical councils binding, the Report goes beyond the Platform, and adopts a most important principle which is not recognized in that instrument, and which, in our view, is entirely inconsistent with its most prominent features. The Platform admits of Lay-ordination, but the Report proceeds upon the principle that ordination is exclusively the work of ministers.

Though we believe that, as a general thing, it is best that Ministers should ordain Ministers, and this they can in all ordinary cases do, even if the right belongs to the church; yet we think it important that, in a system of rules for the government of the churches, this right of theirs ought to be recognized, as it is in the platform. If the churches have a right in all cases to exclude appeals from their decisions in reference to their offending members, as the Report admits;

it can be neither duty nor good policy to establish a permanent and uniform tribunal, beyond the power of the churches, which shall virtually take this right out of their hands. To constitute by agreement a tribunal, to which every member of a church is understood to have the right of appeal from its decisions in every case, and to make the decision of this tribunal *binding*, is to remove the power of discipline from the body in which Christ has placed it, and to give individuals a power which Christ never gave them. If the church place the right of decision in respect to the discipline of its own members, beyond their control, they are *liable* in certain cases, to be obliged to acquiesce in wrong decisions and in decisions which they *know* to be wrong. We see not how this is consistent with the responsibility which rests upon them as the depositaries of all Ecclesiastical power.

A minister ought, in our view, always to be a member of the church of which he is the Pastor, and, like other members, subject to its discipline for all immorality, crime or heresy. We think his own church is a *suitable* body to try him; although they ought as a general thing to seek that instruction and advice in so important matters which are to be obtained from an Ecclesiastical council. We do not think that, in *any* case, the minister has the power of suspending the action of the church, in opposition to the will of the majority. It is his prerogative to decide all questions of order, and his decision is binding until an appeal is taken from it to the whole body and by them reversed. We are happy to agree with the authors of the Report on the general inutility of exparte councils. We think they do more hurt than good. But as we do not consider Ecclesiastical councils, when called to act with respect to the affairs of a particular church, a judicial, but only an advisory body, we are not prepared to adopt, in full, the language of the Report respecting them. We admit "that there are some things in the Platform of a subordinate character which cannot at the present day be carried into practice, and some defects which it is important to supply." We need no ruling Elders in distinction from those who preach, and we do not believe that the Bible makes any distinction between officers of this class. It is our opinion that the rules of church discipline, found in the eighteenth chapter of Matthew are applicable to public as well as private offenses. If this be not a direction respecting the treatment of public offenses, we have none in the New Testament for this class. Besides any offender, whether his crime be public or private, is more likely to be gained by being first approached in a private, affectionate manner, than he is to be at once arraigned before the whole church, and made the subject of public censure. In the process of dealing with offenders given in the eighteenth chapter of Matthew, there is a display of Divine Wisdom so obviously adapted to touch the feelings of the human heart, and win over a fallen brother, that we cannot believe its advantages were designed to be confined to private offenses alone.

We believe that the act of Excommunication may, for prudential reasons, be occasionally delayed for a short time after the offender is proved guilty of an offense of sufficient magnitude to cut him off from the church; and that, during this delay, it would be improper for him to come to the communion; but suspension, as a punishment to be inflicted upon a member, or as the final act of the church in any case, is unknown in the scriptures, and obviously unauthorized by the great Head of the body.—

In the above remarks, we express to you the views of a large majority of our association. In respect to some of the points involved, there are a few contrary minds.

April 8, 1845. "Resolved, that we regard slavery in the Southern States as a great sin; a violation alike of the great principles and the spirit of Christianity, and that it becomes us, as members of the same great christian family, to remonstrate with our brethren at the South in regard to this sin of oppression:" and urge that the General Association correspond with Southern Ecclesiastical bodies on the subject.

Aug. 12, 1846. Voted "that the Am. Protestant Society, aiming as it does, in the spirit of love, to convert the Romanists of our land to the Gospel of Christ, by the dissemination of light and knowledge, is worthy of the confidence, prayer and charities of christian benevolence."

Jan. 12, 1847. A plan of action was adopted respecting agencies of benevolent associations; according to which the claims of the various benevolent societies were placed each under the special care of one of the members, to be presented by him whenever requested within the bounds of this body. The plan was adopted as an experiment for a single year. The following year the plan was dropped, and each pastor was left to adopt his own arrangements.

Aug. 13, 1851. A resolution was passed condemning the use of Tobacco as highly pernicious.

Some other votes of a temporary or local application, have been omitted in this summary.

HOME MISSIONS.

The subject of Domestic Missions has ever had a strong hold upon the sympathies of this association: and not without reason. Of the little group of FOUR who originated the Mass. Miss. Society, *two* were members of this body. Mrs. McFarland notes the fact in these words. "During Election week in May 1799, a number of ministers [Dr. Spring, Dr. Emmons, Mr. Sanford and Father Niles, as they called him] came to my mother's and requested the use of that room to consult together about forming the Mass. Missionary Society. They met four or five times during the week, and then resolved to form the Society."*

* Memoirs of Mrs. McFarland, p. 179.

Dr. Emmons, then in the strength of his influence at home and abroad, was the first President. The first secretary, Dr. Austin, was a member of this body. Of the first two Missionaries sent out, Jacob Cram was its Licentiate, and David Avery a member.

In 1797, two years before the existence of the State Society, the Association virtually resolved itself into a temporary missionary organization, by voting to supply South Mendon, then destitute, one Sabbath each, gratis.

Similar votes have been frequently passed in respect to other destitute parishes. In 1800, a committee examined "the religious state of the people" in Cumberland, Smithfield and Patuxet, R. I., and the association voted to preach once each gratis in the first mentioned place. In 1805, again preached in turn in South Mendon. In 1810, Blackstone was similarly favored with pulpit ministrations. In 1824, committees were chosen to confer with the Rhode Island Domestic Miss. Soc'y, and with the people of Greenwich respecting their 'waste places.' In 1830, the church in Canton was gratuitously supplied.

PUBLICATIONS.

The first publication issued by the Mendon Association, of which any record is made, — and the largest single work they have issued, — is entitled "Evidences of Revealed Religion."

The preliminary steps were taken at a meeting of the Association at Holliston, Oct. 11, 1796, in the following votes:

I. That it is desirable that Mendon Association should publish upon the Evidence of Divine Revelation, with some strictures upon Deistical writers.

The parts were assigned as follows:

I. The need and importance of a Divine Revelation. By Rev. John Robinson, of Westboro.

II. The Spirituality of the Bible. By Rev. David Sanford of Medway.

III. Miracles. By Rev. Nathaniel Emmons of Franklin.

IV. Prophecies. By Rev. Caleb Alexander of Mendon.

V. Strictures upon Deistical Writers. By Rev. John Crane of Northbridge.

At an adjourned meeting, Northbridge, Jan. 10, 1797, the parts were read to the Association: and it was voted to issue them in a volume. Each member in favor of the vote, shared equally in the expenses and profits of the publication. The work of publishing was committed to Rev. Messrs. Alexander, Dickinson and Crane.

A Sermon by Rev. Dr. Emmons, preached before the Association at Upton, Oct. 13, 1813, was published by vote and at the expense of the body. Four hundred copies were printed and circulated. The discourse is the same as appears in his published works, Vol. IV., Sermon XXXIV., entitled "The Law of Paradise."

A sermon by Rev. Nathaniel Howe, founded upon John 1: 31, and preached before the Association at Foxboro', Oct. 5, 1819, was also published by vote of the Association.

The subject of issuing a monthly periodical was introduced to the Association at their meeting in Oct. 21, 1823, by a communication from Mr. Barnum Field, Providence, R. I., then publisher of "The Christian Visitor." A committee of conference reported upon the subject, and the result was a vote to issue a prospectus for a separate magazine. As *all* the members did not second this movement, or wish to be involved in the responsibility of such an undertaking, the imprimatur read as follows: "The Christian Magazine; By members of Mendon Association," rather than, "By Mendon Association." Yet the agency of the body in the existence of "The Christian Magazine" extended thus far, that they voted to publish it and chose the Editors. The members individually contributed to its columns and its subscription list at their pleasure. The work appeared January, 1824, under the Editorial Supervision of Rev. Messrs. J. Ide, C. Park, and E. Fisk: and was continued *four* years, extending to four volumes.

Several tractates, essays and biographic notices of members read before the Association at different times, have been kindly published in the Boston Recorder and New England Puritan, and other religious papers. These articles may be regarded as generally expressing the views and feelings of the body upon the topics so presented.

QUESTIONS FOR DISCUSSION.

In the following list of questions, the date of their adoption for discussion is added, as a suggestive guide to their importance. Those marked with an asterisk were assigned to some one member to write upon. The remainder were discussed orally.

1794. *June 3d.* * Whether the soul after death, does or does not sleep during the intermediate state?

* Whether or not there be any proof, the Bible excepted, that there is another state of existence for man?

1807. *June 9th.* Meaning of "the first resurrection"—Rev. 20: 6. Whether there be sufficient argument to support the doctrine of the intermediate state?

Oct. 13th. Meaning of mens' being rewarded according to their works?

1809. *June 13th.* Is it lawful in any case, for individuals to withdraw from a church without its consent, on account of corruption in doctrine and practice?

What is the ground of moral obligation?

Oct. 10th. Whether our Saviour returned thanks after eating?

At what time did the Jewish dispensation end, and the Christian dispensation commence?

1810. *June 12th.* Do such universal promises as "all flesh shall be saved," and "in him shall all the families of the earth be blessed," etc., embrace all who have lived and shall live in time to come, or only those who are to live on the earth in some future day?

Is it proper, under any existing circumstances, for congregational ministers to baptize by immersion unbaptized persons?

Oct. 9th. Have a plurality of gods been worshipped as gods, or as inferior deities and intercessors between the worshippers and the Supreme Being?

Ought churches to pay any regard to the sentiments and practices of other churches of the same denomination, in dismissing and recommending members to their communion?

Will the first and third persons in the Trinity ever be visible to Saints in Heaven?

1811. *June 11th.* Meaning of probation in this world?

May God reward men in time, and punish them in eternity for the same actions?

Oct. 8th. Meaning of 'the sin of the world' which Christ took away, and how did he take it away?

Why is the punishment of the finally impenitent endless?

1812. *June 9th.* In what does the righteousness of Christ consist?

Oct. 13th. Is there any foundation in the Scriptures for the formation of a Consociation of churches, as an Ecclesiastical body, to which individual churches may appeal for a final decision in cases of discipline?

Is an individual member belonging to a church, to be censured for neglecting the communion, who pleads *conscience* on account of ill treatment which in his opinion he has received by a vote of the church?

Does the Divine Law require men to love their neighbors *as much* as they do themselves?

1813. *June 8th.* Was Christ the Son of God before his incarnation?

Is there any foundation in the Scriptures for the use of the term *Infant Baptism*?

Oct. 12th. Is there any foundation in the Scriptures for *delegates* to vote in the ordination of a minister?

1815. *May 16th.* If delegates are allowed to *vote* with respect to the ordination of ministers, why may they not consistently *assist* in the ordination?

Do ministers ordain *ex officio*, or act under the authority of the churches exclusively?

Oct. 10th. Did John the Baptist require a profession of repentance and faith previous to his administering the ordinance of baptism?

When may a minister be said to have left the ministry?

1816. *June 11th.* What obligations are Christians under to profess religion?

Oct. 8th. * What authority have we for the imposition of hands at an Installation?

Is there Scriptural authority for the use of the sword in any case?

1817. *Oct. 7th.* Was there any difference between the church and society in Corinth?

How long a period will the Millennium continue?

1818. *June 2d.* What was the design of John's Baptism?

* In what will the future punishment of the wicked consist?

Oct. 6th. * Import of the fifth petition in the Lord's prayer?

1819. *June 1st.* Is it agreeable to the Scriptures for a council to ordain a candidate as pastor of a *parish*?

Did the Jewish tythes pay the expenses of civil government as well as of religious worship, or only of the latter?

1821. *June 5th.* Did the Divine nature of Christ suffer on the cross?

Is true faith the *only* condition of salvation?

1822. *June 18th.* What is the true province of reason in ascertaining the doctrines of revelation?

Would it be subservient to the interests of religion for the Massachusetts Convention of Ministers to discuss and decide the question, What constitutes a Christian church?

Oct. 15th. Is 1 John 5 : 7 canonical, or an interpolation?

To what must the ultimate appeal be made in establishing the principles of interpretation?

1823. *June 17th.* When are children too old to be baptized on account of the faith of their parents?

Does native depravity originate from a privative cause?

1824. *April 27th.* Meaning of Pilate's question to Christ, "What is truth?"

As the laws of this State permit individuals to join any ecclesiastical society which they choose, ought our churches and societies to make any exertions to obtain an amendment to the laws, so that our parishes may have the power of refusing such applicants under certain circumstances?

Ought a church member who has committed a public offence worthy of discipline, to be required to make a confession before the congregation?

Oct. 19th. Is the agency of God the same in governing the conduct of holy and unholy creatures?

Can any particular method of ecclesiastical government be supported from the Scriptures?

1825. *April 26th.* Had the Apostles and primitive Christians any apprehension that the end of the world was nigh in their time?

Have the ministers of Christ received authority from him to license candidates, and to ordain them to the ministerial work? And does this authority cease with the ordination?

Oct. 25*th.* * What is the foundation for the common arrangement of the books in the Bible?

* May God both reward and punish a person for the same conduct?

1827. *April* 24*th.* "By man came death," — what death?

* What motives shall be used to induce creatures totally selfish, to embrace the Gospel?

1828. *April* 29*th.* Did our Saviour give thanks after eating?

* What is the penalty of the divine law?

1829. *April* 28*th.* * How are we to understand those passages of the Scriptures which employ the term *fire* in reference to future punishment?

* Is there any rule by which we can determine what proportion of our property ought to be devoted to benevolent and religious purposes?

1830. *April* 27*th.* * What do the Scriptures teach concerning the existence and agency of Devils?

1831. *Aug.* 16*th.* * Are there any *means* of regeneration appointed in the Scriptures to be used by unrenewed sinners?

Oct. 25*th.* * What are the Scriptural means to promote revivals of religion?

1832. *April* 24*th.* * Can man act independently?

* Is it necessary to the moral government of God that there be a penalty to the divine law? If so, is this penalty efficient as a motive to induce sinners to obey?

1833. *Aug.* 20*th.* What is the Scriptural process of church discipline?

1833. *Oct.* 29*th.* * Is it necessary that a complaint entered against a brother in the church should specify *all* the particular acts which it is designed to prove against him, and the *time* when the censurable acts were done?

* Did Christ in the garden sweat drops of real blood?

1835. *April* 28*th.* * Are believers rewarded on the same ground on which they are forgiven?

* Is it expedient for ministers to exchange labors very frequently?

What is the best method of constructing a sermon?

Aug. 18*th.* Is the modern practice of settling ministers for a limited time, beneficial or prejudicial to the interests of religion?

* Does Romans vii. ch. describe the feelings of the impenitent sinner, or of the Christian?

* Does the Holy Spirit renew the hearts of sinners without the use of means? If so, what is the evidence? if not, what are the means?

Oct. 28*th.* * Was the human soul of Christ saved by grace, or was he admitted into heaven on account of having yielded perfect obedience to the divine law?

* Did Christ, in making atonement for sin, suffer in his divine nature?

1837. *April* 25*th.* What is the object of 'laying on of hands,' at ordination?

* Can the *consistency* between divine and human agency in the moral actions of men be seen?

Aug. 15*th.* * Is there any distinction between justification and pardon?

Nov. 21*st.* * Meaning of "whom he did foreknow?"

* What are we to understand by the intercession of Christ, and what is its influence in the salvation of men?

Why, previous to Christ, was transgression followed, to so great an extent, with present penalty?

1838. *April* 24*th*. * What evidence is there that the books contained in the common version of the Bible, are the ones, and the only ones, which can justly claim to be inspired?

1839. *April* 30*th*. What is the meaning of sovereignty when applied to God?

Are protracted meetings on the whole a good measure for promoting religion?

Oct. 29*th*. Have Christians, in any case, a right to defend themselves by force?

* What is the real difference between Arminianism and Calvinism?

Is it desirable that our churches take any action respecting communion with slave-holders, or admitting them to the pulpit?

1840. *Aug.* 18*th*. What is clerical etiquette, to be observed between neighboring ministers?

A man is a member of the church, and his wife is not. He died before his child is baptized. Is that child a subject of baptism? And if so, who is to present it?

Oct. 27*th*. Is the *dedication* of a child by the parents, an essential part of infant baptism?

* What is the doctrine of professed modern Perfectionism? and is it taught in the Bible?

1841. *April* 27*th*. * Is a literal return of the Jews to Palestine predicted in the Scriptures? And if so, what bearing have recent events in the East upon this subject?

* Is the exercise of love or any other affection at the direct command of the will?

Oct. 19*th*. Is any exercise of Christian affection *perfect* in its character?

Is it expedient and advisable to encourage and patronize missionary associations formed on the principle of refusing the contributions of slave-holders?

1842. *April* 19*th*. * What relation do baptized children sustain to the church?

* Can a future state of existence be proved from the Old Testament?

Oct. 18*th*. * Does βαπτίζω mean to purify, without reference to the mode?

1843. *April* 18*th*. * Do the Scriptures teach that there will be a millennium of peculiar holiness and happiness upon *this* earth?

Aug. 15*th*. The duty of the church toward those members who neglect the ordinance of Infant Baptism?

Have ministers a right to ordain for the Gospel ministry independently of the churches?

Oct. 17*th*. * How far is the Cambridge Platform our rule of discipline?

Dec. 19*th*. How far ought the building of meeting-houses at the west to be aided by the churches at the east?

What advice shall a pastor give to the members of his church going south, respecting their communion with slave-holding churches?

1844. *April* 16*th*. What are the *political* duties of pastors at the present time?

Aug. 20*th*. Is it consistent or right for Congregational churches to admit as members those who disbelieve in infant baptism?

Oct. 15*th*. * Ought capital punishment to be abolished?

Dec. 17*th*. What course of proceeding ought our churches to take with those members who have fallen into the errors and irregularities of Millerism?

1845. *April* 8*th*. Is it right for a man to marry his paternal half-brother's daughter?

1845. *Aug.* 12*th.* What is odd-fellowship? and what is the duty of ministers and churches in reference to it?

Oct. 14*th.* * Ought slave-holding to be treated by the churches as other sins?

* What is the Bible view of infant salvation?

1846. *Jan.* 13*th.* * Did Christ suffer in his divine nature in making atonement for sin?

* What is the great end of punishment?

April 14*th.* * Does God experience any degree of suffering in connection with his perfect happiness?

Shall the basis of organization of the General Association be so modified as to admit of a lay delegation?

Aug. 11*th.* * Does the New Testament authorize divorce for any other reason than adultery? Or, if the courts grant a bill of divorce for other reasons, has the party which obtains a bill, a *moral* right to marry again?

Is God *necessarily* a good Being?

Oct. 13*th.* Why cannot a member of a church, of his own accord, leave the church?

* What can we do as ministers of Christ to increase each other's usefulness?

1847. *Jan.* 12*th.* * Is the agency of God universal and particular?

What is our duty towards the "Evangelical Alliance?"

April 13*th.* * Is there a succession of exercises in the Divine Mind?

Oct. 12*th.* Ought a minister to be a member of his own church?

* The significance and use of infant baptism?

1848. *April* 12*th.* * What is the duty of ministers and churches in relation to the order of the Sons of Temperance and other secret societies?

Aug. 22*d.* Is it advisable for our Congregational

churches so to alter their creeds and covenants as to admit persons as members, who deny that infant baptism is a Scriptural rite?

1848. *Oct.* 10*th.* * Orthodoxy, the antagonist of superstition.

Have the majority of a church the right to contravene its articles of faith and covenant, to accommodate individuals, against the protest of a minority?

1849. *Jan.* 9*th.* * Was Melchisedeck a divine person?

Is it advisable to continue our separate county organizations for benevolent purposes?

April 10*th.* * Review of "Dr. Smith on Infant Salvation."

Aug. 14*th.* * Is sin the necessary means of the greatest good?

Oct. 9*th.* Is it right for a Congregational church to dismiss its members, and recommend them to a Methodist church?

1850. *Jan.* 8*th.* Is there any specific rule by which the amount of our Christian charities, or pecuniary benefactions, should be regulated?

* What is the nature of the unpardonable sin?

April 16*th.* Is an individual a proper subject of church discipline who removes from a place where his property remains, and where the Gospel *is supported* by taxation, and who 'signs off' from the parish, in order to avoid such taxation?

Should a pastor leave a notice to be read by an exchange, which he would not give himself? And if so, who takes the responsibility?

Is the prevalence of a universal language during the Millennium predicted, as in Zeph. 3 : 9?

* What is the origin, propriety, and true signification of the benediction, as practised in Christian assemblies?

Aug. 13*th.* Are there any limitations of *age* in respect to the subjects of household baptism?

1850. * Review of the 'Conventional Sermon by Prof. E. A. Park."

Is congregational *sitting* a proper posture in public prayer? And what is ministerial duty in relation to this practice?

Oct. 8th. * The duty of ministers in regard to 'the Fugitive Slave Bill,' or in regard to the fugitive who in distress may come to us for protection?

1851. *Jan. 14th.* * The household *versus* Socialism.

* History of the doctrine of Imputation.

April 15th. Is there any difference between common and special grace? and, if any, what?

Aug. 13th. * What obedience to the husband do the Scriptures enjoin on the wife, and what authority do they give the husband over the wife?

TEXTS OF EXEGETICAL ESSAYS.

As the date of their exhibition is of no consequence, they are arranged in their order of occurrence in the Bible.

Gen. 1 : 1; 4 : 7; 1 : 27; 6 : 14. Psalms, 15 : 5; 68 : 30; 74 : 4. Proverbs, 16 : 7; 25 : 2. Eccl. 7 : 29. Isaiah, 23 : 18; 42 : 19; 53 : 8; with Acts, 8 : 33; 66 : 22. Ezekiel, 24 : 13; 37 : 4. Zephaniah, 3 : 9. Matt. 6 : 10; 11 : 12; 12 : 43–5; 16 : 28; 19 : 14; 26 : 39. Mark, 2 : 27–8. Luke, 10 : 18; 11 : 9; 15 : 7; 18 : 8. John, 1 : 1; 1 : 9; 14 : 21; 16 : 8; 17 : 12; 19 : 11, l. c. Acts, 3 : 21; 8 : 33; with Isa. 53 : 8. Romans, 3 : 4; 5 : 14; 5 : 19; 6 : 23; 7 : 14; 8 : 16; 8 : 19–23; 9 : 3; 11 : 32. I. Corinthians, 3 : 23; 5 : 5; 11 : 3; 15 : 29. II. Corinthians, 5 : 1. Galatians, 4 : 22. Ephesians, 6 : 4. Philippians, 3 : 11–12. II. Thessalonians, 1 : 9. I. Timothy, 5 : 8. Hebrews, 2 : 11; 5 : 7; 13 : 17. James, 2 : 10; I. Peter, 3 : 19. II. Peter, 2 : 1. I. John, 3 : 9. Revelation, 20 : 4–6; 20 : 5.

APPROBATION OF CANDIDATES FOR THE MINISTRY.

At the date of the formation of this Association, the practice of admitting only *approved* candidates to the sacred desk, had been generally adopted. 'In the beginning it was not so.' The brethren of the church at Plymouth, gave leave to any of their number to 'prophesy,' subject to the regulation of the Elders of the church, who thus 'ruled over' them. In the Massachusetts colony, the matter of 'prophesying' early occupied the attention of the court. They first legislated upon the subject of the pastoral office.

In 1651, The church in Malden was *fined* for settling a minister without consulting the neighboring churches. And in 1653, the court *forbade* the settlement of Mr. Powell over the second or north church in Boston, because he was not a learned man. An order was also passed that no minister should be called into office without the approbation and allowance of some of the magistrates as well as the neighboring churches. A similar order was adopted respecting candidates for the ministry.

"1653, *May* 18*th*. Ordered that no person shall begin to preach or prophesy without the approbation of elders belonging to the four next churches or county court."

The church of Woburn, and also of Salem, remonstrated against this order, on the ground that if they, the churches, had the power of election and ordination of ministers, they had the power of approbation also. 1 Cor. XIV. The order was repealed.*

In certain proposals, assented to by delegates of associations at a meeting in Boston 13th Sept. 1705, occur the following recommendation: "That the Candidates of the Ministry undergo a due Tryal by some one or other of the associations

---

* See this interesting petition of the Woburn church in Mass. Hist Coll. Series III. Vol. I, p. 39.

concerning their qualifications for the Evangelical Ministry: and that no particular Pastor or Congregation Imploy any one in occasional preaching who has not been recommended by a testimonial under the hands of some association."*

On this proposition Rev. J. Wise of Ipswich, who so sarcastically reviewed the proposals, makes the following historical comment: "Their degrees, with the express testimony of the college (when particularly desired), are sufficient testimonials of their learning: and the experience of their other good gifts and ministerial qualifications, obtained by converse and their occasional preaching has been the chief test and tryal of our candidates; and by these methods they have been approbated in order to settlement in office-trust: and this has been the custom of the country and churches for near fourscore years,"* — that is, from its settlement.

The practice, however, of approbating candidates by Clerical Associations obtained almost universally, though the other proposals of the meeting above-mentioned failed of adoption. In the Mendon Association, applicants for approbation to preach the Gospel have, from the beginning, been subjected to a thorough examination, as the first certificate already inserted witnesseth.

The *mode* of ascertaining the candidate's qualifications and the *form* of certifying to them have hardly varied during the century.

As to the *mode*, the following vote, passed June 7, 1785, expresses the present practice. "Voted that for the future, when any gentleman shall offer himself to this body, in order for recommendation as a candidate for the Gospel Ministry, the person thus offering himself shall first read a sermon; after which, secondly, there shall be a particular and systematic examination of his knowledge in Divinity, and acquaintance

* See Wise's Church's Quarrel Espoused; and Vindication of the government of the N. E. Churches.

with experimental religion: and thirdly, his design in preaching the Gospel."

The recommendation of convention of Congregational Ministers at Boston, May 26, 1790, met the cordial approval of Mendon Association, and agreement to admit none into their pulpits to preach, except such as had been examined and regularly approbated.

Certificates of approbation, at first, bore the signatures of all the members of the association present. In 1794 they were authenticated by the signatures of the moderator and scribe, and so continue to be. The form adopted 1802, is the latest recorded, and is still in use.

FORM OF RECOMMENDATION OF CANDIDATES FOR THE MINISTRY.

At a meeting of Mendon Association at the house of Rev. ———, in———, on the ——, Mr. ——— appeared, and requested to be recommended by the association to the churches as a preacher of the Gospel, and a candidate for the Christian Ministry. The association received authentic testimonials of his regular membership in the church of Christ, and of his having honorably completed a course of academic education. They examined him with respect to his views and feelings in contemplating to undertake this work, his attainments in the knowledge of the leading doctrines of Christianity, and his personal qualifications to perform the duties which will devolve upon him. Finding him in these several respects a person qualified, the association deemed it expedient to comply with his request: and do thereupon, by these presents, recommend the said Mr. —— —— to the churches, to be employed by them as a candidate for the Gospel Ministry, and to the patronage of the pastors of the churches, for this purpose.

——————— *Moderator.*

——————— *Scribe.*

LICENTIATES.

LIST of persons approbated to preach the Gospel, with the date of their approbation. The numbers refer to the Biographic Index. Those starred became members of the Association, and will be found, by the numbers in parentheses at the end of the name, among the sketches of members.

1. * David Thurston, Nov. 8, 1751, (O. S.) (5.)
2. Moses Taft, Jan. 7, 1752, (O. S.)
3. Cornelius Jones, May 9, 1753.
4. Nathaniel Potter, May, 1754.
5. Joseph Dorr, jr. Aug. 11, 1756.
6. Asaph Rice, Aug. 11, 1756.
7. Benjamin Caryl, Sept. 8, 1761.
8. * Ebenezer Chaplin, June 4, 1764. (9.)
9. Ezekiel Emerson, June 5, 1764.
10. Silas Biglow, July 9, 1766.
11. Alexander Thayer, June 28, 1768.
12. Josiah Reed, June 3, 1777.
13. Elisha Fish, jr., Oct. 30, 1781.
14. Moses Warren, June 7, 1785.
15. Jacob Cram, June 7, 1785.
16. Solomon Aikin, June 7, 1785.
17. Enoch Pond, Oct. 3, 1786.
18. Walter Harris, June 17, 1788.
19. Reed Paige, June 2, 1789.
20. Elias Dudley, June 2, 1789.
21. Herman Daggett, Oct. 7, 1789.
22. Royal Tyler, Oct. 7, 1789.
23. Josiah Holbrook, Oct. 5, 1790.
24. Holloway Fish, Oct. 4, 1791.
25. John Morse, Feb. 14, 1792.
26. * Samuel Judson, June 5, 1792. (22.)
27. Nathaniel Hall, June 5, 1792.

28. John Fitch, June 5, 1792.
29. Eli Smith, Oct. 2, 1792.
30. William Jackson, June 4, 1793.
31. Kiah Bailey, June 3, 1794.
32. Abijah Wines, Jan. 13, 1795.
33. John Smith, Jan. 13, 1795.
34. Nathaniel Ogden, Oct. 14, 1795.
35. John Bowers Preston, Oct. 14, 1795.
36. Joseph Rowell, June 12, 1798.
37. * Nathan Holman, June 12, 1798. (26.)
38. Drury Fairbank, Aug. 15, 1798.
39. Leonard Worcester, March 12, 1799.
40. Joseph Emerson, June 9, 1801.
41. Nathan Waldo, jr. Oct. 13, 1801.
42. Levi Nelson, June 9, 1802.
43. Joseph Cheney, Oct. 13, 1802.
44. Sherman Johnson, Oct. 11, 1803.
45. * David Holman, jr. Oct. 9, 1804. (33.)
46. Gaius Conant, Oct. 9, 1804.
47. * Daniel Thomas, Oct. 9, 1804. (41.)
48. Stephen Chapin, Oct. 9, 1804.
49. Elnathan Walker, June 11, 1805.
50. Algernon Sidney Bailey, Oct. 14, 1806.
51. * Samuel Wood Colburn, Oct. 11, 1808. (35.)
52. Nathaniel Rawson, Jan. 10, 1809.
53. Isaac Perkins Lowe, Jan. 10, 1809.
54. Martin Moore, June 10, 1812.
55. John Burt Wight, Oct. 14, 1812.
56. * Josephus Wheaton, June 14, 1814. (38.)
57. Emerson Paine, June 14, 1814.
58. Enoch Pond, June 14, 1814.
59. * Alvan Cobb, Oct. 11, 1814. (37.)
60. Jonas Perkins, Oct. 11, 1814.
61. Stetson Raymond, Aug. 2, 1815.
62. Lot Bumpas Sullivan, Aug. 2, 1815

63. Moses Partridge, June 11, 1816.
64. John Luke Parkhurst, June 3, 1817.
65. Willard Holbrook, June 3, 1817.
66. Abel Manning, Feb. 9, 1818.
67. William Tyler, Oct. 6, 1818.
68. Jonathan Longley, June 1, 1819.
69. David Brigham, June 1, 1819.
70. Zolva Whitmore, Oct. 5, 1819.
71. * Sewall Harding, Oct. 5, 1819. (61.)
72. Silas Shores, June 6, 1820.
73. John Milton Putnam, June 6, 1820.
74. George Fisher, Oct. 3, 1820.
75. * John Ferguson, June 5, 1821. (42.)
76. * Moses Thacher, June 19, 1822. (43.)
77. Augustus Brown Reed, Oct. 15, 1822.
78. Levi Packard, Oct. 15, 1822.
79. * James Ormsbee Barney, June 17, 1823. (44.)
80. Henry Harrison Fayette Sweet, Oct. 21, 1823.
81. * Tyler Thacher, April 26, 1825. (64.)
82. James Tisdale, Oct. 25, 1825.
83. Lucius Watson Clark, Oct. 31, 1826.
84. Sylvester Graham, Oct. 31, 1826.
85. * Charles Jarvis Warren, Oct. 30, 1827. (47.)
86. Cyrus Whitman Conant, Oct. 30, 1827.
87. William Harlow, Oct. 30, 1827.
88. * Elam Smalley, Oct. 28, 1828. (49.)
89. Gilbert Fay, Oct. 28, 1828.
90. John Forbush, Dec. 31, 1829.
91. Varnum Noyes, April 27, 1830.
92. Isaac Erwin Heaton, Oct. 28, 1834.
93. Thomas Edwards, Aug. 16, 1836.
94. Eli Thurston, Aug. 16, 1836.
95. Charles Turner Torrey, Oct. 25, 1836.
96. Elnathan Davis, Oct. 25, 1836.
97. John Dwight, Jan. 25, 1837.

98. * Mortimer Blake, April 24, 1838. (56.)
99. Edmund Dowse, April 24, 1838.
100. * Charles Chamberlain, Aug. 21, 1838. (75.)
101. * Samuel Hunt, Aug. 21, 1838. (76.)
102. * Daniel Jefferson Poor, Aug. 20, 1839. (55.)
103. William Phipps, jr. Aug. 20, 1839.
104. Jonathan Grout, April 28, 1840.
105. Joseph Homes Bailey, Aug. 16, 1842.
106. * Preston Pond, jr. August 16, 1842. (73.)
107. Richard Cecil Spofford, Aug. 16, 1842.
108. Horace Deane Walker, Oct. 18, 1842.
109. Abraham Jenkins, jr. Aug. 15, 1843.
110. Edward Pratt, Dec. 19, 1843.
111. Malachi Bullard, jr. Dec. 19, 1843.
112. Allen Lincoln, April 16, 1844.
113. William Makepeace Thayer, Oct. 16, 1844.
114. James M. Bacon, Dec. 17, 1844.
115. Josiah Lyman Armes, Aug. 12, 1845.
116. Ezra Newton, jr. April 14, 1846.
117. Hiram Clark Daniels, Aug. 11, 1846.
118. John Wheeler Harding, April 11, 1848.
119. Frederick Augustus Fiske, Aug. 14, 1849.
120. Henry Lobdell, Aug. 13, 1851.
121. John Edwin Corey, Nov. 19, 1851.

MEMBERS.

A List of the members of Mendon Association, with the dates of their admission and dismission. Those *starred* died in connection. Those marked (†) were dismissed on removal elsewhere.

1. * Joseph Dorr,
2. * Nathan Webb,
3. * Amariah Frost,
4. * Elisha Fish.

} Original members, Nov. 8, 1751, O. S.

5. † David Thurston, admitted May, 1754.
6. * David Hall, D. D. ——
7. † Aaron Hutchinson, May 10, 1757.
8. † Caleb Barnum, June 4, 1764.
9. * Ebenezer Chaplin, Oct. 8, 1765.
10. * Isaac Stone, May or June, 1772.
11. * David Sanford, ——
12. * Nathaniel Emmons, D. D., between 1773 and 1781.
13. * Elijah Fitch, ——
14. † Josiah Spaulding, 1772; dismissed 1787.
15. † John Crane, D. D., Oct. 7, 1783; dis. Oct. 6, 1818.*
16. † David Avery, Oct. 3, 1786; dis. 1796.
17. † Caleb Alexander, Oct. 3, 1786; dis. 1803.
18. * Timothy Dickinson, June 1, 1790.
19. † Edmund Mills, June 7, 1791; dis. Oct. 6, 1818.*
20. † John Robinson, June 5, 1792; dismissed 1815.
21. * Nathaniel Howe, June 5, 1792.
22. † Samuel Judson, Oct. 2, 1793; dism. Oct. 6, 1818.*
23. * John Wilder, June 3, 1794.
24. † Benjamin Wood, Oct. 11, 1797; dism. Oct. 6, 1818.*
25. * John Cleveland, March 12, 1799.
26. † Nathan Holman, Dec. 10, 1800; dismissed 1825.
27. † Otis Thompson, "
28. * David Long, June 9, 1801.
29. * Elisha Fiske, June 8, 1802.
30. † Samuel Austin, D. D. " ; dismissed 1805.
31. † William Warren, Oct. 9, 1804.
32. † Preserved Smith, June 15, 1808; dismissed, 1812.
33. † David Holman, June 13, 1809; dism. Oct. 6, 1818.*
34. † Elisha Rockwood, Oct. 9, 1810. " " "
35. † Samuel Wood Colburn. ——
36. Jacob Ide, D. D., May 16, 1815.
37. † Alvan Cobb, " "; dism. April 29, 1834.

* See note, at the end of this list.

38. * Josephus Wheaton, Oct. 8, 1816.
39. Thomas Williams, June 3, 1817; dism. Oct. 25, 1825; and readmitted, April 15, 1851.
40. * Calvin Park, D. D., June 5, 1821.
41. † Daniel Thomas, "
42. † John Ferguson, June 18, 1822.
43. † Moses Thacher, Oct. 21, 1823.
44. † James Ormsbee Barney, Oct. 19, 1824.
45. † Willard Pierce, April 26, 1825.
46. † Charles Fitch, April 25, 1826.
47. † Charles Jarvis Warren, Ap. 29, 1828; dis. Ap. 29, 1834.
48. † Preston Cummings, Oct. 28, 1828.
49. † Elam Smalley, D.D., Oct. 27, 1829; dis. Aug. 19, 1840.
50. † Amos Augustus Phelps, Oct. 26, 1830.
51. † Harrison Greenough Park, Oct. 29, 1833.
52. † Asahel Bigelow, Oct. 28, 1834; dis. Aug. 21, 1838.
53. David Sanford, April 30, 1838.
54. † Tertius Dunning Southworth, Aug. 20, 1839; dis. Oct. 8, 1850.
55. Daniel Jefferson Poor, April 28, 1840.
56. Mortimer Blake, Aug. 18, 1840.
57. † Moses Gill Grosvenor, Oct. 19, 1841.
58. Thomas T. Richmond, April 18, 1843.
59. Timothy Dwight Porter Stone, Aug. 15, 1843.
60. † David R. Barnes, " "
61. Sewall Harding, Oct. 17, 1843.
62. Andrew Hunter Reed, "
63. Horace James, Dec. 19, 1843.
64. † Tyler Thacher, Aug. 20, 1844; dis. Oct. 8, 1850.
65. † Smith B. Goodenow, Dec. 17, 1844; dis. Oct. 12, 1847.
66. Charles Simmons, April 18, 1843.
67. † Calvin White, Aug. 12, 1845.
68. † Oramel W. Cooley, Aug. 22, 1848; dism. Nov. 19, 1851.

69. † Henry Lewis Bullen, April 12, 1848.
70. William Barnes, Oct. 10, 1848.
71. Joshua Thomas Tucker, Aug. 14, 1849.
72. Preston Pond, jr. Jan. 8, 1850.
73. George Harrison Newhall, Oct. 8, 1850.
74. Charles Chamberlain, " "
75. Samuel Hunt, Jan. 14, 1851.
76. John Haskell, " "
77. Asa Hixon, April 15, 1851.

NOTE. In 1818, Oct. 6th, six members obtained a dismission, for the purpose of forming another Association. Their request is thus recorded:

NORTHBRIDGE, OCT. 5, 1818.

BRETHREN,

We, the subscribers, members of Mendon Association, wish, on account of local conveniences, to form another Association by ourselves, and with such others as may wish to unite with us; and ask, that the body with which we are now connected will grant us this request.

At the same time, we wish to have it understood, that we retain the same fraternal affection which has ever subsisted among us. We remain yours, brethren, with affection and esteem,

JOHN CRANE,
EDMUND MILLS,
SAMUEL JUDSON,
BENJAMIN WOOD,
ELISHA ROCKWOOD,
DAVID HOLMAN.

Thus and then originated the Harmony Association.

LIST OF TOWNS,

Which have been ministerially connected with the Mendon Association.

Abington.
Attleboro'.
" East.
Dedham, South.
Dighton.
Douglas.
Dover.
Foxboro'.
Franklin.
Grafton.
Holliston.
Hopkinton.
Mansfield.
Medfield.
Medway, West.
" East.
" Village.
Mendon.
Milford.
Milbury.
Northbridge.
Rehoboth.
Seekonk.
Stoughton.
Sutton.
Taunton, West.
Upton.
Uxbridge.
Walpole.
Westboro'.
Worcester, South.
Wrentham.
" North.

Total, 33.

PRESENT TERRITORIAL EXTENT.

Dover.
Foxboro'.
Franklin.
Holliston.
Mansfield.
Medfield.
Medway, West.
" East.
Medway Village.
Mendon.
Milford.
Walpole.
Wrentham.
" North.

Total, 14.

BIOGRAPHICAL SKETCHES

OF THE

MEMBERS OF MENDON ASSOCIATION.

THE authorities for these sketches are the Quarterly Register, Hist. and Geneal. Register, Panoplist, Mass. Hist. Collections, Ordination and Funeral Sermons in the Library of Brown University, and elsewhere, newspaper obituaries, and an extensive correspondence with the persons themselves, or their successors and descendants. For this last valuable assistance, the compiler would here express his acknowledgments.

He has taken the liberty of rearranging articles, when needful, to adapt them to one common form. Dates are given in the *style* of their own time of occurrence. The sketches are as complete as he had the means of making them, without delaying the publication of the work too long beyond its occasion. And he would take this opportunity to request any *corrections* or *additional information*, which may be with those into whose hands this book may fall, to be forwarded to him, to be placed in the care of the Association for future use. Particularly, *genealogical* items will be valuable.

1. REV. JOSEPH DORR,

Was the youngest son except one, of Rev. Edward and Elizabeth Dorr, and was born in Roxbury about 1689.* He

---

* Rev. Edward Dorr had the following children: 1st. Edward, born

graduated at Harvard 1711, and received the degree of A. M. in course. He was ordained over the church in Mendon, 25 Feb. 1716, and continued in the ministry there until his death, 9 March, 1768, aged 79.

Mr. Dorr's predecessor in the pastoral office, was Rev. Grindal Rawson, (youngest son and child of Edward Rawson, the famous secretary of the Massachusetts Colony from 1650 to 1686,) whose daughter, Mary, he married 9 April, 1724. Her mother was Susanna, daughter of Rev. John Wilson of Medfield, and granddaughter of Rev. John Wilson, the first minister of Boston. By this alliance he also became connected with the celebrated John Hooker, and Edmund Grindal, the renowned Archbishop of Canterbury, of the reign of Queen Elizabeth.*

Mendon Association certainly had good Puritan blood in the *family* of its first moderator.

Mr. Dorr's children were:—

1. Mary, b. 6 June, 1725, the wife of Rev. Moses Taft. (See Licentiates, No. 2.)

2. Joseph Jr., b. 24 May, 1730. (See Licentiates, No. 4.)

3. Katharine, b. 8 March, 1732, and married Rev. Ezekiel Emerson. (See Licentiates, No. 9.)

4. Susanna, b. 4 Sept., 1784, and married Rev. Amariah Frost. [See Members, No. 3.]

Mrs. Dorr was born 22 June, 1699, and died 9 April, 1776, aged 77.

Nov. 15, 1683. 2nd. Ebenezer, b. 25 Jan., 1687. 3d. Joseph, b. about 1689, or 90, (birth not recorded.) 4th. Edward, b. Oct. 19, 1692. *Church Records of Roxbury*. Of the father, no notice has been found. He is not mentioned amongst the ministers of Roxbury by Farmer, and yet his great grandson, E. Frost, M. D., of Meriden, N. H., asserts him to be a clergyman. Was Edward, the minister of Hartford, the maternal uncle of Dr. E. D. Griffin, his eldest son, and did the title of Rev. belong to the son instead of the father?

* Hist. and Geneal. Register, Vol. III, p. 201 and 310.

Rev. Mr. Dorr's character is thus summarily expressed upon his tombstone. "He was endowed with good sense. His temper was mild and placid. He excelled in the virtues of meekness, patience, temperance, sobriety, gravity, benevolence, and charity; was a good scholar, a learned divine, and exemplary Christian."

The above facts are all which an extensive inquiry has elicited respecting the projector and first moderator of our Association. That he sympathized with the revival of 1740, and with Edwardean sentiments, is a rational inference from the fact of his signature to the "testimony" in favor of that work of grace. The ministerial character of his family argues its decided piety and intelligence. Nothing is known of his publications, or of the success of his ministry.

2. REV. NATHAN WEBB

Graduated at Harvard, 1725; was ordained over the church in Uxbridge, 3 February, 1731; and died there in the pastoral office, 14 March, 1772, in the 67th year of his age, and 41st of his ministry. He was consequently born about 1707; where, it has not been ascertained. He married Elizabeth (Pratt?)

His widow subsequently married, November, 1773, Isaac Coit, Esq., a very respectable citizen of Plainfield, Ct., a widower of 59, and without children. He died, still without issue, 23 April, 1776. His widow, formerly Mrs. Webb, then married, 30 November, 1779, a Rev. Mr. Jones of Western.*

The following is the inscription upon Mr. Webb's gravestone: —

* Letter of Rev. R. C. Learned, Canterbury, Ct.

SACRED TO THE MEMORY OF THE

REVEREND AND LEARNED NATHAN WEBB,

PASTOR OF THE CHURCH OF CHRIST,

IN UXBRIDGE:

Who, after a laborious life in the Gospel Ministry, Resigned his Ministerial office in God's Sanctuary for the sublime Employments of Immortality, March 14, 1772; In the 67th year of his age, And the 42nd year of his Ministry.

MEMENTO MORI.*

3. REV. AMARIAH FROST

Was the son of Mr. Samuel and Elizabeth (Rice) Frost, and was born in Framingham, 4 October, 1720. He graduated at Harvard 1740, and A. M., was ordained over the second church in Mendon, (now Milford,) 21 December, 1743, and died 14 March, 1792, aged seventy-two years.

The following interesting document, in his own handwriting, is copied from the church-records of Milford: —

"A record of my genealogy, as far as I can trace it back according to the best accounts received by tradition:

"JOHN FROST of England, in the time of the Nonconformists, wherein a great number were silenced in England, was one of *them.* Two of his sons came to America, — fled for refuge to this then savage wilderness, to escape the more savage oppression and enjoy the freedom of Englishmen. *Samuel Frost,* my father, of Framingham, in the county of Middlesex, and province of Massachusetts Bay, in New England, was a descendant of the fifth generation, *(ut puto).*†

---

* Letter of Rev. J. J. Abbot, Uxbridge.

† Dr. Elias Frost, of Plainfield, N. H., furnishes the following grounds of this "puto."

1. Rev. *John Frost,* the silenced non-conformist, whose two sons, Nicholas and *Edmund,* came to America, about 1635; of whom, Nicholas settled in Portsmouth, N. H.

2. *Edmund Frost* settled at Cambridge, and was ruling elder in Rev.

My mother was a Rice, the daughter of Dea. Rice of Framingham aforesaid, and was descended from the Walkers of England, (mother's side). I, *Amariah Frost*, of Mendon, (Millriver,) now Milford, in the county of Worcester, was born at Framingham, in the county of Middlesex, 4 October, 1720. Married Esther Messinger, daughter of Rev. Henry Messinger, of Wrenthan, county of Suffolk, (now Norfolk,) 27 April, 1747."

By this marriage, Rev. Mr. Frost had five children; the first, Esther, died young. The others were as follows: —

2. Amariah, b. 5 Feb. 1750. H. U. 1770, and preached some time in Ward. He died in Sanford, Me.

3. Sarah, b. 24 May, 1751; and married Rev. Hezekiah Taylor of New Fane, Vt.

4. Olive, b. 19 February, 1753; and married Dr. Samuel Willard, an eminent physician of Uxbridge.

5. Elizabeth, b. 6 September, 1754; and married Dr. Isaac Brigham, of Milford.

Rev. Mr. Frost's wife died 5 January, 1778. He then married Susanna, the youngest daughter of Rev. Joseph Dorr, of Mendon, and had two children. The first, Mary, died young. The second, Elias, was born 10 January, 1782. Fitted for college at Leicester, and with Dr. Crane of North-

---

Thomas Shepard's church; and who had children, — 1. *John*, born in England. 2. James, Dea. at Billerica, and died 12 August, 1711, aged 74. 3. Samuel; and 4. Joseph.

3. *John Frost*, the child immigrant, supposed to have a son, *Thomas*, who took 300 acres of land in Framingham in 1700.

4. *Thomas* Frost had sons, Thomas, jr, and doubtless *Samuel*.

5. *Samuel* Frost, the fifth generation from Rev. John, the non-conformist, and father of Rev. Amariah Frost of Milford. He married Elizabeth Rice, and had seven children. 1. Keziah, born 1 Dec. 1711. 2. Bezaleel, born 8 September, 1713. 3. Samuel, born 13 Dec. 1715, and married Rebecca How. 4. Amasa, born 24 Jan. 1717. 5. *Amariah*, born 4 Oct. 1720. 6. Elizabeth, born 10 May, 1724, and married Isaac Cutler. 7. Lois, 2 Oct. 1732, and married Phinehas Goodenow.

bridge. Graduated at Brown University, 1804. A. M. and M. D. in 1824. He has since extensively practised medicine in Plainfield, N. H., where he now resides.

Rev. Mr. Frost was again deprived of his wife, 21 June, 1783; and he married Mrs. Sarah Adams, who survived him.

Mr. Frost was reputed an excellent man, and one of the most popular preachers of his age. It is a sufficient indication of his reputation, and of his attainments, to state, that he was extensively resorted to as an instructor of young men, fitting for college and for the ministry. A list of his pupils is not preserved. But among them were, his son Amariah, Thomas Haven, son of Rev. Elias Haven of Franklin, and settled in Reading 2d church, and Hezekiah Taylor, afterwards of New Fane; and also Alexander Scammel, one of the aids of General Washington in the Revolution.

None of his works were published, save the charge at the ordination of Mr. T. Dickinson, Holliston, — the last charge he ever gave.

4. REV. ELISHA FISH

Was the son of Mr. Moses Fish, a respectable farmer of Groton, Ct. He was born 1719; graduated at Harvard 1750, and A. M., and was ordained over the church in Upton, 5 June, 1751. He continued in the pastoral office forty-four years, and died 6 August, 1795, aged seventy-six years. He married Hannah Fobes, the daughter of Dea. Fobes of Westboro', by whom he had nine children, six of whom survived him, viz:

1. Martha, married —— Page.
2. Abigail, married Elijah Warren.
3. Elisha, jr., (v. Licentiates, No. 13.)
4. Holloway, (v. Licentiates, No. 24.)
5. Henry, married a Holmes.

6. Eunice, married Rev. Mr. Langdon, and now lives with Wm. Fay of Cincinnati, her son-in-law.

Mr. Fish's characteristics have been thus laconically summed up; "He was a grave and good man of the Puritan stamp; gave himself wholly to the ministry; was soundly orthodox; governed his own household, the church of God, and his own tongue and passions." *

The following extracts from his funeral sermon, by his long-tried and intimate friend, Dr. Emmons, may be considered just: —

"The better to prepare him for His own service, God was pleased to give him, for a long time, most clear and distressing views of the enmity, malignity, and total corruption of the human heart.

"Being persuaded it was his duty to preach the Gospel, he surmounted peculiar difficulties, and obtained a liberal education. And as soon as he had finished his academical course, he immediately offered himself as a candidate to the work, to which his heart had been long and zealously attached.

"Being understandingly and heartily attached to the peculiar doctrines of grace, he made them the common subjects of his public discourses. He made a point of explaining the Gospel, and of giving his hearers a clear, connected, and extensive view of the great scheme of redemption. He possessed the rare talents of a good casuist.

"He annually visited every family in his whole congregation, in order to know the state of his flock.

"He carried his religion into all places and into all companies. His house appeared like a bethel; especially on the Sabbath, for which he maintained and inculcated a most sacred reverence. His veracity and integrity were never, perhaps, so much as called in question.

---

* Letter of Rev. W. Warren, Upton.

"His occasional publications served the cause of liberty and religion. And his vigorous exertions in ecclesiastical councils did essential benefit to the churches of Christ.

"Mr. Fish seldom wrote his sermons.

5. REV. DAVID THURSTON

Was the second son of Daniel and Deborah (Pond) Thurston, of Wrentham, where he was born, 9 May, 1726.* He graduated at the college of New Jersey, Princeton, 1751. He received an invitation to settle in West Medway, 5 March, 1752, which he accepted 29 April, and was ordained 23 June, 1752. Rev. Nathan Bucknam, of the first church, preached the ordination-sermon. Owing to the ill health of Mr. Thurston, and some difficulties, supposed to grow out of the revival of 1740, with which some did not sympathize, he was led to ask a dismission. This event took place 22 Feb. 1769, after he had been settled nearly 17 years. Mr. T. was never resettled. In the spring of 1772, he removed with his family to Oxford, where he purchased a farm, for which he paid £700.†.

He subsequently removed to Auburn, and finally to Sutton, where he died 5 May, 1777. He was the father of five children.

1. Susan, married and died in Oxford, September, 1798. Her children are in New York State.

2. Paul, settled in Harvard; and died September, 1797. Some of his descendants are living in Maine.

3. Elihu, with his brother,

4. Abijah, were in the Continental army. Both belonged

---

* His father was born 20 November, 1693, and was the son of Thomas and Esther Thurston, one of the first settlers of the town.—*Rev. H. James, Wrentham.*

† Rev. L. Wright's Century Sermon.

to the same company, and were killed in the same battle, August, 1777.

5. Nathan, died in Oxford, about 1817, and left a numerous and respectable posterity.*

The inscription on Rev. Mr. Thurston's tombstone in Auburn is as follows, verbatim:

IN MEMORY OF THE

REV. MR. DAVID THURSTON,

WHO DIED MAY 5th 1777,

IN THE 51st YEAR OF HIS AGE.

WAS PASTOR OF THE 2nd CHURCH IN MEDWAY MANY YEARS.

Sweet is the memory of those
For whom Christ died; yea, has arose,
And broke the bonds of Death and hell,
That they with Him in Heaven may dwell.†

During the ministry of Mr. Thurston, 79 persons were admitted to the church, and 23 owned the covenant with reference to baptism.

No materials are in our possession for forming an opinion of Mr. Thurston's literary abilities. He is remembered as not efficient enough to combat and overcome the difficulties in his infant church. He yielded to them, and escaped by resignation. No writings of his are known to exist, as any index to his attainments as a theologian, or skill as a preacher.

6. REV. DAVID HALL, D. D.

Was the son of Joseph Hall‡ and his wife Hannah (Miller) Hall, and was born in Yarmouth, 5 August, 1704;

---

* Letter of Mr. Geo. F. Daniels, Oxford.

† Letter of Mr. D. Green, Auburn.

‡ Dr. Hall descended from John Hall, who came from Coventry in the north of England, about 1630; first settled in Charlestown, then

graduated at Harvard 1724, and A. M., and received the honorary degree of S. T. D., Dartmouth, 1777. In Nov. 1729, Mr. Hall commenced supplying the pulpit in Sutton, just vacated by Rev. Mr. McKinstry. On the 7th of March, the church gave him a call to settle, which the town agreed to March 26th, and he was ordained over the church in Sutton, 15 Oct. 1729. Rev. Mr. Williams, of Weston, preached. He labored here until his death, 8 May, 1789, in his 85th year, and the 60th year of his ministry.

Dr. Hall married, 24 June, 1731, Elizabeth Prescott, daughter of Doct. Jonathan and Rebecca (Bulkley) Prescott of Concord. She was daughter of Peter Bulkley, Esq., and grand-daughter of Rev. Peter Bulkley. They had 12 children.

1. David, born 5 May, 1732; married Mary Barrett of Stowe; merchant in Sutton; removed to Windsor, Vt.; and died in Woodstock, Vt., while on a visit.

2. Elizabeth, born 17 February, 1734. Married to Col. John Hale of Sutton, physician; settled in Hollis, N. H., where she died, over 90 years of age.

3. Rebecca, born 1 September, 1736. Married 30 Oct. 1760, to Rev. Aaron Putnam of Pomfret, Ct.; was killed by a fall from her carriage, 17 July, 1773. Left two children, Rebecca, second wife of Doct. Samuel F. Morse of Sutton, and Aaron P. jr.

4. Mary, born, 14 December, 1738. Married to Col. John Putnam of Sutton, and had eleven children, of whom was Doct. John P. of Upton.

5. Hannah, born 3 August, 1740. Married to Capt. Asa

Yarmouth. He married Miss Larned, or, says another Ms., Bethiah Larnard, and had twelve sons. John, the eldest, had three sons, Joseph, John, and Nathaniel. Joseph married Hannah Miller, daughter of Rev. John Miller, first minister of Yarmouth, and had Joseph, Daniel, Josiah, *David*, above, Hannah, Priscilla, and Margary. — *Letters of Rev. D. B. Hall, Cleaveland, N. Y., and Rev. G. Lyman, Sutton.*

Grosvenor of Pomfret, Ct., and died at Reading, 1834, aged ninety-four.

6. Sarah, born 15 Dec. 1742. Married to Gen. Jonathan Chase of Cornish, N. H., his second wife. Her daughter married to Doct. Smith, Medical Prof. at New Haven, and was the mother of Doct. D. S. C. H. Smith, of Sutton, now resident in Providence, R. I.

7. John, born 3 March, 1745 ; died 14 March following.

8. Benjamin, born 27 Feb. 1746. Married Elizabeth Moseley of Sutton. Died at St. Albans, Vt., at the house of his son, about 1833.

9. Lucy, born 19 March, 1749. Married to Capt. Samuel Pain of Randolph, Vt.

10. Joseph, born 8 September, 1751 ; H. U. 1774 ; married Chloe Grosvenor, daughter of Ebenezer G. of Pomfret, Ct. For 30 years town-clerk, and for 50 years school teacher in Sutton. Died 6 April, 1840, aged 89.

11. Jonathan, born 20 January, 1754. Physician in Pomfret, Ct.

12. Deborah, born 5 March, 1756. Married 9 May, 1776, to Rev. Daniel Grosvenor, of Grafton, brother of Joseph's wife. Died, it is believed, in Petersham. She was mother of Rev. Moses G. Grosvenor. [See Members, No. 57.]

Mrs. Hall, wife of Dr. Hall, died in Sutton, 7 Aug. 1803, aged 89.*

A brief sketch, such alone as this work allows, cannot do justice to the labors and character of Dr. Hall.

At his settlement, the church, of only 49 members, was in a low state, and had just passed through serious troubles with the former minister, a rigid Scotch Presbyterian. Iniquity abounded, and piety was dim. But a mighty work of grace soon began, which resulted in the addition of two hundred and sixty-one members to the church, out of a popu-

---

* Letter of Rev. G. Lyman, Sutton.

lation of about four hundred inhabitants.* Other periods of interest followed at different dates.

With such rich fruits before him, Dr. Hall became an earnest laborer in the vicinity, during the revival of 1740. He was amongst its most powerful instruments; and his labors were greatly blessed. His diary from 1751 and onwards, shows him to have been an eminently spiritual Christian, and full of the one idea of bringing souls to Christ. He was a pungent and popular preacher, and had great power over his hearers.

As an illustration of the subduing influence of his preaching, take his account of a sermon in a private house, where opposition was strongly felt towards him. "When I came there, I seemed welcome to but few. But before the sermon was over, there seemed to fall such a shower as softened every heart. They now discovered wonderful affection; and almost the whole number of Christians present were unable to refrain from some uncommon discoveries of it. I exhorted them after preaching, and the power of God seemed to descend; some careless sinners, especially one young man, were brought under strong convictions. All the prejudice conceived by some brethren against me vanished away; and some of them discovered deep anguish of heart for their sin therein."

It is sufficient commendation of Dr. Hall's public reputation amongst his contemporaries, to allude to the fact that he was the intimate and esteemed friend of Rev. Jonathan Edwards, of Northampton. He was a member of the council called to dismiss the latter, and was afterwards addressed in a letter of confession, by one of President Edwards's opposing parishioners.†

* For an account of this revival, see Tracy's History of the Great Awakening, p. 162. Also, Hist. Sermon of Sutton, by Rev. H. A. Tracy.

† See Life of President Edwards, in his works, Vol. I. p. 42.

When president Bunn of New Jersey college died, Dr. Hall was one of the candidates for the vacancy, to which his friend, President Edwards, was elected.

It may be inferred, as was the fact, that the friend of Edwards and admirer of Whitefield was of the Edwardean school in theology. Although it does not appear that, at any period of his life, he devoted himself, with peculiar closeness, to the study of theology as a science. He however received several young men into his family, and directed their theological studies. Few of his writings are extant. Though frequently requested to publish his discourses, it is not known that more than two were ever committed to press: a thanksgiving sermon on the reduction of Canada, Oct.1760, and a half-century sermon, 1779.

His epitaph is as follows: *

SACRED
TO THE MEMORY OF
REV. DAVID HALL, D. D.
Who was ordained Pastor of the First Church of Christ
in Sutton, Oct. 15, 1729, and was
instant and laborious in the business of his office
until May 8, 1789, when he departed this life
in the eighty-fifth year of his age
and sixtieth of his ministry.
He was venerated in life, and lamented in death.
The grateful people of his charge have erected this stone,
a monument of his virtues and their respect.

7. REV. AARON HUTCHINSON

Was born within the then town of Hebron, Ct., March, 1724, and graduated at Yale, 1747, and A. M. He was also Dean scholar at New Haven, and "took the premium with-

* Letter of Rev. G. Lyman, Sutton.

out a competitor appearing as rival." He received the degree of A. M. from Harvard, 1750; Dartmouth, 1780; and New Jersey, 1794. He was ordained second pastor of the church in Grafton, 6 June, 1750. Rev. Mr. Pumroy of Hebron preached. He was dismissed by the church 18 Nov., 1772, at his own request, though the town refused to concur in the vote, and did not. He continued to reside in Grafton, supplying vacant churches in the neighborhood, until 1775, when he purchased a farm in Pomfret, Vt., and engaged to supply, for *five years*, the towns of Pomfret, Woodstock, and Hartford. On the 4th of July, 1776, he removed, with his family of ten children, to Vermont, and resided on his farm, preaching in the vicinity, often gratuitously, until his death. This occurred 1 Sept., 1800, at the age of seventy-six and a half years. During his long ministerial life, he was never prevented from preaching, by ill health, but two Sabbaths; and one of these was the last Sabbath before he died. He preached at a funeral on Friday; was but poorly able to get home, and died the next Thursday, of a fever.

Mr. Hutchinson was a man of strong natural powers of mind, and was considered a learned man and a good classical scholar by his contemporaries. He was particularly remarkable for an extraordinary memory. It was of him that the remark was made, 'If the Bible were destroyed, he could rewrite it from memory.' This, however, was more than true. He could very nearly tell where *any* text was to be found. He could repeat the whole of the New Testament.* He often entered the pulpit and went through the whole service without opening a book of any kind. He appointed his hymns and recited them, as well as passages of Scripture, with entire confidence in his memory, and without mistake.

Mr. Hutchinson is known at this day chiefly as one of the polemic writers of the last century. His controversy with

---

* Letter of Hon. Titus Hutchinson, Woodstock, Vt.

Rev. Dr. Tucker, of the First church, Newbury, on some of the points of Arminianism, presents him as a high-toned Calvinist, a zealous defender of the faith, and a vigorous writer. In his personal habits, Mr. Hutchinson had many eccentricities. "He was without grace or polish in his manners, and his freedom, though he probably was not conscious of it himself, must often have verged upon rudeness." He instructed many youth in his family. Tradition avers that "his method was to teach Latin and Greek, and probably other branches, as he wrought in the field, his pupils being required to follow him as he followed the plough. His classical attainments and strong memory enabled him thus to cultivate mind and mold at the same time. Both soils, we doubt not (says the author we quote), were well tilled, though we may innocently conjecture that the master at the plough-handle would, now and then, be guilty of an ungrammatical apocope, as the share was caught with frequent jerks among the roots and rocks of the rough new country. None but an accomplished linguist, we are sure, could, under such circumstances, have administered Greek to the student and English to the cattle, in due proportion and proper order, without confusion.*

Several printed sermons of Mr. Hutchinson are to be found, viz.

Valor for the Truth. Newburyport, 27 April, 1767.

Sermon at Grafton, 23 Oct., 1768, (Sabbath after the execution of Arthur, at Worcester).

Two Sermons at Grafton 15 Nov., 1772 (the last to his people).

Sermon at Pelham, 28 Dec., 1773.

These sermons show him to have been a preacher of much more than common power and influence.

Mr. Hutchinson married Miss Margary Carter, a native of

---

* See "Church Record," by Rev. E. B. Willson, Grafton.

of his own town Hebron, Ct. She died 8 Aug., 1819, in her ninetieth year. Their *ten* children were as follows.

1. Margary, m. Mr. Samuel Wadsworth, of Henniker, N. H.

2. Mary, m. —— Aldrich. He died in the army, soon after the revolutionary war commenced. She died in Pomfret, Vt., June, 1789.

3. Aaron, Jr., H. U., 1770. Preached till his voice failed; then studied law and settled in Lebanon, N. H., where he died, 1843.

4. William Samuel. Settled first in Pomfret; then Pike, Pa.

5. Susanna, unm., d. in Pomfret, July, 1848.

6. Joanna, m. Mr. Phinehas Davis, S. Stanstead, Canada.

7. Alexander, a retired merchant, still lives in Woodstock, Vt.

8. Sarah, m. John McKenzie ; died, 1844.

9. Oliver, a merchant; died, October, 1800.

10. Titus, grad. Vermont U. 1811. Lawyer and judge; still living in Woodstock.

Two of the above children still live: Alexander, who will be eighty-eight next July 4th, and Titus, who will be eighty-one next April 29th. The others all died at an advanced age.

Inscription upon the gravestone of Rev. Mr. Hutchinson.

Here lie the relicts of
REV. AARON HUTCHINSON.
He died Sept. 27, 1800, in the seventy-ninth year of his age,
and fiftieth of his ministry.
His days he passed in health, religion, and domestic virtue;
nor did his sun go down till night.*

* Letter of Hon. Titus Hutchinson, Woodstock, Vt.

8. REV. CALEB BARNUM,

Was the son of Thomas and Deborah Barnum,* and was born in Danbury, Ct., 30 June, 1737, graduated Princeton, N. J. 1757, and A. M. at Harvard 1768. He received a call to settle over the second church in Wrentham, now Franklin, 28 Oct., 1759, and was ordained 4 June, 1760. Rev. Philips Payson of Walpole, preached the sermon. Difficulties arose, and Mr. Barnum felt it his duty to ask a dismission; to which the church reluctantly consented, and he was dismissed, 6 March, 1768. After his departure from Franklin, he recieved an invitation to the pastoral office in Taunton, and was installed there, 2 Feb., 1769. The war of the colonies awakened his strongest sympathies, and he applied for a chaplaincy in the army. He enlisted 3 May, 1775, left Taunton, and was chaplain, first to Col. Walker's regiment, and then to the XXIV Regiment, Col. John Greaton commander, at that time stationed at Boston. This latter connection began 10 Feb., 1776. After the evacuation of Boston, he accompanied his regiment to New York, then to Montreal, where he was inoculated for the small pox. He shared with fortitude in the disastrous retreat from Canada. At Ticonderoga he was seized with a bilious disorder, which so impaired his health that he obtained a discharge on the 24 July, and commenced his return homewards. But on his reaching Pittsfield, Aug.

---

* Thomas Barnum was either son or grandson of Thomas, one of the first settlers of Norwalk, Ct.; where he is found from 1662 to 1682, or later, when he removed to Danbury. Had 5 sons, Thomas b. 1663, John 1677, Ebenezer 1682, the others born in Danbury, date unknown, as the records were burnt by the British in the war. Thomas, the elder, was appointed by the town in 1681, "to keep decorum during the exercise on the Sabbath and at other public meetings, and to keep a *small stick* with which moderately to correct the disorderly." *Rev. S. H. Emery.*

2, he was arrested by an accession of his disorder. He wrestled with his disease until he fell, 23 Aug. 1776, at the age of 39. A sermon was preached at his funeral, from John 14: 28, by Rev. Thomas Allen, then minister of Pittsfield.

Mr. Barnum left behind him a wife and seven children. He married, 13 June, 1761, Priscilla, daughter of Rev. Caleb Rice of Sturbridge. His wife was sister of Col. Nathan Rice of Hingham, afterwards Aid-de-camp to Gen. Lincoln in the Southern campaign.

He had three sons and five daughters, one of which died in infancy.

1. Caleb, b. 11 April, 1762: m. Nancy Paine of Thetford, Vt.
2. Priscilla, b. 1 April, 1764: m. Capt. David Vickery of Taunton.
3. Deborah, b. 27 Oct., 1766: m. Thomas S. Bailies of Dighton.
4. George, b. 25 May, 1768: m. Sally Cutler of Warren.
5. Mary, died young.
6. Thomas, b. 30 Oct., 1772: m. Sally Abraham of New York.
7. Anna, b. 30 Dec., 1773: m. Rufus Child of Woodstock, Ct. She is the only child living, and is entirely blind; resides in Taunton.
8. Polly, b. 11 Oct., 1775: m. Rev. Peter Nourse of Ellsworth, Me.

The changeful life of Rev. Mr. Barnum, like that of many others, presents numerous points of interest. He was a man of noble impressive aspect, — dignified yet affable, — uniting the paternal mildness of the clergyman with the grace and polish of the gentleman. Yet he had a bold, fearless spirit, which bore him unflinchingly through hardships and opposition. His dismission from Franklin is said to have been primarily owing to a misunderstanding between two members of the church about a few cranberries. The amount of trespass was thought by him who felt injured, to be not more than *two* dollars: which sum Mr. B. offered to pay himself, if the complainant would rest. When this offer was known, the minister was blamed as trying to shield the guilty.* And so a bone was found for the inclined to growl over. The introduction of Dr. Watts's Version of the Psalms, furnished another question of dispute.

Mr. Barnum's connection in Taunton was also marked by differences with some of his parishioners. Yet in both connections, his friends were very strongly his, and they were in decided majorities.

During Mr. Barnum's ministry in Franklin, forty-seven were added to the church, though there was no general revival of religion. In Taunton, the thrilling events of the revolutionary war occupied all minds, and the pastor entered most cordially and enthusiastically into the cause of freedom. He announced the news of the skirmish at Lexington from the pulpit, and gave his people, thereupon, an eloquent exhortation to firmness and patriotism. His manuscript sermons, several of which are in possession of the writer, show him to be vigorous, bold, and unshrinking in his presentation of the Gospel, yet affectionate and persuasive in its practical application. He must have been an efficient and moving preacher. Nothing of his is known to have been published. His closing moments, so painful to him in their circumstances, were sustained by the hopes of the Gospel. Rev. Mr. Allen, of Pittsfield, where he died, thus speaks of him: "Not a repining word was uttered by him. He received the report of his physician, of the great hazard of his case, with equable firmness and composure of mind. Such sweetness of temper, such tranquillity of spirit, such serenity and peace in the near view of death and eternity, — such patience under pain, and entire submission to God's disposing will, which appeared in him,

* Cent. Sermon of Franklin, by Rev. E. Smalley, D. D.

manifested at once the power of those supports and consolations which he enjoyed, and the excellence of the Christian religion.

"Being asked his present views, in the approach of death, as to the goodness of the American cause, in which he had been engaged, and by means of which he was now about to die, replied, 'He had no doubt of the justice and goodness of that cause, and that had he a thousand lives, he should be willing to lay them all down in it.'"*

9. REV. EBENEZER CHAPLIN

Was the son of Benjamin Chaplin.† His mother was an Alden. He was born in that part of Pomfret, Ct., which is now called Hampton, 16 Sept., 1733. He graduated at Yale College, 1763, and A. M.; studied divinity with Rev. Dr. Hall of Sutton, and was ordained over the Second church in Sutton, now Millbury, 14 Nov., 1764; dismissed 6 March, 1792. He afterwards lived with his children, being wealthy; and finally died at Hardwick, 13 Dec., 1822, aged nearly 90.

Mr. Chaplin married Miss Mary Morse, of Holliston, by whom he had seven children: 1. Mary, died at 23 years. 2. Sarah, m. Rev. Thomas Holt, second minister of Hardwick, and the only survivor of the family, now at the age of 89. Mr. Chaplin died in her family. 3. Aaron Morse died, aged 18. 4. Ebenezer, m. Abigail Griswold, of Athol, where he was physician, and died May, 1844. 5. and 6.

* Letter of Rev. T. Allen to Pittsfield Representatives, Aug. 26, 1776.

† He came from England, killed an Indian, and was hunted, in revenge, through the wilderness. Finally settled in Pomfret, Ct. and had eight children. Benjamin, the oldest son, lived in Mansfield, Ct., and was deacon of the church, to which he gave a large sum of money. Hence that part of the town was called Chaplin, in acknowledgment of the gift. The other children were, Joseph, Nathan, John, William, Mary, Tammy, and Ebenezer, above.

Ichabod and Anna, died young. 7. Benjamin, physician in Dixfield, Me., where he died, Dec. 1836. He married Miss Sally Towne, of Ward, now Auburn.*

"Mr. Chaplin was a man of strong mental powers, a good textuary, a fair reasoner, and possessed no inconsiderable share of originality in his colloquial powers and style of writing." He published several controversial works, on doctrinal subjects; among them, a volume "on the Sacraments." His ministry in Millbury was not marked by any remarkable success.

10. REV. ISAAC STONE

Was born in Shrewsbury, 17 March, 1748. He was the only son and eldest of four children of Dea. Jonas and Rachel (Rice) Stone, of Framingham, afterwards of Shrewsbury.† His mother was a woman distinguished for her piety, maternal fidelity, and prayerfulness. It was parental solicitude which early led him to Christ and to the ministry as his vocation. At fifteen, he commenced the study of the languages, under Rev. Mr., afterwards Dr., Sumner, of Shrewsbury. At sixteen, he united with the church. In 1765, he went to Chelsea, and completed his preparation for college with Rev. Mr. Payson, and graduated at Cambridge, 1770, and A. M. in course.

He preached a while in Temple, N. H., and in Ashburnham and Franklin in this State, and came to Douglas as candidate, 31 March, 1771. He was ordained there, 30 Oct., 1771, and was dismissed, at his own request, 28 Oct., 1805, having been settled thirty-four years.

---

* Letter of A. E. Knight, Esq., Hardwick.

† Mr. Stone descended from John Stone, Elder in the church at Cambridge. Elder John Stone's son Nathaniel was father of Isaac Stone of Framingham, whose son was Dea. Jonas Stone, father of the above.

He continued still to reside in Douglas and preached occasionally, and for a considerable time in Whitingham and Reedsboro', Vt., until old age impaired his faculties. He spent the close of his life with his children, in Oxford, where at length he died, 22 Feb., 1837, in his 89th year.

Mr. Stone married Miss Susanna Goddard, daughter of Benjamin Goddard of Shrewsbury, 27 October, 1773, and had six children, four of whom still live.

1. His eldest son, a very active and useful man, died in early life.

2. Susanna, married Mr. John Larned of Webster, and has three children living.

3. Luke R., Deacon in the Congregational Church, Oxford.

4. Grace, married a Mr. Hill of Douglas, and has three children.

5. Submit, married a Mr. Balcom of Douglas, and has nine children.

The wife of Mr. Stone died 28 April, 1837, aged 92 years, 8 months, and 13 days.

This worthy pair lived together nearly sixty-four years, died within two months of each other, and are both interred in one grave in the old burying-ground in Oxford.

Mr. Stone's ministry in Douglas was charaeterized, not by striking and brilliant exhibitions, but by quiet, steady, unobtrusive labor, under which the walls of Zion rise, firmly cemented and compacted, if less rapidly than under such impulses as mark some other men's labors.

11. REV. DAVID SANFORD

Was the third son of Elihu and Rachel (Strong) Sanford, of New Milford, Ct., where he was born, 11 December, 1737. He was named after David Brainerd; to whom his father was especially attached. He graduated at Yale College 1755, and A. M.; and commenced the study of divinity with

Rev. Dr. Bellamy. But, under that godly and faithful instructor, he found himself to be wanting in the essential qualification of a new heart; and he relinquished the business of the ministry, and settled down as a farmer in Great Barrington, near to his brother-in-law, Rev. Dr. Hopkins. Not long afterwards, he became a subject of Divine grace.

The doctrines of the 'new divinity,' as Hopkinsianism was at first termed, peculiarly excited the native depravity of Mr. Sanford, and Dr. Hopkins became the object of his dislike. The settlement of their wives' patrimony was an occasion of showing this dislike, in a very aggravating manner; which, on one evening, overcame Dr. Hopkins's gentleness, and led him to use very sharp language. Mr. S. rejoiced that the mighty had fallen; but on opening his door to a gentle knock in the grey dawn of the next morning, the Dr. stood tearful before him. He requested that the family might be called together, and then acknowledged his resentful words on the preceding evening, implored forgiveness for them, and consented to any reasonable division his brother might propose. Mr. S. was overwhelmed. He knew that he had inveigled the unsuspecting Christian into that resentment; and he saw that a pious heart was nobler than worldly tact. He bowed to the power of the Gospel so tenderly exhibited, and became a child of God. He soon after recommenced and completed his studies, and entered the ministry.*

He received a call to Medway, west parish, 28 Dec. 1772, which he accepted, and was settled, 14 April, 1773. Rev. Dr. West, of Stockbridge, preached on the occasion. During his ministry in Medway, he was appointed chaplain in the army, and served a short time in the beginning of the war.†

---

* See more fully, Prof. Park's Memoir of Hopkins, p. 61.

† Mr. Sanford's commission is inserted as a specimen of such documents. It is a fine specimen of chirography:—

In 1807, he received a stroke of paralysis, which instantly terminated his public labors. He lived, however, in a distressed state, until 7 April, 1810, when he died in his 73d year.

Mr. Sanford married, 4 August, 1757, Miss Bathsheba Ingersol, daughter of Moses Ingersol, then of Great Barrington, and sister to the wife of Rev. S. Hopkins, D. D. She was born 5 June, 1738. They had ten children.

SEAL.

The Committee of the Council of Massachusetts Bay, To DAVID SANFORD, Gentleman, Greeting:

WE being informed of your exemplary life and manners, and reposing especial trust in your abilities and good conduct, Do by these presents constitute and appoint you the said David Sanford to be Chaplain of the Regiment whereof Lemuel Robinson is Colonel, raised by this Colony to reinforce the American army, until the first day of April next. You are therefore carefully and diligently to inculcate on the minds of the soldiers of said Regiment, as well by example as precept, the duties of Religion and morality, and a fervent love to their country in all other respects, and to discharge the duty of a Chaplain in said Regiment, observing from time to time such Orders and Instructions as you shall receive from your superior officers, according to military Rules and discipline established by the American Congress, — in pursuance of the trust reposed in you, for which this shall be a sufficient Warrant.

Given under our hands and the seal of the said Colony, at Watertown, the twenty-third day of January, and in the sixteenth year of the reign of his Majesty King George the Third.

By command of the Major part of the Council.

PEREZ MORTON D. SECY.

W. SEVER.
B. GREENLEAF.
J. WINTHROP.
J. CUSHING.
JAMES PRESCOTT.
JOHN WHETCOMB.
JED. FOSTER.
MOSES GILL.
I. PALMER.
CHAS. CHAUNCEY.
S. HOLTON.
MICHAEL FARLEY.
JABEZ FISHER.
JOHN TAYLOR.
B. WHITE.

1. David, b. 6 January, 1760; private in continental army, and d. in Great Barrington 19 July, 1841.

2. Philo, b. 7 Sept. 1761; married Lydia Whiting of Medway, and lived together over fifty years.

3. Clarissa, b. 20 Nov. 1763; married to Rev. John Morse. (See Licentiates, No. 25.)

4. Elihu, b. 28 Jan. 1766; married, first, Hannah Metcalf, Franklin; second, Miss Betsey Fisher of Belchertown. He died in Oxford.

5. Ichabod, b. 18 Oct. 1768; still lives in Belchertown, father of Rev. W. H. Sanford of Boylston.

6. Bathsheba, b. 14 Feb. 1770; married to Rev. Ethan Smith, of Haverhill, N. H., and author of the "Key to Revelation." She died at Pompey Hill, N. Y., 5 April, 1835.

7. Stephen, b. March, 1773.

8. Moses, b. 7 Nov. 1775; was a lawyer.

9. Electa, b. 13 March, 1778.

10. Samuel, b. 29 January, 1780; married Miss Betsey Wight, daughter of Doct. Aaron Wight, of Medway. He was a physician.

Mr. Sanford's ministry, until near its close, was rendered uncomfortable and marred in its results, by the existence of an unhappy difference between the two churches in Medway, which prevented mutual fellowship and communion. But he lived to see the breach healed, and communion renewed. He was permitted to enjoy several seasons of religious interest, in one of which, in the winter of 1784, nearly one hundred were brought to Christ.

No list of his published books has been obtained, although he appeared occasionally as an author. It is but just to say of him, that in his doctrinal views, he sympathized mainly with his early teachers and later associates in the ministry, while he held some views upon the extent of the atonement and of redemption, as did Mr. Avery of Wrentham, different from his brethren of the Association. The difference, if rightly understood at this time, was rather metaphysical than practical, and only sharpened the discussions of the clerical gatherings of the Association.

The character of Mr. Sanford is thus set forth by one who was his intimate friend and acquaintance for forty years.*

"The Author of nature endowed Mr. Sanford with a rich variety of rare and superior talents. He possessed a quick apprehension, a clear and sound judgment, a lively imagination, and an uncommon knowledge of human nature. These intellectual powers, sanctified by Divine grace, fitted him to shine with peculiar lustre in every branch of his ministerial office. But perhaps he appeared to the best advantage as a speaker. He had a piercing eye, a significant countenance, a majestic appearance, and a strong, clear, melodious voice, which he was able to modulate with ease and propriety. He was able to move any passion which he wished to move, whether love or hatred, hope or fear, joy or sorrow. He knew every avenue to the human heart, and could make the deepest impressions upon it. He preached with great plainness and fidelity, and usually extempore. In private discourse he had a peculiar talent at explaining Scripture, detecting error, and vindicating truth. He was often called to attend the ordination of ministers, and oftener still to attend ecclesiastical councils, where he displayed great ability and had powerful influence."

12. REV. NATHANAEL EMMONS, D. D.

Was the sixth son and twelfth and youngest child of Dea. Samuel, jr. and Ruth (Cone) Emmons.† He was born in East

* See Funeral Sermon, by Rev. N. Emmons, D. D.

† Samuel Emmons, grandfather of Dr. E., migrated from Cambridge and joined the church in E. Haddam, with his wife, 15 October, 1705. He had three sons, Samuel, Nathanael, and Jonathan, and two more children born in E. Haddam, Ebenezer and Mehitabel.

Haddam, Ct., 1 May, 1745, (N. S.). Graduated at Yale College, 1767, and A. M.; also, at Dartmouth, 1786, and D. D. 1798 at Dartmouth. He professed religion in 1769, and commenced the study of theology with Rev. Nathan Strong of Coventry, Ct., and completed the usual course with Rev. John Smalley, D. D. of Berlin. He was licensed by the Hartford South Association, 3 Oct. 1769, and ordained over the church in Franklin, 21 April, 1773; having been hired to supply the pulpit from 14 December preceding.

Discouraged by the little apparent fruit of his labors, he twice asked a dismission; viz. 21 January, 1781, and 20 May, 1784; which were each most wisely refused by his attached people. In 1827, May 13, he was seized with faintness while in the middle of his sermon, and carried to

---

Dea. Samuel jr. married Ruth Cone, 14 Sept. 1721. Nathanael married Elizabeth Mills. Samuel jr. lived at a village called Bashan (Union Factory). His twelve children were,

1. Dorothy, b. 16 Sept. 1722; m. Enoch Arnold of Millington.
2. Elizabeth, b. 6 March, 1724; m. Peter Spencer of Millington.
3. Ebenezer, b. 18 Sept. 1725.
4. Samuel jr., b. 20 Nov. 1727.
5. Mary, b. 6 Feb. 1730; not married.
6. Daniel.
7. Infant son.
8. Jonathan.
9. Hannah; married a Cowdry of Colchester.
10. Ruth; married Abner Chapman of Colchester.
11. Sybel.
12. Nathanael, b. 1 May, 1745.

Dea. E. had a second wife, Rachel. Her tombstone is, "Mrs. Rachel, wife of Ens. Samuel Jones, 2d, wife of Dr. Benjamin Kneeland, 3d, wife of Mr. Nathaniel Mann, 4th, wife of Samuel Emmons, died 25 Feb. 1776." Dea. E. died about 1767.

The minister of Dr. Emmons's boyhood was Rev. Timothy Symmes. He had two sons, John Cleves and Timothy. John C. Symmes was judge in N. J., and his daughter was wife of Gen. W. H. Harrison. His second son, Timothy, was father to Capt. John C. Symmes, famous for his "Theory of the Earth."

his house. He so far recovered as to finish his sermon on the following Sabbath. But this was the last sermon he preached. The second Sabbath following, May 27, 1827, he sent a note resigning his pastoral office, and requesting a meeting called immediately to provide for a supply of the pulpit. Though speedily recovering his former vigor, he would not recall his determination; meaning, he said, 'to retire while he had *sense* enough to do it.' His retirement was spent in converse, reading, and revision of some of his sermons. He died 23 September, 1840, in the 96th year of his age, and the 68th from the commencement of his ministry in Franklin.

A granite pyramid on a granite base is raised to his memory in the centre of Franklin common, — over which he went to the house of God for nearly seventy years, — and bears this simple inscription: —

N. EMMONS, D. D.
AGED 96.

His tomb-stone over his grave in the church-yard, where his dust rests with that of his family, is inscribed as follows:

TO THE MEMORY OF
REV. NATHANAEL EMMONS, D.D.
PASTOR OF THE CHURCH IN FRANKLIN:
BORN MAY 1, 1745.
ORDAINED APRIL 21, 1773.
DIED SEPTEMBER 23, 1840,
In the 96th year of his age, and the 68th of his ministry.

THE TRUTHS OF THE GOSPEL,
And the duties of his sacred calling,
WERE HIS DELIGHT.
He "meditated on these things, gave himself wholly to them,
AND HIS PROFITING APPEARED TO ALL."

In 1775, April 6, Dr. Emmons married Deliverance French, of Braintree. She died 22 June, 1778, and their two infant sons soon followed, on the same day, 8 Sept. 1778. He again married, 4 November, 1779, Martha, daughter of Rev. Chester Williams, of Hadley,* by whom he had two sons and four daughters.

1. Martha, married Willard Gay, Esq. of Dedham.
2. Deliverance, died 3 June, 1813.
3. Sarah, died January, 1823.
4. Mary, married Rev. Jacob Ide, D. D., and still survives. Of the sons, the eldest,

Williams, graduated B. U. 1805; tutor until 1808; married Eunice Wilde of Dedham, and is now judge in Augusta, Maine.

2. Erastus, Maj. aid-de-camp to Gen. Crane; died 13 March, 1820. Mrs. Emmons died 2 August, 1829, and Dr. E. married Mrs. Abigail M. Mills, 18 Sept. 1831. She was daughter of Capt. Judah Moore, sister of Rev. Z. S. Moore, D. D., President of Amherst College, and the widow of Rev. Winslow Packard, of Wilmington, Vt., and afterwards widow of Rev. Edmund Mills, of Sutton. She now resides in Auburn Dale, Newton, still able to attend and enjoy the public worship of God, although 90 years of age.

Of the labors and character of Dr. Emmons, it is unnecessary to speak. His published works, more extensively circulated than this brief notice can be, are sufficient exponents of his character and sentiments.†

* Rev. C. Williams left five children, three of them daughters. His widow was married to Rev. Samuel Hopkins, his successor, who had nine children. Of this family of fourteen children, were Rev. Nathaniel Williams, of Brimfield, and the wives of Rev. Dr. Emmons, of Rev. Dr. Spring of Newburyport, of Rev. Leonard Worcester of Peacham, Vt., of Rev. Dr. Austin of Worcester, and Rev. Wm. Riddell of Bernardstown.

† As a valuable contribution towards a *complete* idea of Dr. Emmons's intellectual character, and as an interesting literary morceau, the

Of his labors, the following extract, — taken from the records of the Association, — may be interesting: —

"He attended *thirty* councils called for advice. He received *seventy-five* calls to attend ordinations and installations, as a member of councils, in *six* different States, *fifty-four* of which he attended. At *twenty-five* of these, he was the preacher. His publications during his ministry were, *four* dissertations on important subjects; nearly *sixty* single occasional sermons, delivered in different places, and published by request of hearers; and *one hundred and thirty-one* sermons in six detached volumes. In addition to these, he wrote largely for several of the periodicals of the day, some of which were almost wholly sustained by him. And such were his industry and resolution, that, together with all these labors and all his parochial duties, including his weekly preparations for the sanctuary, he read all the distinguished books of his day which came within his reach. And he generally had under his tuition one or more students in theology, till the infirmities of age rendered it necessary for him to decline the labor. The whole number of students

author ventures to insert the following poetic effusion. They are the *only* rhyme which Dr. E. is known to have written.

"My thoughts I can with ease disclose
In plain, and pure, and perfect prose;
But give me e'er so much of time,
I cannot make a single rhyme.
No reason I could ever find
Why nature did so frame my mind,
But that it were to check my pride,
And give me reason for my guide.
This guide ne'er led a man astray,
Who heard its voice and did obey.
But there is something I deem higher,
To which I always will aspire, —
To lead mankind to fear and love
The God who lives and reigns above."

whom he thus assisted in their preparation for the ministerial office, was *eighty-six*."

As was the custom in his day, Dr. Emmons seldom visited his parishioners, unless they were sick or in affliction. In the latter part of his ministry, the writer remembers that he called annually, and perhaps oftener, when the members of the family were assembled, enquiries made after the temporal and spiritual welfare, and maxims of wisdom dropped, which are still remembered. Also, in May annually, the children were invited to meet him in their respective school-houses, where they were 'catechised,' and exhorted, and prayed with, by this venerable puritan minister. Those gatherings, and his appearance and words are forever fresh in recollection. The portrait of him in his published works very exactly reflects the image engraven in the minds of that generation; lacking, may be, the vivacious flash of quick intelligence and sympathy. The 'works' themselves have engraved his theological likeness upon a multitude of minds, and will continue to multiply resemblances until earthly teachers cease, and we sit down together at the feet of Him in whom are hid all treasures of wisdom and knowledge.

A list of Dr. Emmons's students, as found amongst his papers, is here inserted. They are not recorded in the order of time, and were therefore probably written down towards the close of his life, from memory. The list does not evidently include all who resorted to him for theological instruction. Some of these were with him but a short time: at the beginning or close of their preparation for the ministry. Some did not enter the ministry at all, but studied for their own benefit. The list is copied without alteration; their place of settlement is added, when known. Those *starred* were approbated by this Association, and will be found in their proper place: —

* Josiah Reed, Uxbridge.
Daniel Farrington, Wrentham ; never settled.
* Jacob Cram, Hampton Falls.
* Read Page, Hardwick.
* Walter Harris, New Lebanon, N. H.
* Elias Dudley, Newport, N. H.
Ariel Parish, Plainfield, Ct.: settled in Manchester.
* Royal Tyler, Uxbridge.
Pierson Thurston, Lancaster; s. in Somersworth, N. H., and St. Johnsbury, Vt.
Thomas Moore, Lancaster; s. in Wiscasset, Me.?
Nathan Church, South Hadley ; s. in Bridgton, Me.
* Herman Daggett, Wrentham.
* Josiah Holbrook, Wrentham.
James Tufts, Oakham; s. in Wolfsboro', N. H., and Dover, N. H.
Josiah Graves, Sunderland; deacon in Amherst.
* John Fitch, Hopkinton.
Eleazer Taft, Waltham.
Phinehas Taft, Braintree; died before settlement.
* Nathaniel Hall, Sutton.
William Riddell, Colerain; s. in Bristol, Me.
John Smith, Palmer; s. in Haverill, N. H.
* Eli Smith, Belchertown.
* Abijah Wines, Newport, N. H.
* John Bowers Preston, N. Jersey.
* Nathaniel Ogden, N. Jersey.
Thomas Thompson, Newbury.
John Simpkins, Boston; s. in Brewster.
* Samuel Judson, Woodbury, Ct.
* John Morse, Medway.
Jonathan Ward, Plymouth, N. H.; s. in Brentwood, N. H.
* William Jackson, Wallingford, N. H.
* Enoch Pond, Wrentham.

Caleb Blake, Wrentham; s. in Westford.
* Kiah Bailey, Haverill, N. H.
Calvin Chaddock, Oakham; s. in Hanover.
* Nathaniel Howe, Linebrook.
Timothy Clark, Wallingford, Ct.; s. in Greenfield, N. H.
* Benjamin Wood, New Lebanon, N. H.
* Nathan Holman, Sutton.
* Joseph Rowell, Newton, N. H.
* Drury Fairbanks, Holliston.
Samuel Fowler Dickinson, Amherst; Lawyer in Amherst.
William Salisbury, Braintree; s. in N. Y. State.
* Joseph Emerson, Hollis, N. H.
Oliver Ayers, Franklin, Ct.; s. in Augusta, N. Y.
Samuel Brown, Kingston, N. H.
* Joseph Cheney, Holden.
* Nathan Waldo, Orange, N. H.
Abel Farley, Hollis, N. H.; s. in Manchester, N. H.
* Levi Nelson, Milford.
* William Warren, New Ipswich, N. H.
Edward Whipple, New Braintree: s, at Charlton and Shrewsbury.
David Jewett, Hollis, N. H.; s. in Gloucester.
Gordon Johnson, Farmington, Ct.; s. at West Killingly, Ct.
Nathaniel Kendrick, Hanover, N. H.
* Gaius Conant, Braintree.
——— Spalding, Westford; s. in Penobscot, Me.?
Truman Baldwin, Granville; s. at Pompey, N. Y.
Luke Wood, Somers, Ct; s. in Waterbury, and Westford, Ct.
* Thomas Williams, Pomfret, Ct.
George Hall, E. Haddam, Ct.; s. at Cherry Valley, N. Y.

Roswell R. Swan, Stonington, Ct.; s. in Norwalk, Ct.
* Stephen Chapin, Milford.
Bela Kellogg, Amherst; s. 2d Ch. Avon, Ct.
* David Holman, Sutton.
——— Fisher, ———, N. H.
Christopher Webb, Weymouth; Mass. Senate, died in Weymouth.
Artemas Dean, Taunton; s. in Rome, N. Y.
* Sherman Johnson, Southboro'.
Bancroft Fowler, Pittsfield; Prof. at Bangor.
Dickinson Fowler, Amherst.
Ebenezer Burgess, Wareham; s. at Dedham.
* John B. Wight, Bristol, R. I.
* Elnathan Walker, Taunton.
Thaddeus Osgood, ———; Missionary in Canada.
* Enoch Pond, North Wrentham.
* Emerson Paine, Mansfield.
Alexander Metcalf Fisher, Franklin; Math. Prof. at Yale College.
* Willard Holbrook, Sutton.
* Moses Partridge, Bellingham.
* William Tyler, Pawtucket.
* Abel Manning, Holden.
* Sewall Harding, Medway.
* David Brigham, Westborough.
* Zolva Whitmore, East Haddam, Ct.
* Jonathan Longley, Boylston.

13. REV. ELIJAH FITCH,

The son of Capt. John Fitch, was born in Windham, Ct., 1746, graduated at Yale college, 1765, and A. M.; and also at Harvard, 1770. He preached in Franklin some time after Mr. Barnum's dismission; but settled, ultimately, in Hopkinton, 15 Jan., 1772, as colleague with Rev. Samuel Barrett. In Dec. 11, Mr. Barrett died, and left Mr. Fitch sole pastor of the church, which office he filled until his death, 16 Dec., 1788, in his 43d year and the 17th of his ministry.

Mr. Fitch married Hannah Fuller, who survived him and died 7 Feb., 1824, aged 80. He left five children alive at his death.

1. A daughter, who died about 1793.
2. John, Rev. (see Licentiates, No. 28).
3. A daughter, resident at Hopkinton.
4. Elijah, Dea. in Hopkinton, d. 27 Apl., 1847, aged 68.
5. Betsey, married Rev. Nathanael Rawson (Licentiates, No. 52).

Mr. Fitch "was a man of great powers of mind. He possessed a sound judgment. He was somewhat reserved in mixed companies, but in the pulpit he was remarkably eloquent. He was unassuming; a man of meekness and candor; a man of humility and benevolence; he was patient, industrious, and persevering. His life spent in one continual series of exertion for the good of his church, people, and family. He was not rigid in his religious opinions; he was considered a moderate Calvinist.

"No man ever more feelingly participated in the happiness or misery of his fellow men, than he; or better filled the several offices of pastor, husband, parent, friend, neighbor, and townsman." He was a fine scholar and poet. He left a poem, of several cantos, in blank verse, entitled the 'Beauties of Religion,' addressed to the young, which contains passages of poetic merit. He published a Sermon on the Evacuation of Boston, 1776.

"Two years before his death, he was unable to preach through the winter. But in the spring he partially recovered, and was able to preach until the April preceding his death.*

* Century Sermon, by Rev. N. Howe, fourth edition.

14. REV. JOSIAH SPALDING

Was born in Plainfield, Ct., 10 Jan., 1751, graduated at Yale college, 1778, and A. M., approbated to preach the Gospel, 1780. He was ordained at Uxbridge, 11 Sept., 1782, and, on account of some dissatisfaction in the church, was dismissed 23 Oct., 1787. The council say : "they view Mr. Spalding's Christian character in a fair and amiable light, and hope Christ will use him as an instrument of speedily building up his Gospel and promoting his cause in the world."

Mr. Spalding was next installed in Worthington, 21 Aug., 1788, and dismissed March, 1794. He left there with the reputation of being 'sound in doctrine, but very eccentric.'* He was next settled in Buckland, in 1794, where he remained until his death, 8 May, 1823, at the age of 72 years, 41 of which he spent in the ministry; viz. 5 years in Uxbridge, 6½ in Worthington, and 28½ years in Buckland.

"His ministry in Buckland," says his successor, "was a successful one. There were several seasons of special religious interest during his ministry, the last of which was the year before he died, when there was probably the most powerful revival ever enjoyed among this people. In 1799, there were 17 admitted to the church at one time; in 1807, 12 at one time; and 8 at one time in the following year; 16 were admitted at once in 1816, and in 1822, 65 were admitted, among which number was Miss Mary Lyon.

"Mr. Spalding was a sound doctrinal preacher, who instructed his people well in the great truths of the Bible, and laid the foundations so thoroughly that they remain to this day. The fruits of his ministry still exist in the church, and they form its strongest pillars. Unitarianism never found a place here (in Buckland), and we need not look any farther than to the labors of such a man, to account for it.

* Letter of Rev. J. W. Bisbee, Worthington.

"As a preacher, his manner was rather dull and uninteresting; but what he lacked in manner, he made up in matter.

"On his death-bed, he was visited by some of his people, who came to confess some wrong they had done him. He felt that he could not die without an interview. When it was over, he said he could die in peace. "His memory still lives among the people. They looked up to him as their father; and when they now speak of him, they usually give him the title of 'father.'

Mr. Spalding published several sermons during his ministry. He also issued a volume entitled, "Universalism destroys itself," which is among the references in the Andover Course of Theological Study. It enters into a minute and extensive examination of the original words used in the Scriptures in reference to the duration of future punishment. It cost much labor, at a time when few helps existed for such researches. He had another work in readiness at his death, but the manuscript is now lost.

Mr. Spalding married Martha Williams, daughter of Judge Williams, of Taunton, who died a few months before him. They had *five* children, — four daughters, and one son, Josiah. Three of the daughters married and left descendants. But a melancholy interest gathers over the son. "Bearing his father's name, the pride of his parents, and designed by them for the ministry, he has been a raving maniac for forty-four years. He is now almost 65. For some two years after he became deranged, he was not confined; but his father's life was repeatedly endangered, and he was chained for some two years. For the last forty years, he has been shut up in a cage. No clothing can be kept on him. He remains constantly in a sitting posture, with a blanket wrapped about him, and only leans back against the cage when he sleeps. He has remained in this position so long, that his limbs cannot be straightened.

"Before he became deranged, he had been for many months in an interesting state of mind, and his parents entertained a hope for him. He was nearly or quite prepared to enter college, and was teaching school when the first signs of insanity appeared. He appears to become more and more demented."* Strange are the ways of Providence! and contradictory now; but radiant hereafter, and admirable to the student in heaven!

15. REV. JOHN CRANE, D. D.

The son of John and Rachel (Terry) Crane, was born in Norton, 26 March, 1756. His parents belonged to the society of Friends.† He graduated at Harvard, 1780, and A. M.; also A. M., 1792, and S. T. D., 1803, from Brown University; studied theology with Dr. Emmons; and, in 1782, was invited by the society in Northbridge to preach as a candidate. Soon after, a church was gathered, and he received a regular call to settle over the church and society, in the work of the ministry. He accepted it, and was ordained over the first church in Northbridge, 25 June, 1783. He died in the ministry, 31 Aug. 1836, aged 80 years, and in the 54th of his pastorate.‡

Dr. Crane married Miss Rachel Taft, of Northbridge; by whom he had three children, daughters. The eldest, Rachel, was married to Rev. Ezekiel Rich.

The second, Susan, was married to Abel Jaquis, Esq., of

---

* Letter of Rev. A. B. Smith, Buckland.

† John Crane Sen. was born in Berkley, 1732, moved to Norton about 1750, and died April, 1800. His wife was of Freetown. She died, 1821.

Their children were John (above), George, b. 8 Nov., 1758, Rachel, b. 12 Sept., 1761, Calver, b. 13 May, 1764, Hannah, b. 18 June, 1766, Terry, b. 28 April, 1774.

‡ "Dr. C. resigned his charge, 14 March, 1832, but continued nominal pastor, until his death. On the first Sabbath in May, 1835, — about a year before his death,—he preached his last sermon in the old meeting-house, in which he had ministered for half a century (just before it was taken down), from this text: "The prayers of David, the son of Jesse, are ended."—*Rev. W. Bates, Northbridge.*

Worcester. The third, Hannah, was married to Rev. John Taylor, late of Shutesbury, but who now leads a private life in Northbridge, on the paternal farm.*

"Dr. Crane had a strong and penetrating and well cultivated mind. He was cordially attached the great and distinguishing doctrines of the Gospel, and never shunned to declare the whole council of God." "It was a settled maxim with him, always to preach the truth in that clear, plain and simple style which even children could understand. He says in one of his sermons, "I have aimed to preach the doctrines of the Gospel in as plain a manner as I could. I have tried to make Divine truth bear upon the heart and the conscience. I have studied to send away my hearers dissatisfied with themselves."

"Dr. Crane was not only a plain, practical and pungent preacher, but he was decidedly orthodox. He embraced substantially, what have been called the doctrines of the Reformation. The free moral agency of man, the entire depravity of the human heart, the Sovereignty of God in the election of grace, the necessity of regeneration by the Spirit of God, the perseverance of the Saints, the resurrection of the dead, and a general and final judgment, formed the great outlines of that system which he believed and preached. This system of doctrines he believed, not merely because they had been embraced and ably advocated by Luther and Calvin and Edwards and Bellamy and Hopkins and Dwight and Emmons: but because they appeared to him to be the great truths taught by the Lord Jesus Christ and his inspired Apostles."†

* At was the fashion of those times, Dr. Crane carried on a large farm, on which, during the latter part of his ministry, he engaged daily with his hired men. For many years, his cider-mill was *the only one in the parish*, and all his people were dependent on him for their cider! Happy the minister who could so easily cut off such supplies !!

† Extract from Funeral Sermon by Rev. D. Holman, Douglas, in B. Recorder, No. 1141.

"Dr. Crane was very active and laborious. Besides his pastoral and ministerial labors, he instructed many youth at a school in his own house, which he kept for many years. In his half-century sermon he says, 'The fifty years which I have passed in this place have been full of labor and hurry. I was employed more than thirty years in teaching youth. I have instructed more than a hundred young men in their preparation for admission to college.* I have written about four thousand sermons, and probably delivered about two hundred extempore discourses.'"

Several revivals marked his ministry. In 1800, 27 were added to the church; in 1809, 28 were added. In 1829–30, about 30 were joined to the followers of Christ. In 1831, almost 70 were gathered into the fold.

"Dr. Crane published several occasional discourses, which show not only strength of mind and maturity of judgment, but also a familiar acquaintance with the Holy Scriptures, and the great and essential truths of our holy religion." His chapter in the 'Mendon Evidences,' indicates the extent of his studies and the power of his logic. The titles of some of his published productions are as follows: —

1. Thanksgiving Sermon, 1800. 2. Two Fast Sermons on Civil Liberty. 3. Ordination Sermon of Rev. Calvin Park, D. D., at Franklin, 1815. 4. Ordination Sermon of Rev. Ezekiel Rich. 5. Ordination Sermon of Rev. John Taylor, at Shutesbury. 6. Two Sermons on the Nature and Design of John's Baptism. 7. Lecture on Sacred Music, at Sutton. 8. Fourth of July Oration, at Douglas. 9. "Reasons why I am not a Baptist: By Bickerstaff."

---

* Among them were Rev. Dr. Hawes, of Hartford, Ct., Rev. Willard Preston, D. D., of Savannah, Ga., and Rev. Cyrus Kingsbury, Missionary to the Choctaws. Dr. Crane represented the town of Northbridge for several years in the General Court.

16. REV. DAVID AVERY

Was born 5 April, 1746, in that part of Norwich, Ct., now forming the town of Franklin. His parents were John and Lydia (Smith) Avery.* He was converted to God at about twenty years of age, under the preaching of Whitefield. Fitted for college at Dr. Wheelock's school, in Lebanon, Ct. Entered Yale College a year in advance, and graduated 1769, A. M. in course, and also at Dartmouth, 1773. Employed in his vacations teaching Indian schools. Studied theology with Rev. Dr. E. Wheelock of Dartmouth Coll. Preached a short time on Long Island as a licentiate. Was soon ordained, probably at Dartmouth, 29 August, 1771, as missionary to the Oneida Indians, and colleague with Rev. Mr. Kirkland, father of President Kirkland of Harvard University.

He was compelled to leave this field of labor by a bad fall upon the ice, when he returned to New England. After preaching in different places, he was installed at Gageboro', now Windsor, 25 March, 1773, and dismissed 14 April, 1777,† to go as chaplain in the army. On his return he was settled at Bennington, Vt., 3 May, 1780, and dismissed 17 June, 1783; again settled at Wrentham, 25 May, 1786; and

* The first of the paternal line in New England was John Avery, a Scotchman, who with his wife and children, — four sons and several daughters, — settled in Truro, where he died. Two of the sons settled in Connecticut, from one of which Rev. Mr. A. descended. John Avery, former Secretary of the state of Massachusetts, and also Rev. Dr. Griffin, President of Wms. Coll., were cousins of Rev. David Avery. See Letter of W. H. Smith, Esq., Prov. R. I. The first minister of Truro was Rev. John Avery, son of Robert, and grandson of Doct. William Avery of Dedham. Was he the same person? See notice of the Avery family, by W. R. Deane, Boston.

† His commission was dated 18 April, 1776. He resigned it 1 Feb. 1780. He was attached to Col. Sherborn's regiment, Continental army. Served from 15 Feb., 1777, to 5 March, 1780. — *State Records.*

after many councils and much difficulty, dismissed 21 April, 1794. He still preached to a congregation at North Wrentham, where a church was organized in 1795. He left previous to 1798, and removed his family to a farm belonging to his wife in Mansfield, now Chaplin, Ct., and employed himself in preaching in vacant places in Connecticut, Massachusetts, and Vermont. He performed two missionary tours in the western frontiers of New York, and one in Maine, under the direction of the Massachusetts Domestic Missionary Society.* He afterwards gathered a new church and society, called the Union Church, in Chaplin, Ct., to which he preached from 1798 to 1801. In 1817, October 28, he visited his daughter, Mrs. Hewett, then resident in Shepardstown, Va., where, and in the vicinity, he preached a few weeks. He received a cordial and unanimous call to settle in Middletown, fifteen miles from Shepardstown, where he was taken (on the evening of a day of fasting preparatory to his installation) with the typhus fever, of which he died. He was buried on the week of his intended installation, the clergy of the invited council officiating as his bearers.

Mr. Avery married, 10 Oct., 1782, Hannah Chaplin, daughter of Dea. Benjamin Chaplin, of Mansfield, Ct. Her mother was Mary Paine, cousin of Judge Robert Treat Paine of Boston, and aunt of Judge Elijah Paine of Vermont. They had four children: 1. Mary C., married to William H. Smith, Esq., and still living at Providence, R. I.

2. David, jr.; graduated at Brown University; lawyer; married Miss Morgan, and resides in Hampton, Ct.

3. Hannah, married to Chester D. Clarke, merchant of Utica, N. Y.

4. Lydia S., married to Lieut. Thomas Hewitt, U. S. Army; and resided in Shepardstown, Va., where both deceased.

* Rev. David Avery and Rev. Jacob Cram, (Licentiate, No. 15,) were the first missionaries commissioned by the Society.

The following list comprises his publications: 1. Thanksgiving Sermon, preached before the Army, 1777. 2. Sermon, on bridling the Tongue, Wrentham, 1779. 3. Funeral Sermon of his Father-in-Law, Dea. Benjamin Chaplin, 1795. 4. Funeral Sermon of Mr. Walter Moore.

Mr. Avery is said to have been tall, portly, commanding in presence, with a prominent Roman countenance. His natural disposition was generous and warm-hearted. His manners were frank, cordial, humble, and dignified. He was emphatically a gentleman of the old school; and when he thought occasion demanded, rigid in adherence to his opinions. He was an Edwardean in sentiment, and a Whitefieldian in warmth of manner: although he differed from the Hopkinsians on some minor points. He preached extemporaneously from short notes. His language was copious, and at times too diffuse. His voice was so clear and sonorous, and his articulation so distinct, that it was a common saying in the army, that every soldier in a brigade could hear all that he said.

His ministry on Long Island in 1771 appears to have been remarkably successful. His private diary for that year exhibits earnest longings to be useful, and in such fields of labor as God should see fit.

"Jan. 1, 1771. Preached at Sag Harbor, a new-year's sermon. People somewhat solemn. I earnestly desire to begin the year with God, and in entire dedication to Him." — "Lord, let me spend and be spent for thee. Dispose of me as thou pleasest; send me where thou pleasest; let me have no will of mine own, — or let my will be thy will.

"2. Preached to-day to a solemn assembly. Had some intimations of God's presence.

"3. This evening preached to a very solemn assembly. Numbers of the youth in tears and sighs.

"6. Preached to an attentive audience on the stoutness of the natural heart. Isa. 46: 12."

The journal of his chaplaincy contains many facts of interest. His connection with the army of Washington was intimate and of considerable continuance. When the news of the battle of Lexington reached Gageboro', Mr. Avery's parishioners assembled in arms, formed themselves into a company, elected him for their captain, and on Saturday, 22 April, after devoutly asking God's blessing on the enterprise, marched for Cambridge. They spent the Sabbath at Northampton, and attended public worship. Mr. Avery preached in the afternoon from Neh. 4: 14. Monday, marched on, and arrived at Cambridge, Saturday, 29, where they were honorably received and congratulated by the troops assembled. Next day, Sabbath, Rev. Dr. Langdon, a chaplain in the army, preached on a temporary stage erected in the college area from 1 Tim. 6: 12. In the P. M. Mr. Avery preached from Neh. 4: 14. Monday, Mr. A. commenced a regular course of morning and evening prayer with the regiment to which he belonged. Tuesday, commenced visiting and praying with the sick and wounded regulars in the hospitals.

May 11. A Province Fast. Preached on Cambridge Common.

29. Went volunteer with an expedition to Noddle's Island. A brisk skirmish. Stood guard two hours that night after praying with the expedition.

July 20. Continental fast day. Preached to the troops.

27. Read to the troops the Declaration of War by Congress against General Gage.

Nov. 14. "My people, (of Gageboro',) consented that I should engage in the next campaign, and the neighboring ministers kindly agreed to supply my pulpit two-thirds of the time of my absence."

Dec. 31. Exhorted the troops to repent of their past sins, and begin the new year with new hearts and lives, and to be faithful in the service of God and their country."

Mr. Avery often acted as physician and assistant surgeon. He was at the taking of Burgoyne, the capture of the Hessians at Trenton, and in the battle of Princeton. When settled at Bennington, at the request of the Governor and Council of Vermont, he took the field with General Allen, and was in the battle of Bennington, and assisted in dressing the wounds of the soldiery.

Mr. Avery had *fourteen* cousins of the name of Avery in Groton Fort, who were all massacred except one, and he had a musket ball pass through the left side of his head, carrying his left eye with it. He lived to be more than a hundred years old.*

17. REV. CALEB ALEXANDER

Was born in Northfield, 22 July, 1755. Graduated at Yale College 1777, and studied theology with Rev. Ephraim Judson, of Taunton. He was ordained at New Marlboro', 28 February, 1781, and dismissed 28 June, 1782. Installed at Mendon, 12 April, 1786. In 1801, he was appointed by the Massachusetts Missionary Society, to visit the churches and Indians in Western New York. On his return, he was dismissed from his charge in Mendon, 7 December, 1802, and reëntered the western field as teacher, for which work he had eminent abilities. He first located in Fairfield, Herkimer Co., N. Y., where he was elected Preceptor of Fairfield Academy, just erected. Under his direction it became a prominent resort for education. In 1812, he removed to Onondaga, Onondaga Co., to take charge of a newly-established academy there. He was also greatly instrumental in the establishment of Hamilton College and Auburn Theological Seminary. During the time, he preached almost every Sabbath in adjoining places, and gathered many now flourishing churches in the region.

---

* Letter of W. H. Smith, Esq., Providence, R. I.

He died at Onondaga, N. Y., 12 April, 1828, aged 72 years, 8 months, and 20 days. His epitaph is as follows:—

HIS INDUSTRY AND ZEAL,
IN THE CAUSE OF LITERATURE AND RELIGION,
WERE UNTIRING AND BENEVOLENT.
"PRECIOUS IN THE SIGHT OF THE LORD IS THE DEATH OF HIS SAINTS."

The following extracts are from an obituary notice of Mr. Alexander, published in the Onondaga Register for April 16, 1828:

"Rev. Mr. Alexander graduated at New Haven College, fifty-one years since; and after obtaining a theological education, and being for a few years pastor of a church, he chose for his future life the equally laborious employment of a teacher. For this employment he was admirably fitted. Being himself an excellent scholar, he excelled in this department of usefulness, and may be considered as the founder of several important literary institutions. Many of the distinguished men in each of the professions in this State have been brought up under his instructions. His literary labors, considering the nature of his official duties, have been astonishing. As the correspondent of scientific and religious periodicals, and as the author of several systems of education, translations, and essays on various subjects, he has long been well known to the world. But this is not all. As a steward of the mysteries of the Gospel, he was a 'scribe well instructed.' Clear and distinguishing in his views of divine truth, he manifested to all that, amid his complicated labors, the Bible had never been neglected; and we have seldom seen a man so familiar with its doctrines, and so capable of making the Scripture the interpreter of itself. The last years of his life, after having retired from its active duties, were devoted to the Bible; and the treasures of divine knowledge he had gathered from it were truly wonderful."

Mr. Alexander married Miss Lucina Strong, daughter of his predecessor at New Marlboro', Rev. Thomas Strong. She died in Onondaga, 24 Nov., 1847, aged 91. They had seven children:

1. William H., now living in Syracuse, N. Y.
2. Fanny, married —— Smith of Rocton, Herkimer Co.
3. Elizabeth, married —— Groesbuck of Buffalo.
4. Sylvia, married a Sheldon, of Buffalo.
5. Laura, wife of Rev. D. C. Lansing, D. D., of Brooklyn, deceased.
6. Sophia, wife of W. Raynor, of Syracuse, deceased.
7. Sarah, of Onondaga.*

Mr. Alexander published many works. Among them are "Essay on the Deity of Christ, with Strictures upon Emlyn, 1791. Translation of Virgil. Latin, Greek, and English Grammars." And several occasional Sermons.

18. REV. TIMOTHY DICKINSON,

The son of Nathan and Esther Dickinson, was born at Amherst, 25 June, 1761.† He lived with his parents and

---

* Letter of W. H. Alexander, Esq., Syracuse, N. Y.

† The ancestral line is traceable to Nathaniel of Weathersfield, Ct., as early as 1638. He signed the agreement of the Hadley Settlers at the house of "Goodman Ward," in Hartford, 18 April, 1659, and moved to Hadley within the year after. He died at Hadley, 16 June, 1676. He had nine children.

II. Samuel, the eldest son of Nathaniel, born 1638, and married Martha Bridgman of Springfield, and lived at Hatfield. He died 30 Nov., 1711: had nine children.

III. Ebenezer, the sixth son, born 2 Feb. 1680; married Hannah Frary, and lived at Hatfield. Died 16 May, 1730. Had seven children.

IV. Nathan, the third son, born 30 May, 1712; married, 1. Thankful Warner; 2. Joanna Leonard; 3. Judith Hosmer. Died 7 Aug., 1796. Had thirteen children. He moved to Amherst, 1742.

labored upon a farm until sixteen years of age, when he enlisted as a private soldier in the Continental Militia. He served in the army about fifteen months. Urged by the developments of depravity so visible in the camp, he determined to secure a public education, that he might combat it more successfully. He fitted for college under Rev. Dr. Dwight, afterwards President of Yale College, then teaching a private school in Northampton. He graduated at Dartmouth College 1785, and A. M.; and then, for one year, took charge of "Moore's Charity School," connected with the College. He studied theology with Rev. David Tappan, D. D., then of Newbury, afterwards Divinity Professor in Harvard University. He preached at Exeter, N. H., and at Hopkinton, N. H.; and finally, he received an unanimous invitation to settle in Holliston, 13 Nov., 1788. He was the thirteenth candidate after the dismission of Rev. Joshua Prentiss. He was ordained and settled 18 Feb., 1789. He died in the ministry, 6 July, 1813, aged fifty-two years, having been a pastor twenty-four years.

Mr. Dickinson married Margaret, the eldest daughter of Rev. J. Prentiss, his predecessor, and had seven children, five of whom survived him, and two became physicians. His children were, —

1. Nancy.

2. Joshua Prentiss, graduated Brown, 1811, and M. D. at Cambridge, 1816. Lives in Bangor, Me.

3. Thomas.

4. Edwards, graduated Harvard, 1818, and M. D. 1823. Died at Holliston, 1831.

5. Irene. 6. John. 7. Esther.

Mr. Dickinson published several occasional sermons;

V. Nathan, jr., born 19 Oct. 1735; married Esther Fowler; 2. m. Jerusha Blodgett, daughter of Dea. Ebenezer Dickinson. He died 3 Aug., 1825. He had eight children, of whom Rev. Timothy D., above, was the eldest. — *Letter of Rev. L. M. Boltwood, Amherst.*

among them a sermon preached before the Mass. Missionary Society, 1811.

Mr. Dickinson became a subject of Divine grace during a remarkable revival of religion, in his first year at college. He had the reputation of a correct classical scholar, and was diligent and persevering in his studies.

"As a preacher, he was plain, faithful, and affectionate. And as he firmly believed in those doctrines which are usually denominated the doctrines of grace, he felt it his duty often plainly and affectionately to state and illustrate them. No considerations of popularity or self-interest could deter him from a plain and frequent exhibition of those truths which are so offensive to the carnal mind."*

"He had a clear, strong, and pleasant voice, which enabled him to speak with peculiar propriety and energy; and as he aimed to draw the attention of his hearers to his subject, rather than to himself, so he seldom failed of deeply impressing their hearts and consciences."

"He loved to converse upon religious subjects, and greatly excelled in private discourse with his people. In some Christian and ministerial virtues, he shone with a peculiar lustre. He was among the most zealous ministers and Christians to spread the Gospel, and to extend the kingdom of Christ through the world."† He was one of the founders of the Massachusetts Missionary Society, and one of its trustees. His boldness in preaching the offensive doctrines of the Gospel produced much disturbance and alienation, insomuch that a council was once called, 4 June, 1804, to dissolve the connection. But harmony was ultimately restored, and his closing labors were performed in quiet, and to the general edification of his people.

---

* Panoplist, June, 1814.

† Funeral Sermon, by Dr. Emmons.

19. REV. EDMUND MILLS

Was born in Kent, Ct., 1752; graduated at Yale College 1775. He preached in various places, was invited to settle in Westboro', but finally accepted a call from the church in Sutton, as successor of Rev. Dr. Hall, where he was ordained 23 June, 1790. The sermon was preached by his brother, Samuel John Mills of Torringford, father to S. J. Mills, of missionary celebrity. He remained here until his death, 7 Nov. 1825, aged 73 years, having ministered 35 years 5 months.

Mr. Mills married Mrs. Abigail M. Packard, widow of Rev. Winslow Packard, of Wilmington, Vt., and afterwards wife of Rev. Dr. Emmons.

He left five children, three sons and two daughters. The eldest, E. J. Mills, Esq., resides in Sutton. 2. Lewis, is of the firm of Dodge, Tucker & Co., merchants, Boston. 3. Henry, is in trade at Watertown. The eldest daughter is married to William Whittlesey, Esq., of Auburndale. The second is widow of the late N. Whittlesey of West Newton, brother to the last named.

The beginning of Mr. Mills's ministry encountered the rank spirit of infidelity which followed the French Revolution, and blighted so many places in New England. But his wise and vigorous exhibitions of truth annihilated the influence and existence of an infidel club in the town, and secured the triumph of the Gospel. In 1810, the church was reduced to 55 members; but an extensive revival raised the church, and increased it to 125 members. Another season of refreshing was enjoyed ten years after, when between 40 and 50 were added to the church.

"Mr. Mills was an uncommon man. His erect and commanding person, the dignity and urbanity of his manners, his great sensibility and kindness of heart, fitted him in an admirable degree to gain the respect and good will of all who knew him.

"He was a man universally beloved and admired; and to this day is mentioned with veneration.

"He possessed great originality of mind, a fine taste, and a cultivated intellect. These, together with a warm heart, enabled him in the pulpit to command and rivet the attention of his hearers. He was distinguished for appropriateness in all his performances. Upon unusual occasions, he was ready at a moment's notice to perform any part assigned him, with propriety and effect. It was upon such occasions more than any other that he appeared the man he was. He always excelled where others failed. He was fitted by nature and by grace to gain influence and preserve it.

"His piety was of the contemplative cast. He loved retirement. He was a sound divine. The great doctrines of the Reformation as set forth by Calvin, received his most hearty assent. He was a faithful and affectionate pastor. His last prayers were for his family and his people."*

20. REV. JOHN ROBINSON

Was the son of Ichabod and Lydia (Brown) Robinson,† and was born in Lebanon, Ct., April, 1760. He graduated

---

* Tracy's Historical Sermon of Sutton.

† The father of Rev. John R., above, is supposed to be the son of Rev. John Robinson of Duxbury, who *had* a son of the same name. If so, his ancestral line is as follows:

1. William Robinson, Dorchester, 1636, *Farmer*. Supposed by some, but without positive proof, to be son of Rev. John Robinson, of Leyden. None of the name in this country, have *proved* their descent from the famous Nonconformist.

2. James, son of William.

3. Rev. John, born at Dorchester, 17 April, 1675; H. U. 1695; ordained at Duxbury, 5 June, 1702; dismissed in 1739; removed to Lebanon, Ct., and died 14 Nov. 1745. He married Hannah, daughter

at Yale College 1780, and was settled in Westboro' 14 Jan. 1789; dismissed, 1 Oct. 1807. He continued to reside in Westboro' some years after his dismission, preaching occasionally, but ultimately removed to Lebanon, his native place, where he died suddenly, dropping dead in the street, 2 May, 1832, aged 72. He was never resettled, and preached but little, being of the uncommon class of dismissed ministers, able to live without the pittances of occasional supplies.

His residence in Lebanon was marked by a controversy with the church, the result of which was, rightfully or wrongfully, his exclusion from the sacramental table.

The first wife of Mr. Robinson was a native of Westboro', by whom he had two children, who reached maturity. The oldest, Melinda, a young Christian of hopeful promise, died at the age of 23. The other, John A. Robinson, is a very eminent and wealthy merchant in New York city.

His second wife, a widow, still resides in Lebanon, Ct.*

21. REV. NATHANAEL HOWE

Was the third son of Capt. Abraham and Lucy (Appleton) Howe, of Ipswich, Linebrook parish, where he was born, 6

---

of his predecessor, Rev. Ichabod Wiswall, 31 Jan. 1705. His wife and daughter Mary, aged 16, were drowned on a passage to Boston, 22 Sept. 1722. His other children were, Hannah, Althea, Betsey, John, and Ichabod. John, jr., born 16 April, 1715, married a Hinckley of Lebanon, Ct., Teacher in Portsmouth, N. H., and died in Norwich, North Concord parish, 21 Aug. 1784.

4. Ichabod, born 12 Dec. 1720. His son William, born at Lebanon, 15 Aug. 1754, ordained at Southington, Ct., 1780, and died 15 Aug. 1825. He was the father of Rev. Edward Robinson, D. D., author of Biblical Researches, etc.

5. Rev. John, of Westboro', probably son of Ichabod.

W. R. Deane, Boston.

* Letter of D. S. Woodworth, Esq., Lebanon, Ct.

Oct. 1764. He prepared for college at Dummer Academy, Byfield, under Mr. Samuel Moody, and afterwards studied with Rev. George Leslie, his pastor, and Rev. E. Bradford, of Ipswich. With the latter he experienced religion and united with his church. He entered the junior class at Nassau Hall, Princeton, N. J., Dr. Weatherspoon from Scotland being then President; remained one year, and graduated at Harvard University 1786, and A. M.

After teaching school a while in his native town, he commenced the study of theology with Rev. Dr. Hart of Ct., which he completed with Rev. Dr. Emmons. He preached at Londonderry and Francestown, N. H., and at Hampton, Ct., and at Grafton, where he declined a call to settle. He commenced preaching at Hopkinton, 16 Jan. 1791, and in May was invited unanimously by the church to settlement. The town concurred, on condition of retaining the half-way covenant system. Mr. Howe refused any personal agency in its operation, but engaged to exchange with ministers who would administer it in his absence to such as desired.

The town assented, 18 July, and he was settled, 5 Oct. 1791. Rev. E. Bradford, of Ipswich, preached the sermon. In April, 1830, it was proposed to him, on account of increasing infirmities, to have a colleague pastor; and accordingly Rev. Amos A. Phelps was so settled as colleague 14 Sept. 1830, and continued until his dismission, 1 May, 1832. In 1833, Rev. Jeffries Hall was ordained colleague, and continued in the office until after Mr. Howe's death. With both these gentlemen Mr. H. lived on the most friendly terms. His last sermon was preached at Franklin, 25 Dec. 1836. Text, Gal. 1: 10.* His last public service was the installing prayer of Rev. D. Brigham, at Framingham. He died in peace and hope, 15 Feb. 1837, in the 73d year of his age,

---

* His vivid description of "popular preachers," and parsonages on wheels, at that time, are still quoted to this day, in F.

and 46th of his ministry. His funeral sermon was preached by Rev. J. Ide, D. D., of Medway.

Mr. Howe married Olive Jones, daughter of Col. John Jones, of Hopkinton, son of Col. John of Boston, who came to H. 1727. She died 10 Dec. 1843, "as distinguished as her husband." They had *four* children:

1. Appleton, H. U. 1815, M. D., and State Senator; also Major Gen. 1st Div. Mass. Militia; resides in Weymouth.

2. Eliza, died 1815, aged 21.

3. Mary, married Rev. Samuel Russell, Boylston; died 1836.

4. Lucy Ann, married John Fitch, son of Dea. Elijah F., and grandson of Rev. Elijah Fitch, of Hopkinton.

There is little need, for the present generation, of any portraiture of Mr. Howe's character, in these brief sketches. And there is every prospect that its impressive features will be perpetuated in his celebrated Century Sermon, and its valuable illustrative notes, which has now reached its fourth edition, and been translated into foreign languages.

He is especially remembered for his fervency and appropriateness in prayer; his originality and raciness of expression in his sermons; and his earnest sympathy with his subject in their delivery; — for his generosity, often eccentric in its exhibition, and his unflinching utterance of truth, let it fall where it might. "He was rightly named Nathanael, an Israelite, indeed, in whom there is no guile!"*

His publications were, —

1. A Funeral Sermon, 1808.

2. A Century Sermon, 24 Dec. 1815.

3. A Sermon on the Design of John's Baptism, preached before the Mendon Association, Foxboro', 1819.

4. A Reply to Dr. Baldwin on John's Baptism, 1820.

---

* See Century Sermon, and notes by E. Nason, A. M.; fourth edition, from which the above sketch is digested.

5. A Catechism, with Miscellaneous Questions, and a Chapter of Proverbs, for the Children under his Pastoral Care, 1834.

22. REV. SAMUEL JUDSON

Was born 8 December, 1767, in Woodbury, Ct. Graduated at Yale College 1790 and A. M., and was ordained over the church in Uxbridge, 17 Oct. 1792. He was dismissed on account of ill health in 1832, and soon died, 11 Nov. 1832, aged 65 years.

Mr. Judson married Sally Bartlett, daughter of Mr. Walter P. and Elizabeth (Norris) Bartlett, of Salem. They had five children, three sons and two daughters. The oldest son, Walter P. Bartlett, grad. B. U. 1818, A. M.; and M. D. at Harvard, 1821. He practised medicine in Bridgewater until his health failed; went to New Orleans, and died there 1825. The second son resides in Connecticut. Their eldest daughter married the late Rev. Albert Cole, of Bluehill, Me. The youngest son and daughter are active Christians in Uxbridge.

"Mr. Judson was sound in the faith, a consistent minister of the Gospel, an excellent pastor, and highly respected and beloved by his people."*

He gave a thousand dollars to found a scholarship for the education of pious young men. Not long before his death, his church were exiled from the house of their fathers; but he lived long enough to see a new house dedicated to the worship of the Triune God, and a godly successor of like faith to his own ordained.

---

* Letter of Miss S. J., Uxbridge.

23. REV. JOHN WILDER

Was born in Templeton, 12 March, 1758.* He was the son of Mr. Jonas and Elizabeth Wilder, and removed with them to Lancaster, in 1776. He graduated at Dartmouth, 1784, and A. M.; studied theology with Rev. Dr. Hart, of Preston, Ct., and was ordained in Attleboro', 27 Jan'y, 1790. He was dismissed 28 Nov., 1822, and died in Attleboro', 9 Feb. 1836, aged 78 years.

Mr. Wilder married Esther Tyler, daughter of Col. Samuel Tyler, of Preston, Ct. Mrs. Wilder died, 19 Jan. 1811.† He married Mrs. Elizabeth Austin, of New Hartford, Ct., sister to the late Dr. E. D. Griffin. She died at Austinburgh, March, 1847, aged 72. His children were:

1. Esther, died at the age of 18. (Funeral Sermon: Dr. Emmons's Works, Vol. III, p. 93.)
2. Eliza, m. Hon. Lemuel May, Esq., S. Attleboro': d. 1831 aged 39.
3. Julia, resides in Jewett's City, Ct.
4. John, Rev., grad. Brown Univ. 1822, settled in Charleton 1828, died March, 1844. He m. Mary W., d. of Nehemiah Jones, Esq., Raynham. He was a talented and useful minister of the Gospel.
5. Jonas, a distinguished school teacher in Brighton; died 1838, m. Miss P. Hyde, d. of Capt. Samuel H. of Newton: See obit. in B. Recorder, 22 June, '38.
6. Samuel T., grad. Brown Univ. 1825; Lawyer in Rochester, N. Y., where he died 1837, aged 37.
7. Charles B., merchant in Boston; m. Mary A., d. of Mr. Ebenezer Guild, S. Attleboro'.
8. Betsey B., resides in Lowell.

---

* Rev. L. Sabin, Templeton.

† See her Funeral Sermon, Dr. Emmons's works, Vol. III, p. 104.

9. Amy Ann, m. Rev. J. W. Smith, of Eaton Rapids, Mich., where she died, in 1846, aged 37.

10. Joseph A., Merchant, Philadelphia; m. Mary, d. of Capt. Henry Smith, of Dedham.

11. Richard E., school teacher, in Kentucky.

12. George G., Merchant, in Boston; m. Martha, d. of Mr. Benjamin Swan, of Fitchburg.

The funeral sermon of Mr. Wilder, by Rev. E. Fiske, of Wrentham, was printed, and exhibits him as an able, firm preacher of the Hopkinsian school, and eminently useful in his work.

Mr. Wilder's ministry succeeded a long vacancy of eight years, in the pastoral office, following the death of Rev. Habijah Weld; in which time so much difference of opinion about candidates prevailed, that the church appointed a "Fast on account of present difficulties." Upon his settlement, these differences disappeared, and unanimity marked the thirty-two years of his pastoral connection with them, in which time the church grew, and was strengthened.

Mr. Wilder was a faithful pastor, a clear and convincing preacher, and respected by his people to the end of his life. His memory is gratefully preserved by them to this day.

He published several sermons, among which are, Funeral Sermon of Dea. Lane, also of Hon. Elisha May; Fast Sermon, 1805; Sermon on "The Coming of The Lord;" Address before the Attleboro' Agricultural Society.

24. REV. BENJAMIN WOOD

Was the son of Joseph and Ellen (Palmer) Wood, and was born in Lebanon, N. H., 15 Sept., 1772. He was the eleventh of twelve children, seven sons and five daughters, ten of whom reached maturity. The eldest son was the late Samuel Wood D. D., of Boscawen, N. H. The youngest is now a clergyman in the State of New York. His parents at the first resided in Mansfield, Ct., and removed to Lebanon, N. H. 1767.

He fitted for college with his brother Samuel, and graduated at Dartmouth, 1793, and A. M. He commenced Theology with his brother, then settled at Boscawen, and completed his course with Rev. Dr. Emmons. He first preached in Upton, 14 June,1795; on December 17, received an unanimous call to settle there, which he accepted, 12 March, and was ordained in Upton 1 June, 1796. He was urged to take charge of the newly organized Central Church in Worcester in 1820, but he refused; and, according to his then reply, "I shall leave my bones in Upton," adhered to his first choice until his death, 24 April, 1849, aged 76.

Mr. Wood married Miss Betsey Dustin, of Haverhill, a descendant of the Mrs. Dustin taken by the Indians. His second wife was Miss Almira Howe; she died 16 Sept., 1845, after a sickness of six years.

He had seven children; Betsy, Palmer, Fanny, Philena, Maria, Willard, and Hannah.

During the fifty three years of Mr. Wood's labors in Upton, eight distinct seasons of refreshing were enjoyed, which resulted in the addition of over four hundred members to the church. He lived to see a new house of worship opened. When the old pulpit was forsaken, he felt it was time that the voice which had spoken from it half a century should be silent. His last sermon was preached on the last Sabbath in March before his death, and was addressed to the youth. Then he laid down to die. To a clerical brother, he expressed his dying faith, "I have been examining the doctrines which I preached, to see if any of them may be spared: but I cannot part with one. They are all precious; They are all links in a golden chain."

"Mr. Wood was a man of great excellence. He was a gentleman and a Christian. His vivacity and kindness of disposition, associated with his piety, made religion in him appear with peculiar beauty.

"He was a sound and discriminating theologian; a faithful, efficient, and popular preacher. He was eminently a doctrinal preacher. There was an aptness and vivacity in his instructions, a clearness in his statements and reasoning that, aside from any peculiarity of voice and manner, would have made him an interesting and popular preacher."*

25. REV. JOHN CLEAVELAND, JR.

Was born in Ipswich, 17 Jan. 1749–50. He was the son of Rev. John Cleaveland, of the Fourth church, Chebacco parish, Ipswich, now Essex. His father was born in Canterbury, Ct., 1722; Yale Coll. 1745; and was chaplain four years in the French war, at Louisburg and Ticonderoga.† The subject of this sketch, with his younger brother, commenced preparation for Yale college; but the father being unable to support both in college, decided to treat both alike, and give them the best education he could. On this account, he never graduated. For a time, he served as soldier in the war of the Revolution;‡ but left, and resumed his studies in private, and qualified himself for the ministry. He received an honorary A. M., Union Coll., 1803. He was ordained at Stoneham, 19 Oct., 1785, and dismissed 23 Oct. 1794; was installed over the Second or North church in Wrentham, 6 June, 1798; where he died, 1 Feb., 1815, aged 65 years, after a wasting sickness by consumption. While at Stoneham,

* See Extract from his Funeral Sermon, in B. Recorder.

† He was son of Josiah and Abigail Cleaveland, and b. 11April,1722. Ordained at Chebacco, 25 July, 1747; m. 1. Mary, dau. of Parker Dodge, 31 July, 1747. 2d. Mary, widow of Capt. John Foster, of Manchester, Sept. 1769.—*Hist. Ipswich*, p. 263.

‡ John Cleaveland served as chaplain in Col. Little's regiment, xvii Foot, Cont. Army, enlisted 1 July, 1775.

he married Miss Abigail Adams of Canterbury, Ct. She died of small pox, in 1793. His second wife was Miss Elizabeth Evans, of Stoneham. She was not pious, but afterwards became eminently so.* She afterwards became the wife of Rev. Dr. Harris, of Dunbarton, N. H.

While Mr. Cleaveland was in Wrentham, several seasons of religious interest were enjoyed amongst his people, and a large proportion of them were converted to God. They were days of brightness and prosperity to that part of the Lord's vineyard.

Mr. Cleaveland was grave and sedate. "He possessed a singular talent at turning conversation to some useful subject, and at making pertinent and serious remarks with ease and propriety.

"He dwelt much, in his preaching, upon experimental religion. His discourses were more solid than brilliant, more sentimental than declamatory ; and better adapted to assist the memory, enlighten the understanding, and awaken the conscience, and penetrate the heart, than to excite the admiration, or gratify the vain curiosity of his hearers."†

He published a few occasional sermons : one, 'War,' preached fast-day, 1812.

Mr. Cleaveland invariably devoted two afternoons, weekly, to systematic visitation of his people, and the rest of the week as systematically to study.

He was remarkably punctual ; so much so, that when he found he was likely to arrive at the meeting-house five minutes too soon, he would walk his horse, so as invariably to reach the door within *three* minutes of the time. He had also an almost prophetic induction of future events. By calm colla-

---

* This marriage with a non-professor, troubled some pious minds at Stoneham, and occasioned his dismission; without the least charge, however, to the pastor or his wife.

† See Funeral Sermon, by Rev. Dr. Emmons.

tion of Scripture with history, he very fully predicted, to confidential friends, half a century ago, just such improvements in education and facilities for travel as are now taking place.

As Mr. C. had no children, he adopted two as daughters: Miss Nancy Felt, now Mrs. J. C. Proctor, of Boston, and Miss Mary Robishaw, now of Walpole; natives of Wrentham.

26. REV. NATHAN HOLMAN

Was the third son of Mr. David and Lucy (Thurston) Holman, and was born in that part of Sutton now called Millbury, 17 May, 1769. He descended from Solomon Holman of Newbury.*

He labored upon his father's farm until his 21st year, when his ardent thirst for knowledge set him determinately at work to procure a liberal education. He had no funds of his own, and could expect but little direct assistance from his father, who had a family of twelve children to provide for;

* The Holman family migrated from Wales to the Bermuda Islands, between 1670 and 1690. It included three sons born in Wales. Two of the sons, Solomon and John, were seized by a press-gang and brought to Newburyport. There they succeeded in escaping from the British ship. John, the younger, settled in North Carolina. Solomon settled in Newbury, married a Miss Barton, of Old York, and had four sons and three daughters, viz. Solomon, Edward, Thomas, and John; Anna m. Richard Waters, Rachel m. Samuel Waters, and Sarah m. Abel Chase. Solomon, Edward, and Thomas settled in Sutton, before 1732. They were among the original proprietors of Millbury.

Edward m. Hannah Emory of Newbury, and had eleven children, — six sons and five daughters.

David, his third son, m. Lucy Thurston, of Uxbridge, — an orphan from infancy, and had twelve children. Eight sons and one daughter reached maturity.

Nathan, above, was their third son.—*Letter of Rev. David Holman, Douglas, brother of Nathan.*

but by uncommon adherence to his cherished purpose, he succeeded. He graduated at Brown university, 1797, and A. M., with distinguished honors; and immediately commenced the study of theology with Rev. Edmund Mills of Sutton. He spent the close of his course with Rev. Dr. Emmons.

After approbation, he preached in several places with great success, and received several calls to settle in the ministry. Early in 1800, he commenced preaching in East Attleboro', and was ordained there, 15 Oct. 1800, the successor of Rev. Ebenezer Lazell. After laboring nearly 21 years, he was, to the regret of his people, dismissed, 22 May, 1821.* He still resided in Attleboro', supplying destitute pulpits as he was able, while he lived. He died suddenly, 28 Oct., 1844, at the age of 75 years. His monument is conspicuous in the burying-ground, north of the meeting-house where he spent his strength, — a plain pyramidal shaft, with the brief inscription, above the usual dates:

"LOOK TO GOD."

Mr. Holman married Miss Lettice, daughter of Mr. Samuel Morey, of Norton. She died 6 March, 1848. They had three children:

1. Samuel Morey. Married Miss Lincoln, of Norton, and lives in Attleboro'.

2. David Emory. Married Miss Jane Bolcom. Resides in Attleboro'.

---

* The real cause of his dismission, (undivulged at the time, as appears from his papers,) was two-fold: 1. His objection to the introduction of *wind* instruments, in sacred music, on the Sabbath. 2. His not proposing a relinquishment of some part of his salary. He asked a dismission, April 12. At two church-meetings, *not one* was in favor of granting his request. At the third, only *two*. The rest of the church present, 28, refused to act. Accordingly, the request was declared granted.

3. Mary Hodges, the wife of Col. M. Stone, of Norton. At the time of Mr. Holman's settlement in Attleboro', the church was in a very reduced state. There had been but *nine* additions for eighteen years. There were but ten active male members, and none of these under fifty years. A deep interest in religion marked the commencement of his ministry. He says in a sermon, "From the first sermon preached by me in this pulpit, some dated those serious impressions upon their minds, which resulted in hopeful conversion." During the first two years of his ministry, forty-three were added to the church. Then for twelve years religion declined, and only twelve were added. In 1814, his labors were blessed with another and very extensive outpouring of the Holy Spirit. The work continued two years, and resulted in the addition of one hundred and thirty-four to the church.

This revival seemed to give new life to the church, and wrought a great change in the morals and habits of the people. Many deeply interesting facts are remembered of this surprising work of grace. As a specimen, "a pious father travelled some thirty miles to bring home an absent child, saying, 'it is my duty to place my children where God is.' Next day she attended a conference, and the 30 Hymn II Book, of Watts was sung:—

'Come, we who love the Lord,
And let our joys be known,' etc.

She arose and sung the first and second stanzas with others. When they began the third,

'Let those refuse to sing,
Who never knew their God,'—

she dropped upon her seat, and knew no peace till she found it in believing."*

* Historical Sketches, by Rev. J. Crane, p. 41.

Mr. Holman thus speaks of the religious experience of the subjects of this work of grace. Their relations "were particularly Scriptural, and truly orthodox. In general, those who have united with the church for twenty years past have fully embraced the system of doctrine, which is called Hopkinsian."

It is perhaps needless to say that Mr. Holman believed and preached the same system of Divine truth.

He was a clear, plain and discriminating preacher of the doctrines of grace. As a pastor, he was eminently adapted to labor in seasons of religious interest. The writer well remembers his serious appeals in public, and his faithful exhortations, and wise directions in the inquiry-meeting, during a revival of religion in Franklin, where he supplied the pulpit after Dr. Emmons's resignation. He had ever a peculiar and impressive solemnity in the pulpit, especially in his prayers, which seldom failed to impart itself to the assembly.

His manners and habits were marked by regularity, precision, firmness and industry.* He had by nature a kind and benevolent disposition, and in all his intercourse, as a pastor, citizen, husband and father, the law of kindness was written on his heart.

His style as a writer was pure and chaste. His productions are marked by unity of subject, and every sentence tells upon the final impression. They abound in terse apothegms.

---

* The *Loom* by which Mr. H. procured the means of his education was still kept in working order in his garret at Attleboro,' on which he plied the shuttle almost daily during his ministry. The first suit of clothes says one of his sons, which he wore to meeting, when a boy, were of his father's weaving. As evidence of Mr. H's perseverance, it is said that he studied Latin and Greek while at work in the field ; setting open his book on the wall at one side of the plot of ground, and conning his declensions and paradigms, while he followed the plough, the hoe, or the scythe across and back. He thus *worked* his way through the farm and the classics at the same time.

Many sentences, heard from his lips twenty years ago, are still fresh in mind, even to the exact phraseology.

Mr. Holman published several occasional sermons and addresses. The publication of a volume from his manuscripts, has been contemplated.

27. REV. OTIS THOMPSON

Is the son of Nathaniel Thompson, and was born in Middleboro', 14 Sept., 1776. He graduated at Brown University 1798, and A. M. For the two years following his graduation, he filled the office of tutor to the College; the last year in connection with Rev. E. Fisk, of Wrentham. He pursued the study of theology while instructing in the University, and was ordained over the church in Rehoboth, 24 Sept., 1800. He continued in this connection until his dismission, 30 Oct. 1832. He afterwards preached in various places, until 1840, when he removed to the state of New York, and took charge of a church in Litchfield, Herkimer Co., N. Y.; which charge he relinquished in 1849. Since the latter date, he has resided in North Abington, his present abiding place.

Mr. Thompson married Miss Rachel Chandler of Plympton, by whom he had nine children, six of whom survive. Of his four daughters, one was married to Rev. Tyler Thacher, now of California; one to Rev. Origen Batchellor, once editor of the Anti-Universalist; one to a Mr. Carpenter, of Auburndale; and one to Mr. Lewis Kent, of Boston. None of his sons are in the ministry. His wife died in 1827, and he married Miss Charlotte Fales, of Bristol, R. I. She died in 1849. His present wife was Miss Polly Shaw, of North Abington.

Mr. Thompson is chiefly known as an experienced and skilful theological instructor and writer.

During his ministry he superintended the theological

studies of fifteen candidates for the ministry, eleven of whom are noticed in these sketches.*

The chief of Mr. Thompson's publications are the following: —

1. "A Review of Rev. Thomas Andros's Essay on Divine Efficiency." 12mo., 1821.

2. "The Hopkinsian Magazine," a monthly, and making four volumes in eight years, 1824–32.

3. "Sermons, Doctrinal and Practical." Vol. I. 12mo. pp. 336, 1850.

4. 16 Funeral Sermons, 6 Ordination Sermons, 3 Fast and Thanksgiving Sermons, 5 Occasional Sermons, making 30 pamphlets.

These works show the author to be an acute metaphysical thinker, a discriminating writer, and a thorough, consistent Hopkinsian, who understands his position and his definitions, and leaves no obstacle to prevent others from doing the same. Though now the *oldest* of the living clergymen who have been connected with this body, and though his earthly tabernacle trembles under the load of years, his mind shows no indications of yielding to the pressure of age.

28. REV. DAVID LONG

Was the son of Mr. Enoch and Abigail Long, and was born in Newbury 3 Feb., 1772. At the age of five years, he removed with his parents to Hopkinton, N. H. He became

* The following is a list of Mr. Thompson's students. Those starred are elsewhere mentioned. * Daniel Thomas. Jason Chamberlain, Prof. in Vermont University, deceased. * Alvan Cobb. * Jonas Perkins. * Stetson Raymond. * Lot B. Sullivan. * Josephus Wheaton. * Augustus B. Read. Jabez Porter, never settled, deceased. * Silas Shores. * Moses Thacher. *Tyler Thacher. * Elam Smalley. Ebenezer W. Robinson, Lisbon, Ct. Stephen S. Harrison, Bloomingdale, Ill.

a subject of Divine grace in his nineteenth year, and united with the church under Rev. Jacob Cram. He fitted for college under the eye of Rev. Mr. Paige of Hopkinton, N. H., and Rev. Dr. Wood of Boscawen; and entered the sophomore class of 1795 at Dartmouth College, and graduated 1798, and A. M. He studied theology with Rev. Walter Harris, D. D., of Dunbarton, N. H. He received invitations to settle in the ministry, both at Deering, N. H., and at Manchester, Mass., but declined them. He came to Milford in 1800, and was ordained there 20 May, 1801. He continued in the pastoral office until 1844, when he resigned to a successor. He remained in Milford until his death, which event occurred while he was on a visit to a sick daughter, at Hartford, Ct., 13 March, 1850. He was 78 years old, and had been nearly 49 years in the ministry.

Mr. Long married Miss Lois Howe in 1794, who died in a few months. He married a second time, 4 June, 1804, Miss Rebecca Curtis of Worcester, by whom he had *four* children. The mother died 24 June, 1824. None of the children are now alive. The daughter, at whose house Mr. Long closed his days, Mrs. Maria A., wife of Mr. Hoyt Freeman, of Hartford, Ct., followed him in three weeks. The only child who survived him, Claudius B. Long, died in 1851. Mr. Long married a third time, 17 April, 1826, Miss Sophia Rice, of Marlboro', who still lives.

"Mr. Long was a firm believer in the distinguishing doctrines of the Gospel, as they were taught and believed by our Pilgrim Fathers. (He was an intelligent Hopkinsian.)

"His sermons were able, well studied, and correctly written; not so remarkable for their brilliancy as for their depth of thought and weight of matter. In his delivery, there was more of that distinctness, moderation, and solemnity, which the philosophic and patient thinker prizes, than that rapidity of utterance, animation of feeling, and energy of manner, which are pleasing to all, and deemed indispensable by some, with whom the chief object of preaching is animal excitement.

"There was a beautiful correspondence between the truths which he taught and the principles by which his own conduct was governed. Integrity and uprightness were leading features in his character. When he once made a promise, everybody expected he would fulfil it. He *would* do right at all events.

"There were repeated revivals among his people during his ministry. But he gathered men by individuals rather than by multitudes into the church; and his success lay rather in establishing Christians in the faith once delivered to the saints, in inculcating the duties which devolved upon them as the professed disciples of Christ, and in disciplining their minds for their holy warfare, than in rapidly increasing their number. There are comparatively few men that have done more for the kingdom of Christ, in similar circumstances."*

Mr. Long published but one sermon, on the return of an artillery company from the war of 1812.

29. REV. ELISHA FISK

Was the son of Robert and Mary (Hall) Fisk, and was born in that part of Holliston now included in West Medway, 3 Sept., 1769.† At a year and a half of age his parents

* See Funeral Sermon, by Rev. Dr. Ide; also, Obituary in Assoc. Records.

† Mr. Fisk descended from William Fisk, brother of Rev. John Fisk, minister of Chelmsford, where he died 14 Jan., 1676. William Fisk arrived 1637, admitted freeman 1642, member of the church, Salem, 2 July, 1641; removed to Wenham, where he was town clerk, and rep. from 1647 to 1650, and died 1654. His widow married a Rix, of Salem. His grandson, Daniel, removed from Wenham to Upton in 1748, and died about 1761. He had eight children. Samuel, one of

removed to Upton, where he spent his youth, and where he became a child of God, under the ministry of Rev. Elisha Fish; whose name differed from his own by but a single letter. At five years of age he had read the Bible through. He set himself to gain a liberal education with reference to the ministry, and by dint of perseverance, entered Brown University, and graduated 1795, and A. M. He was tutor the three years following. While here, he was approbated to preach the Gospel.

He preached the first time in Wrentham, on the first Sabbath in May, 1798. It was the first sermon he wrote, and the text was Gen. 1 : 1. It proved to be the first of a long series of discourses to that people. Nov. 6th, he received a call to settle amongst them. The prospect was dark indeed, but circumstances appeared to make duty very plain. He was the *forty-ninth* candidate, and but the second who had received a call. Imagining the interminable catalogue which might follow if he declined, he decided to break this non-apostolic succession, and accepted the invitation, 25 April. He was ordained over the first church in Wrentham 12 June, 1799. Rev. Dr. Hitchcock of Providence preached the sermon. After occupying the field alone nearly 45 years, he proposed that a colleague should be settled, and Rev. Horace James was inducted into this office 1 November, 1843. Mr. Fisk still continued to preach almost every Sabbath at home, in surrounding vacant places, or in the pulpits of his brethren.

The last Sabbath he spent on earth was employed in preaching the Gospel and breaking the sacramental bread

---

the sons, removed to Shelburne, and was the ancestor of Rev. Pliny Fisk. Daniel, the oldest son, born about 1723, married Zelpah Tyler, and had five children. Of them, Robert, born 24 February, 1746, married Mary Hall, and had four children. The eldest was Elisha Fisk, above. — *Letter of M. Plimpton, Esq., Boston.*

to the church in Attleboro'. It was an intensely cold day in December, and the fatigue and exposure of riding in an open sleigh some ten miles was more than a human frame of over four score years standing could endure. A cold and fever was the result, running into a lethargic state, in which the ever-busy spirit, having put its weary partner of dust to sleep, softly withdrew to the presence of God. He died 7 Jan., 1851, in the 82d year of his age, and 52d of his ministry, and was buried on the day of the regular meeting of the Association at his house. It was appointed to be there at his request, and he had anticipated its coming with great satisfaction, — not imagining that they should be convened for his funeral!

Mr. Fisk married first, Lydia, daughter of John and Susanna Robinson of Milford. She died 11 July, 1805, leaving two children. He next married Mrs. Margaret Brown, daughter of Capt. Benjamin and Hepsibah (Blake) Shepherd, of Wrentham. She died 30 April, 1850. His children were, —

1. Mary Hall, married Rev. George Fisher, Harvard, and died 29 April, 1852, aged 51.

2. Charles Robinson, grad. Brown University 1824, and now a clergyman in Illinois.

3. Charlotte Brown, daughter of his second wife, by a former husband, who married Rev. Amos A. Phelps of Boston, and died Aug., 1838.

4. Emily Frances, married to Capt. Wm. Sturtevant, of New Bedford.

5. William Jones, died in 1830, aged 16.

6. Frederick Augustus, Rev. (See Licentiates, No. 119).

7. Harriet Josephine, wife of Rev. Erasmus D. Moore, of Boston.

At the time of Mr. Fisk's ordination, the church was reduced to *ten* members; and "they were divided in their religious opinions, and in many instances strongly excited against each other, on account of the different positions which they had taken in the controversy with his predecessor, Rev. Mr. Avery. Of an observing mind, careful and conciliating in his conversation and manners, interesting and popular in his pulpit performances, he succeeded, as few other men would, in uniting and holding together very discordant materials, not only at the commencement of his ministry, but through the vicissitudes of more than fifty years. He gained and kept the enviable reputation of *peace-maker*."*

He was blessed with several seasons of refreshing from the presence of the Lord. In 1805, 51 were added to the church. In 1815 and 16, 64 made profession of religion. In 1821, 43 were gathered in. Again, 58 joined in 1832. The whole number of admissions during his *sole* ministry was 432.

Mr. Fisk possessed an iron constitution, and great perseverance, and was able to labor, even in his advanced age, beyond the ability of many young men. He frequently took long walks of five and even ten miles on his exchanges. He travelled much on foot over his extensive parish. He was seldom unable to preach; but two Sabbaths in forty years. He was seldom absent, or even tardy, at Associational meetings. He attended over one hundred and fifty ecclesiastical councils; and did a large part of the editing of the "Christian Magazine," during its four years' continuance; and was in all ministerial labors abundant.

"Mr. Fisk was sound in doctrine, fervent in his devotions, and active and laborious in his efforts to do good. He ex-

---

* Funeral Sermon, by Rev. Dr. Storrs, Braintree. As a fact illustrative of Mr. Fisk's reputation, the celebrated Hannah Adams once said, that another question should be added to well-known interrogatories in the New England Primer, 'Who is the first man,' etc., viz.: 'Who is the most prudent man? . Parson Fisk, of Wrentham.'

celled in the carefulness and prudence with which he was accustomed to feel his way through difficulties, and to compose conflicting elements just ready to burst into a storm.

"He had a fondness for society, was eminently social in his tastes, and acceptable in company. His vivacity and interest in young people rendered him a pleasant friend to all. His attachment to his ministerial brethren, and enjoyment in their society, was unbounded."*

Mr. Fisk lived long enough to pass through the regular and usual phases of a pastor's life; which may be divided into the attractive novelty of the first settlement, the period of common-place regard, of indifference, of burdened uneasiness, of reviving veneration, and, if he live long enough to celebrate his jubilee, the period of *rare relics*, of whose possession his people will be justly proud.

Mr. Fisk will be remembered chiefly, for the heavenly fervor and unction of his prayers, and for his lively interest in children and youth. His apt sayings to them, have a warrant of immortality in their memories for at least half a century to come.

Mr. Fisk published several sermons; among them are, 1. Address on removing the bodies of Dea. Tho. Mann and wife into a tomb, 1813; 2. Ord. Sermon of Rev. Martin Moore, at Natick, 1814; 3. Sermon before the Norfolk Co. Education Society, 1819; 4. Funeral Sermon of Maj. Erastus Emmons, 1820; 5. Sermon before the Mass. Soc. for the promotion of Christian Knowledge, 1822; 6. Funeral Sermon of Mrs. David Fisher, Esq., 1827; 7. Do. Rev. John Wilder, 1836; 8. Two Sermons on the 47th anniversary of his settlement, 1846; 9. Semi-centennial Sermon of his settlement, 1849.

---

* Obituary Notice in Assoc. Records.

30. REV. SAMUEL AUSTIN, D. D.

Was born at New Haven, Ct., 7 Oct., 1760. He was the eldest son and child of Samuel and Lydia (Wolcot) Austin. At the age of sixteen he took his father's place in the army, who had been drafted as a soldier, and did military duty in New York. When the British took possession of the city, he obtained a discharge and returned home. He taught school two or three years, and then commenced studying law with Judge Chauncey, of New Haven. But he soon dropped his professional studies, and began upon the classics. In one year he fitted himself for the Sophomore Class, which he entered at Yale College, 1781. In the same year he joined the College Church. He graduated 1783, with the highest honors of the college, in a class of forty-two members, and was also a Dean scholar. He recieved A. M. in course from his alma mater, and also from New Jersey, 1785, and D. D. 1807 from Williams College. After graduation, he commenced the study of Theology with Rev. Jonathan Edwards, D. D., then settled in New Haven. At the same time, he taught an English and Grammar school. In 1784, he took charge of the academy at Norwich.

He was approbated to preach the Gospel, 12 Oct, 1784, by the New London Association, and on the following Sabbath, preached his first sermon in Chelsea, now Norwich City. Soon after, he preached in New York, and received an unanimous invitation from the Middle Dutch Church, to settle as colleague with Rev. Dr. Livingston. He declined on account of scruples at the half-way covenant there practised. He also declined a call to settle in Hampton, Ct. In 1786, he was invited by the society of Fairhaven in New Haven, and was ordained there 9 Nov., 1786. His class-mate, afterwards Dr. Morse, of Charlestown, was ordained Evangelist at the same time. After three years, the society was remerged in

Dr. Edwards's society, and Mr. Austin resigned, 19 Jan., 1790. The first society in Worcester, hearing of his intention to leave, sent him an invitation to resettle with them. He was installed over the first church in Worcester, 29 Sept., 1790. In 1815, he was invited to the presidency of the University of Vermont, at Burlington, Vt. Into this office, he was inducted, 26 July, 1815. He continued at this post about six years, — encountering great difficulties in resuscitating and sustaining the institution, — and resigned in 1821. Hearing of the feeble and destitute state of the church in Newport, over which Dr. Hopkins was once pastor, he offered to come and supply them, an offer which they gladly accepted. He was installed at Newport, 25 July, 1821. But his health admonished him to seek a less laborious post, and he resigned the pastoral charge in 1825, and withdrew to the family of John W. Hubbard, Esq, of Worcester, son of Mrs. Austin's sister, and whom they had brought up from a child. But this quiet retreat was broken up suddenly, by Mr. Hubbard's death. The inroads of aggravated disease, affliction, and perplexities in the settlement of his nephew's estate, induced upon Dr. Austin a deep melancholy passing into a temporary insanity, to which he had an inherited constitutional tendency, that clouded his remaining days.

He spent the year 1827 with his brother-in-law, Mr. John Hopkins, of Northampton. In 1828, he went to reside with his nephew, Rev. Samuel H. Riddell, of Glastonbury, Ct., where he died 4 Dec., 1830, in his 71st year.

Dr. Austin married, 14 Sept., 1788, Miss Jerusha Hopkins, daughter of Rev. Dr. Samuel Hopkins, of Hadley.* She survived him. They had no children.

Intellectually, Dr. Austin sustained a high rank among scholars. His powers of conception and imagination, to-

* See Note on Dr. Emmons, No. 12.

gether with comparison and association of ideas, were unusually developed. As a writer, his style was nervous, copious, and unstudied. Its faults were those of redundance, diffuseness, and occasional negligence. As a preacher, he ranked among the most able, eloquent, and popular of American divines. His manner in the pulpit was solemn, dignified, and commanding. The tones of his voice were full and flexible; his enunciation, free and emphatic.

His doctrinal tenets were thoroughly Calvinistic; in general accordance with those of Edwards, Bellamy, and Hopkins. And these he "heartily and earnestly inculcated upon his hearers." He instructed many students in theology, among whom may be mentioned Dr. Samuel Worcester, of Salem, and Rev. Leonard Worcester, of Peacham, Vt., who imbibed here the missionary spirit, bearing fruit so rich at this day.

Dr. Austin issued several publications; among them the following:

1. A View of the Church. 2. Lectures on Baptism: a review of Merrill's Sermons, 1805. 3. Reply to Merrill's Twelve Lectures, 1806. 4. Dissertations on the several fundamental articles of Christian Theology, 1826. Also, the following sermons: on Disinterested Love, 1790. Funeral sermon on a Mr. and Miss Smith, of Exeter, N. H., 1790. On Death of Miss Hannah Blair, 1794. Thanksgiving Sermon, 1797. Ordination Sermon of Rev. Samuel Worcester, 1798. Of Rev. Leonard Worcester, 1800. Of Rev. Warren Fay and Rev. J. M. Whiton, 1808. Dedication at Hadley, 1808. Fast Sermon, 1811. Two Fast Sermons, 1812. Dedication Sermon, at Worcester, 1823. Sermon before the Mass. Miss. Soc., 1803. Fourth of July Address, at Worcester, 1825.*

* Abridged from his Memoir, in Quart. Reg. Vol. IX. p. 201.

31. REV. WILLIAM WARREN

Was born in New Ipswich, N. H. Graduated at Dartmouth, 1800; studied theology with Rev. Dr. Emmons, and was ordained, at Dighton, in 1802; dismissed in 1815; and removed to the state of New York, where he entirely resigned the duties and designations of the ministry, and turned to the practice of medicine. The date and place of his death have not been ascertained.

Mr. Warren married a daughter of Capt. John Davis, of Dighton, and left a large family of children, five of whom are living.

Mr. Warren was endowed, by nature, with uncommon mental abilities, and was one of the most popular preachers in Bristol county. His eminently social qualities made him a welcome visitor amongst his people, who delighted to show their hospitality in the way universal half a century ago. The pastor, thus *cordially* treated, formed intemperate habits, which incapacitated him for the functions of the ministry, and compelled him to resort to another calling and another region; a painful fruit of those usages which cannot be too speedily expelled from every vocation and every region of society where they still linger.

32. REV. PRESERVED SMITH

Was the son of Elder Ebenezer Smith, Baptist minister of Ashfield, and his wife Remember (Ellis) Smith, daughter of Richard Ellis, who came from Ireland, 1617.* He was

* He was sixth in descent from Rev. Henry Smith, of England. Settled in Weathersfield, Ct., 1641, and died 1648; who, tradition avers, had a son born on the passage, which was called *Preserved*, a name still retained. His father was a Baptist preacher 72 years, and died at the age of 90. The Elder, when to be married, took his lady behind him, on horseback, from Ashfield, — then Huntstown, — to Deerfield, there

born in Ashfield, 25 June, 1759; and, at an early age, became a member of the Baptist church.

He had a great thirst for knowledge, and taught himself in arithmetic, with chalk and a piece of bark. The sight of a Latin grammar, determined him to learn the language.

When the revolutionary war began, he entered the army and served five campaigns as a soldier. He was present at the surrender of Burgoyne. He left the army at the age of nineteen, 'bought his time' of his father, purchased a piece of ground, paid for it with the first crop, sold it at an advance, and with the proceeds, set himself to carry into effect his early resolves for an education.

He fitted for college with Rev. Messrs. Hubbard of Shelburne and Murdock of Pawlet, Vt. He entered Brown University one year in advance, and graduated in 1786; studied theology with Rev. John Emerson, of Conway, and was approbated by the Hampshire Association in the spring of 1787.

He was ordained at Rowe, Nov. 1787, and dismissed May, 1804. After declining an invitation to resettle in Whitingham and Guilford, Vt., he was installed over the first and second churches in Mendon, 2 Oct., 1805. In 1812, the people of Rowe invited him to return to them. His attachments to his former parishioners, and the labor of two churches, attended besides with some unpleasant differences, at the latter place, induced him to accept, and he was dismissed from Mendon, 20 Oct., 1812, and in Dec. was resettled at Rowe, where he remained until July, 1832, when his age induced him to resign. He died at Warwick, 15 Aug., 1834, aged 75.

Mr. Smith married, 1 Jan., 1788, Miss Eunice Wells, daughter of Col. David Wells of Shelburne. Born in Col-

---

being no minister or magistrate nearer, to perform the ceremony; and his father rode another horse, before him, with a gun, to keep off the Indians. This was in 1756.

chester, Ct., 12 May, 1764; removed to Shelburne with the family in 1771, and died 13 July, 1847, aged 83. They had two children.

1. Preserved, jr., born 1 Aug., 1789. Grad. B. U. 1812. Rev. settled at Warwick 30 years; at Pembroke, 4 years; now in Deerfield.

2. Royal Wells, born 8 Sept., 1799. Grad. Wms. College, 1818. Died while preparing for the ministry, 1820.

Mr. Smith issued but few publications. Two Masonic discourses previous to 1800, and a farewell discourse, 1804.

"He was a great student through life; and, in the last twenty years of his ministry, much devoted to the study of the Scriptures, especially in the original, and various translations. His sermons were mostly extemporaneous, rarely writing them in full; and they were replete with fresh thoughts from his richly-stored mind.

"His theological views for many years might be termed *Trinitarian-Arminian;* but towards the close of his ministry, he discarded the Trinitarian dogma, yet he did not like to be called Unitarian. He thought that the name given to the disciples at Antioch is the true name by which the followers of Christ ought to be called.

"Mathematics and astronomy were his favorite studies for relaxation. For controversial theology he had no taste. His love of free inquiry led him to advocate freedom of action, and oppose combinations for their tendency to abuse of power. In manner, he was affectionate and sincere; in conversation, affable, entertaining, and full of anecdote,—and serene in his old age."*

* Abridged from a biographical sketch of Rev. P. Smith, Greenfield, 1852, in pamphlet.

33. REV. DAVID HOLMAN

Was born in Sutton, now Millbury, 13 December, 1777. He is the son of Mr. David and Lucy (Thurston) Holman, and brother of Rev. Nathan Holman, and descendant of Solomon Holman, one of the original proprietors and settlers of Sutton.* He experienced the power of the Holy Spirit while preparing for college; entered Brown University, sophomore class, and graduated 1803, and A. M. After graduation, he taught in an academy in Cumberland, R. I.; then studied theology, first with his brother, Rev. N. Holman, of Attleboro', and finally with Rev. Dr. Emmons. He afterwards had charge, for six months, of the grammar-school in Worcester.

He was ordained over the church in Douglas, 19 October, 1808, and dismissed 17 August, 1842, on account of the feeble state of his health, and the inability of the society to raise his support. After a separation of some six years, during which time he preached in vacant parishes, Mr. Holman was recalled, and now, for three years, has been the stated supply of the people for whom he labored as pastor for thirty-four years; — a rare instance of reunion, and highly commendatory of both him and them.

Mr. Holman married Miss Clarissa Packard, daughter of Rev. Winslow Packard, of Wilmington, and of Abigail (Moore) Packard, afterwards wife of Rev. Dr. Emmons. They had six children, of whom five reached maturity, and two still live.

1. Daniel W., married Elizabeth Aldrich of Mendon, and was suddenly killed by a wheel in a factory, at about thirty years of age.

2. Mary Anne, was married to Samuel Waters, son of Elder S. Waters of Millbury, and died at Chelmsford.

---

* See Rev. N. Holman, Sketches of Members, No. 26.

3. Florella Mills, was the wife of Rev. Jonathan Grout, now of Coolville, Ohio, and died in Westboro'.

4. Edward More, married Sarah, daughter of Capt. Peter Butler, of Oxford, and is now Civil Engineer in Worcester.

5. Daughter residing with her parents.

Mrs. Holman died 14 November, 1823.

His second wife was Miss Lois Adams, daughter of Lieut. Abner Adams, of Northbridge. She died 9 September, 1831; and he married Miss Sarah Cannon of Greenwich, daughter of Mr. Cornelius and Mary Cannon, and sister of Rev. Josiah Cannon of Gill, and of Rev. Frederic E. Cannon of Geneva, N. Y.

Mr. Holman furnishes the following incidents for insertion in this sketch: —

"I worked on the paternal farm until about twenty-one. My advantages for even a common school education were very small. About eight weeks in the winter, in an old smoky school-house, with a teacher that would be called, at this day, an *ignoramus*, comprised them all. I had good and salutary religious instruction in my father's family. My parents were pious. The Bible was read daily, and prayer was offered. The Catechism, next to the Bible, was the text-book of the family, and from it, every Sabbath, lessons of instruction were imparted to us. When I became of age, I was influenced and encouraged to obtain a liberal education. But to accomplish this, I must rely mainly upon my own resources."

The church in Douglas, at the date of his settlement, was in a very weak and feeble state. It embraced 27 members, 9 males and 18 females, — most of them very aged and infirm. He says, "They had never been accustomed to occasional meetings. As to revivals, they had heard but little said about them since the days of Edwards and Whitefield. But during the first year of my ministry here, God in mercy granted a time of refreshing from his presence. It was the beginning of a series of revivals, which, during my ministry, brought into the church 226 members. About 70 have been dismissed, including about 35 to form the church in East Douglas." In his farewell sermon to his people, Mr. Holman says, "During these 34 years, we have enjoyed no less than *seven* revivals, besides some intervening drops of mercy. In 1809, 18 were added to the church. In 1813 and 14, 10 were added. In 1819 and 20, 18 were joined. In 1824, we were favored with an extraordinary and signal display of God's power and grace. The whole town, together with the surrounding region, seemed to be shaken." Soon after the death of the pastor's wife the work commenced. The Spirit of the Lord came down with great power. Sinners were pricked in the heart, and the cries of the wounded were soon succeeded by the songs of the redeemed. Business was in a great measure laid aside. The brethren went from house to house, praying and exhorting the people. Our meetings were crowded, still, and solemn. Divine truth preached seemed to be pressed upon the conscience and heart by the Spirit of God. There was no noise, no crying out. There was opposition. But a number of the most bitter and violent opposers were overcome, and hopefully converted. During the year, we have reason to believe, as many as 150 were converted.

34. REV. ELISHA ROCKWOOD

Was born in Chesterfield, N. H., 9 May, 1778. He was the oldest son of Elisha and Abigail (Stone) Rockwood, and had two sisters older, and three brothers younger, all of whom lived to have families.* He fitted for college at Chesterfield

* Rev. Mr. Rockwood's direct ancestral line is as follows:—

1. Nicholas Rockett, or Rockwood, of Wrentham, probably in Medfield, 1661, and the son of Richard Rockett, of Dorchester, prior to

Academy, and graduated at Dartmouth, 1802, A. M.; and also at Harvard. He then taught an academy at Plymouth two years, and was tutor in Dartmouth College two years, from 1804 to 1806. In 1804, he hopefully experienced religion, and united with the church in Chesterfield in 1805. He studied theology while tutor, and was approbated by the Londonderry Presbytery in 1806. He preached afterwards in Woodstock and Barnard, Vt.; in Bernardston, Springfield, Ashfield, Brimfield, and Dorchester, and was ordained in Westboro', 28 Oct., 1808. He was dismissed 11 March, 1835, and preached as a supply in Attleboro', Weymouth, and Sherborn; in York, and South Berwick, Me., and was installed in Swansey, N. H., 16 Nov., 1836, where he still officiates as pastor.

During Mr. Rockwood's ministry in Westboro', there were precious seasons of revival, and 354 were added to the church.

Mr. Rockwood married, 2 Oct., 1809, Susanna B. Parkman, daughter of Breck Parkman, Esq., by whom he had five children.

1. Elisha Parkman, died aged 16½ years.

2. William Otis, married Helen Mar More, of Illinois, and lives in Shelbyville, Indiana.

1636, (see Dr. Harris's List of Settlers,) who is supposed to have come from England.

2. Nathaniel Rockwood, of Wrentham, born 1665, and married Joanna Ellis, 1698. His youngest son was

3. Elisha Rockwood, born Wrentham, 1716; married Elizabeth Adams of Sherborn, 1738, and soon removed to Groton, and settled as clothier and farmer. Hie oldest son was

4. Elisha Rockwood, born in Groton, 1740; married Abigail Stone, of Groton, 1771; removed to Chesterfield, N. H., amongst the first settlers; joined with the church, and died there, — he in his 92d and she in her 63d year. Their third child, and oldest son, was

5. Elisha Rockwood, the subject of the above sketch. — *Letter of Rev. E. Rockwood, Swansey, N. H.*

3. Susan Brigham, was married to Dea. C. C. Denny, of Keene, N. H., and died in 1843, leaving one son, Henry Rockwood Denny.

4. Hannah Abagail, is the wife of Dexter Brigham, Jr., of the firm of Harnden & Co., Boston.

5. Robert Breck, died at 3 days old.

Mrs. Rockwood died at Westboro', 4 June, 1836, and he married Mrs. Emily W. Herrick, relict of Rev. Osgood Herrick, late of Millbury. She still lives.

Mr. Rockwood has published several sermons: 1. Ordination Sermon of Rev. Cyrus Mann, Westminster. 2. A Century Sermon, in Westboro', 1808. 3. A Dedicatory Sermon. 4. Farewell Sermon at W., 1835. 5. Funeral Sermon of Rev. John Sabin, 1845.

35. REV. SAMUEL W. COLBURN

Is the son of Mr. Asa Colburn, of Lebanon, N. H. His mother was sister of Rev. Dr. S. Wood of Boscawen, N. H., by whom he was adopted and educated. Graduated at Dartmouth, 1808; ordained in West Taunton, 29 August, 1809, and dismissed in feeble health, 9 Dec. 1812. As health permitted, he labored some time as missionary in R. I. Installed in East Abington, 3d ch., 13 Oct., 1813; dismissed 5 Feb., 1830. Several years agent of the Am. Doct. Tract and Book Society. Preached a year at Newark, N. J., two years at West Attleboro', and three years at Sandwich. From July 1835 to July 1838 were spent at Little Compton, R. I. His present residence is South Weymouth. He has published several occasional sermons. The Doctrinal Tracts, Nos. 9 and 16, are from his pen.

Mr. Colburn married Miss Ruth Cogswell, daughter of Nehemiah and Ruth Cogswell, of Boscawen, N. H., and has three children. One is the wife of Mr. Albert Reed, of New York; the second married Mr. Theron V. Shaw, South

Weymouth; and the third is wife to Mr. B. A. Smith, Principal of Leicester Academy.*

36. REV. JACOB IDE, D. D.,

The son of Mr. Jacob Ide, of Attleborough, was born in Attleborough, 1786.† He graduated at Brown University, 1809, and A. M., whence he received the honorary degree of S. T. D., 1827; and studied theology at Andover, where he was graduated, 1812. He was ordained over the church in West Medway, 2 November, 1814, and there still continues.

Dr. Ide married Mary Emmons, daughter of Rev. N. Emmons, D. D., of Franklin. Of his children, the oldest son living, Jacob, Jr., graduated at Amherst College, 1848; and is preparing for the ministry. His youngest daughter, Mary, was married to Rev. Charles T. Torrey.

Dr. Ide was one of the editors of the "Christian Magazine," published in the Association, and enriched its pages with his communications. He has published several occasional discourses, and edited a new and uniform edition of Dr. Emmons's Works, to which he prefixed an able exhibition of the life of the author. He has also superintended the theological studies, wholly or in part, of forty-one candidates for the ministry.‡

---

* Letter of Rev. S. W. Colburn, South Weymouth.

† His New England ancestry originates in Nicholas Ide, Rehoboth, 1645. Nicholas, Jr., b. Nov., 1654., m. Mary Ormsby and had 7 ch. Jacob, his second son, m. Sarah Perry and had 2 ch., Sarah, and Jacob, b. 26 Sept., 1723. He was father of Jacob, and grandfather to Rev. Jacob Ide, D. D., above.

‡ His students are, Rev. Messrs. *Sewall Harding, *David Brigham, *Zolva Whitmore, *John M. Putnam, *George Fisher, *Henry H. F. Swett, *James O. Barney, *Levi Packard, —— Cone, of E. Haddam, Ct., M. S. Hagar, —— Morrell, of Boscawen, N.

37. REV. ALVAN COBB

Is the son of Timothy and Deborah (Church) Cobb, and is a native of Carver.* He graduated at Brown University, 1813, and A. M.; and studied theology with Rev. Otis Thompson, of Rehoboth. He was ordained over the church in West Taunton, 19 April, 1815, where he still labors.

Mr. Cobb married Mary, daughter of Hon. Elijah and Rebecca Ingraham, of Pawtucket. She died 13 September, 1846, having had *two* children, one of whom survives. He next married Miss Abiah F. Homer, of Boston.

Mr. Cobb's chief publications are: 1. Funeral Sermon of Mrs. Rebecca Talbot, N. Y., 1825. 2. Sermon on "Forefathers' Day," Plymouth, 1831. 3. Ordination Sermon of Rev. C. Simmons, Attleborough, 1832. 4. Funeral Sermon of Mrs. Hannah Walker, Taunton, 1838. 5 Ordination Sermon of Rev. David Tilton, Edgartown, M. V., 1835. 6. Funeral Sermon of Rev. Joseph H. Bailey, Dighton, 1844. 7. Doctrinal Tract, No. 23,—besides many articles in periodicals.

Mr. Cobb has had charge of the theological instruction of *nine* students.†

H., * Gilbert Fay, * Lucius W. Clark, * Cyrus W. Conant, Charles R. Fisk, * Varnum Noyes, * John Forbush, * Isaac E. Heaton, * Ch's T. Torrey, * Eli Thurston, * Thomas Edwards, * John Dwight, * Edmund Dowse, * Charles Chamberlain, * Daniel J. Poor, Samuel Vial, * Samuel Hunt, * Abram Jenkins, Jr., * Richard C. Spofford, * Joseph H. Bailey, * William Phipps, Jr., * Jonathan Grout, * William M. Thayer, * Preston Pond, Jr., * Horace D. Walker, * Allen Lincoln, William S. Leavett, Asa Bullard, * Malachi Bullard, * James M. Bacon, Jacob Ide, Jr. Some of these remained but a short time. Those starred are elsewhere mentioned.

* His ancestry are found in Plymouth Colony. His grandfather, Nathan, was brother to Ebenezer Cobb, of Kingston, who attained the age of one hundred and eight.

† They are Rev. Messrs. * Silas Shores, * James Tisdale, * Charles

38. REV. JOSEPHUS WHEATON

Was born in Rehoboth, 16 March, 1788, and was the son of Joseph Wheaton, Esq. He early evinced a strong thirst for knowledge, and by his own ingenuity and perseverance obtained the trade of shoemaker, the avails of which enabled him to obtain an education. He entered the Sophomore class in Brown University, and graduated in 1812, one of the best scholars in his class; among whom was Rev. C. Kingsbury, missionary to the Choctaws, his room-mate and dear friend. He made profession of religion while in college; and after graduation, studied for the ministry with Rev. Otis Thompson, of his native town. At the same time he had, for a while, the preceptorship of George-street Academy, Providence; and was tutor in the college from 1813 to 1815. He was approbated while in the University, and commenced supplying the pulpit in Holliston, vacated by the death of Rev. Mr. Dickinson. He was ordained pastor of the Church in Holliston, 6 December, 1815. Rev. Otis Thompson preached the sermon. A pulmonary disease soon made its appearance, with which he contended about three years. The latter part of the time he was blind — until he died, 4 February, 1825, at nearly the age of thirty-seven, and in the tenth year of his ministry.

Mr. Wheaton married first, Mary, the only daughter of Daniel and Sarah Ide, of Franklin. Her father died in her infancy, and she was brought up in the family of Peter Hunt, Esq., of Seekonk, to whom her mother was married. This alliance continued only from January, 1816 to July, 1817, when Mrs. Wheaton died of consumption. Mr. Wheaton's second wife was Miss Abby Fales, whom he left

---

J. Warren, Martin Cushman, Michael Burdette, David Tilton, H. Augustus Woodman, —— Robinson, * Thomas T. Richmond. The starred are included in this volume.

a widow with three children. She was subsequently married to Dea. Benjamin Shepherd, of Wrentham, 15 November, 1838, and died in Wrentham. Their children were,

1. Francis, grad. Brown, 1840, and now practising Law.

2. Henry Stewart, grad. Brown, 1841, now a Lawyer in California.

3. Mary and Louisa.

Mr. Wheaton excelled in an intimate acquaintance with the classics, and his talents as an instructor, drew many youth to him for qualification for college.

"As a preacher he was instructive, animated, and animating. His delivery was uncommonly rapid, yet natural, and made him a highly acceptable preacher. His conciliating deportment, amiable temper, and dignified, yet unaffected manners won the affections of those who were not always pleased with his theological sentiments, which closely resemble those of his predecessor, and were decidedly what are termed Hopkinsian. He united his people when they were not a little discordant, and retained their respect, confidence, and affection, to the close of his life. Humility was the distinguishing feature of his piety: and it shone with brightness during his long and painful sickness."

Mr. Wheaton published several occasional sermons. Among them: 1. A Fast Sermon, on the Equality of Mankind, and the Evils of Slavery: 1820.

2. A Funeral Sermon of Miss Sarah Emmons: 1823.

3. Dedication Sermon of the meeting-house, Holliston, 5 Nov., 1823.

39. REV. THOMAS WILLIAMS,

The son of Joseph Williams,* was born in Pomfret, Ct., 5 Nov., 1779, graduated at Yale College, 1800, and A. M. in

* His immigrant Ancestor was Robert Williams, of Roxbury, from

course: also A. M. at Brown Univ., 1814. After graduation, he taught a Colored school in Boston, of a hundred scholars. In 1804, May, he was approbated to preach, by the Windham Evangelical Association, when he returned to Boston, and officiated as chaplain to the almshouse. At the close of his engagement, he went as a missionary to Otsego, Delaware Co., N. Y., under the direction of the Conn. Dom. Miss. Society. On his return, he was ordained in Providence, R. I., 1 Jan., 1807. Spent six weeks with Rev. Dr. Emmons, reading Ecclesiastical writers, and then acted as stated supply to the Richmond St. Church, in Providence, until 1816, when he removed to Foxboro', where he was installed, 16 Nov., 1816, and continued until 24 Oct., 1821. He preached in Attleboro' from 29 Sept., 1824, until 11 Dec., 1827; in Hebronville, in the same town, until April, 1832; then in Barrington, R. I., until 1838; since which last date, he has resided in Providence, laboring in destitute parishes. He has never viewed himself as regularly settled over any individual Church, but as set apart to do the work of an Evangelist, or "Job work," as he significantly terms it.

Mr. Williams was one of the originators of the Evan. Consociation of Rhode Island, drafted its articles of Faith and Rules, and was the first scribe of the body.

Mr. Williams married Miss Ruth Hale, of Newbury, and has had seven children. His second son, Nathan Ritter, graduated at Yale, and was ordained at Shrewsbury, 28 Feb., 1849.

Mr. Williams has published several volumes and pamphlets. The following list is nearly complete.

1. Volume of *ten* sermons on Election, Hartford, 1810.

Norwich, England. Freeman, 1638. He had four sons. Samuel, Dea. in Roxbury; Isaac, settled in Newton, ancestor of the founder of Wms. Coll.; Stephen, Thomas. The ancestral line is, Robert, 2. Dea. Samuel, 3. Samuel, Jr., 4. William, one of the first settlers in Pomfret, Ct., and brother to the first minister, 5. Joseph, 6. Rev. Thomas, above.

2. Sermon on the peace between the U. S. and Great Britain, 1815.

3. Sermon on the National Thanksgiving for peace, 1815.

4. Ordination Sermon of Rev. Emerson Paine, 14 Feb., 1816.

5. Sermon on Psalmody, 1817; another in 1823.

6. Dedication Sermon at Foxboro', 1 Jan., 1823.

7. Volume of seven sermons, Providence, 1823.

8. Funeral Sermon of Mrs. Chloe Read, Attleboro', 1826.

9. On the effects of the Gospel on the day of Pentecost.

10. Volume of twelve sermons, Providence, 1832.

11. Sermon on Rhode Island Protestantism, 1836.

12. "Domestic Chaplain,"— twenty-four short sermons, Hartford, 1839.

13. Funeral Sermon of Rev. Dr. Emmons, 1840.

14. Discourse on the Battle of the Great Day, 1849.

15. Sermon on Theological and Evangelical Orthodoxy, 1850.

16. Discourse on the Life and Death of Oliver Shaw, 1851.

17. Volume on the Official Character of Dr. Emmons, 1851.

Mr. Williams also contributed very many articles in the Conn. Ev. Magazine and Panoplist.

40. REV. CALVIN PARK, D. D.

Was the son of Nathan Park, and was born in Northbridge, 11 Sept., 1774. He graduated at Brown University, 1797, and A. M.; and from which he received the degree of S. T. D., 1818. He studied theology with Rev. Dr. Austin of Worcester. In 1800, he accepted the office of Tutor in his Alma Mater, which office he filled until 1804, when he was elected Professor of Languages. In 1811, he took the chair of Moral Philosophy and Metaphysics, and continued in it until his resignation, 1825.

He preached, from the beginning of his connection with the college, in destitute churches in the vicinity, but he was not ordained until 1815, May 17 ; when, at his request, the Mendon Association convened at Franklin, and he was there inducted into the sacred office, as Evangelist. Rev. Dr. Crane, of his native town, preached the sermon. After the resignation of his professorship, he commenced preaching to the Evangelical church in Stoughton. He was installed as pastor, 13 Dec., 1826. In 1840, he resigned the pastoral charge, but still resided in the town until his death, 5 Jan., 1847, the same day on which died his near and well-loved brother in the ministry, Rev. Daniel Thomas of Abington, in the 73d year of his age. His last words were: "It is well that we are not always to live."

Dr. Park married Miss Abigail Ware of Wrentham, the daughter of Mr. Nathaniel and Abigail Ware. He had three children :

1. Harrison G., Rev., now in Burlington. (See Members, No. 51).

2. Edwards A., Rev., S. T. D. and Divinity Professor in Andover Theological Seminary. He married Miss Maria Edwards, daughter of Wm. Edwards, of Hunter, Greene Co., N. Y., and recently deceased at Brooklyn.

3. Calvin E., Rev., and pastor of the Congregational Church in West Boxford. He married Miss Harriet T., daughter of Joseph Pope of Portland, Me., deceased.

The following extract from a biographical sketch of Dr. Park, on the Records of this Association, is deemed pertinent and truthful:—

"As a teacher, he was apt, faithful, and thorough. If any under his care were not good scholars, the fault was not in him. He possessed a clear, discriminating mind, and sound judgment. He was not satisfied with looking at the mere surface of things, but disposed to examine elements and principles; and was one who could see effects in their causes.

"As to character and habits, he was correct, stable, conscientious, pious, and devout. Although he had great sensibility and quickness of feeling, yet his passions were under control. No one, it is presumed, ever found confidence in him misplaced.

"His mind was of a meditative and pensive cast. As a moralist and divine, he had no superior. His views of the great doctrines of the Gospel were strictly Calvinistic. They were his own; made so not by adoption, but by a careful examination of evidence. He knew what and why he believed. So rooted and grounded was he in the truth, that he was not shaken by any of the new or plausible theories which came up in the religious community.

"As a preacher, he was clear, definite, instructive, solemn, and impressive. He fully and faithfully preached what he believed. His aim in his sermons was at the understanding, conscience, and heart of his hearers. But few preachers, with his compass of voice, or even with a much greater, could keep an audience more still and attentive.

"He was not a man of noise and display, but of sound thought and close reasoning. He felt, and he made his hearers feel."

41. REV. DANIEL THOMAS,

The son of Daniel Thomas, was born in Middleboro', 1779, and graduated at Brown University, 1803, and A. M. He studied theology with Rev. O. Thompson, of Rehoboth, and was ordained over the second church in Abington, south parish, 1 June, 1808. He successfully labored there until his dismission, 1842. He died 5 Jan., 1847, in the 68th year of his age.

Mr. Thomas was never married. He was betrothed in the early part of his ministry, to a very lovely and respectable lady of his own parish. But she became sick and was confined to her bed, most of the time for thirty-seven years. This prevented their union; and yet it showed the strength of its bond, that he remained true, affectionate, indulgent, and gentle in the trial, and never sought another, considering his engagement morally binding, and a prevention to any other connection.

In person, he was tall, spare, and, in the latter part of his life, emaciated by toil and disease. He had a dark, kindling eye, a swelling, symmetrical forehead; and in his whole appearance chaste, neat, immaculate. "Without spot" was his apparel; "without spot or wrinkle" his sermon.

"He was a clear, intelligent preacher. Everybody understood him, — some much better than they desired. He did not make spiritual confectionary of his sermons, and spice them so sparingly with Gospel truth as just to keep them from being fatal, so that the enemies might take the preparation, not knowing what it was. Nor did he whip down the high doctrines of sovereignty, decrees, election, depravity, the law and the atonement into delicious rhetorical sillabub, so that the 'babes in Christ' might take unconsciously what they knew not. He gave them the 'sincere milk of the Word,' and made them distinctly understand what it was.

"He was a poet. He was pleasantly facetious, and his wit was sensible, adding life, cheerfulness, and power to great principles.

"His character might not inappropriately be compared for chasteness and beauty to a Grecian pillar of Parian marble, — pure, symmetrical, finished.

"Having been in feeble health for more than a year, on the 10th of December, he was taken suddenly more ill, and laid down to die. His mind was clouded, and his mental faculties seemed to be paralized. Reason struggled hard to retain her seat, and at intervals would assert her sway. But it was evident she had yielded her empire to disease. In the midst of this mental darkness, there was the man, the Christian, the minister, meek, patient, gentle, holy. On the morning of January 5, he faintly whispered, 'I am going home,' and ceased to breathe. Rev. Mr. Couch, of North Bridgewater, preached his funeral sermon; and his dust was committed to the earth, the same day with the remains of his long and intimately acquainted friend and neighbor, Rev. Dr. Park, of Stoughton."*

Mr. Thomas published a few occasional sermons and poems.

42. REV. JOHN FERGUSON

Was born 9 Dec., 1788, in Dunse, Berwickshire, Scotland. He is the oldest son of Mr. John Ferguson, a native of the same town in 1739.† His mother's maiden name was Ann Briggs, a native of Little Compton, R. I. Both his parents died in Newport, R. I., and each at the age of 85.

At 20 years of age, and while residing in Providence, R. I., he began preparing for the ministry, under the direction of Rev. C. Park, D. D., then professor in the college. He did not graduate, but received an honorary A. M. from Amherst College in 1837.

He was ordained at East Attleboro', as successor of Rev. N. Holman, 27 Feb., 1822, was dismissed 25 March, 1835. Installed at Whately, 16 March, 1836, and dismissed, 17 June, 1840. He preached about two years in Lanesboro', and has since been engaged by the Am. Tract Society, as

---

* Extract from Funeral Sermon, in Puritan Recorder.

† The grandfather of Rev. Mr. Ferguson was a native of the Highlands of Scotland. He belonged to the Scotch Greys, — a regiment of heavy cavalry, — and was under the Duke of Marlborough in all his wars. He was brother to Rev. — Ferguson, minister of the parish of Logierait, in Perthshire, who was the father of Doct. Adam Ferguson, the historian, and predecessor of Dugald Stewart in the chair of Philosophy, at Edinburgh. He died in 1742. Mr. F. above, is the only male representative of his family, excepting his own children.

General Agent for New Hampshire and Vermont. His residence is at Whately.

Mr. Ferguson married first, Mary V., daughter of Benjamin Hammett, of Newport, R. I. His present wife was Margaret Snow Eddy, daughter of William Eddy, of Providence, R. I. He has had eleven children, eight of whom are living; viz.: John; Mary H., m. to Mr. Stockbridge, Whately; Peter; William E.; George R., grad. Amherst Coll., 1849; Margaret E., Teacher in the Young Ladies' Institute, Pittsfield; James A., and Abby Park.

Mr. Ferguson has published several sermons, and a memoir of Dr. S. Hopkins, of Newport, R. I., for Sabbath Schools.

43. REV. MOSES THACHER

Is the son of Obadiah and Elizabeth (Richardson) Thacher, and was born in Princeton, 14 Nov., 1795.* Fitted for

* His immigrant ancestor was Rev. Thomas Thacher, son of Rev. Peter Thacher, of Sarum, or Salsbury, England. He was born 1 May, 1620, arrived in Boston, 4 June, 1635, ord. at Weymouth, 2 Jan., 1645, inst. pastor of the Old South Church, Boston, 16 Feb., 1670, and d. 16 Oct., 1678, aged 58. He m. a daughter of Rev. Ralph Partridge, of Duxbury. His son, *Rev. Peter*, b. at Salem, 18 July, 1651, ord. at Milton 1 June, 1681, and d. 27 Dec., 1727, aged 77. He m. Theodora, daughter of Rev. John Oxenbridge, of the first church, Boston. He m. 2nd., the widow of Rev. John Bailey, and 3d., the widow of Rev. Joshua Gee, both of Boston. He had 9 ch.; The sixth, was *Rev. Peter*, b. 9 Oct., 1688, ord. at Middleboro', 2 Nov., 1709, and d. 22 April, 1744, aged 56. He m. Mary, sister of Rev. Thomas Prince, of the Old South Ch., Boston; he had ten ch. The eldest was *Rev. Peter*, ord. in East Attleboro', 30 Nov., 1748, and died 13 Sept., 1785, aged 70. He m. Bethiah, daughter of Obadiah Carpenter, of Attleboro', and had ten ch.; one of whom was *Obadiah*, father to *Rev. Moses* above. Of the last two generations of this family, six are in the ministry, and over one hundred now living members of the church. Eighteen of them joined the church in Harford, Pa., on *one* Sabbath, in 1808. See Farmer, History of Middleboro' and Daggett's Attleboro', and Letter of Rev. M. Thacher.

college, partly, with Rev. N. Holman, and graduated at Brown University, 1821, and A. M. He studied Divinity with Rev. O. Thompson, of Rehoboth, and was ordained at North Wrentham, 20 Aug., 1823, and dismissed, 30 Oct., 1832. A portion of the church withdrew, and was constituted a separate church over whom he was installed, 20 Feb., 1833. In 1838, he left New England for the Middle States, and was installed at Wysox, Pa., 29 April, 1840. Afterwards he was settled four and a half years at Virgil, Cortlandt Co., N. Y., and is now pastor of the church in Genoa, Cayuga Co., N. Y.

Mr. Thacher married Henrietta, daughter of Stephen and Lurana Wilmarth, of Attleboro', and has several children.

Mr. Thacher has published: 1. Funeral Sermon of Mr. Shubael Pratt, of Foxboro', 1822; 2. do. of Mrs. Naomi F. Harlow, wife of Rev. William Harlow, of North Wrentham, 1823; 3. do. on the death of his mother, 1823; 4. New England Telegraph as a weekly religious paper, for four years, from Jan., 1831, and two years as a monthly magazine; 5. several Tractates upon Free Masonry; 6. on Household Baptism; 7. Confession of Faith in Scriptural Quotations.

44. REV. JAMES O. BARNEY

Is a native of Providence, R. I., where he was born 30 Sept., 1795. His parents were Cromwell and Lydia P. (Grinnell) Barney. At the age of fourteen, he was seized with a strong desire to visit foreign countries, and shipped as a sailor to gratify this wish. His seafaring life, though short, — being terminated by the Embargo Act, and the war with England, — had its share of peril and suffering. Once he was shipwrecked, once on short allowance, and once nearly drowned at sea in a long-boat. He then went to Attleboro' to learn a trade, where he was conquered to Christ by the powerful revival of 1815, under Rev. N. Holman. He joined the church, 2 July, 1815, and began his preparation for the ministry; graduated at Brown University 1821, and A. M.; and studied divinity with Rev. Prof. C. Park, and Rev. Dr. Ide. He was ordained at Seekonk, 4 Feb., 1824, and was dismissed, 13 May, 1850, to act as Seamen's Chaplain, and to supply the pulpit of the Fourth Cong. Church in the city of Providence. He returned 1 June, 1852, to his former charge, retaining, however, a partial chaplaincy among seamen at the port.

Mr. Barney married Eliza Lathe, daughter of Mr. Zephaniah Lathe, of Charlton, and has four children. Eliza L., the oldest, is married to Mr. James Walker, grad. Amherst Coll., 1844, and teacher of a high school in Taunton.

45. REV. WILLARD PIERCE

Is a native of Stoughton, where he was born 15 March, 1790. He was the son of Seth Pierce, Jr. His mother was Alice, daughter of Timothy and Elizabeth Gay, of Stoughton. Being one of a large family of children, and of parents not abundant in "goods," he left home before eleven years of age to win his own support. His only wealth, was a mind richly stored with the Assembly's Catechism, Watts's Cradle Hymns, and what was of more value, followed by a pious mother's prayers. Not only did he get his own living, but, while a mere lad, and before he began his apprenticeship, he remitted a hundred dollars to his parents. Soon after leaving his trade, — a carpenter, — he fell and broke his arm. He returned home in discouragement, with his arm slung to his neck, and having nothing else to do, he attended a religious meeting. A revival was commencing, and one of its early fruits, was the disabled carpenter. By advice of Rev. Dr. Strong, of Randolph, where he learned his trade, he was advised to commence a course of study: and the Dr. offered to teach him at seventy-five cents per week, and be remunerated in carpenter's work at a dollar a day. The plan was agreed to, with pecuniary prospects on the part of the student sufficiently dark to appal the stoutest heart. It took three days' work weekly to pay his board and tuition, and the rest was given to study, as labor engagements permitted. Yet he kept pace with a class-mate, who studied all the time, and at the close, was admitted to college, while the student was rejected.

Dr. Strong had a large number of private students, and but one rule of tuition, to charge each for the whole week, whether present or absent. Such a settlement in the present case was very onerous upon a poor youth who had spent half his time in work, to pay for the other half. The Dr. wished to favor his poor pupil, but then the rule, it could not be broken! An ingenious solution of the difficulty was proposed by the student, in the present case: viz. *to settle both bills by the same rule*, of charging for the whole week, whether he had studied or worked but a part of it, which with tuition at seventy-five cents per week, and work at a dollar a day, would evidently make a sensible difference in the settlement. The Dr. laughed heartily, and agreed to settle by the actual quantity received and rendered, and offered to furnish a hundred dollars to the young collegian, if he should want it. In two short months, the Dr. was in his grave.

Mr. Pierce graduated at Brown University, 1818, and A. M. He was ordained over the church in Foxboro', 17 November, 1824, and was dismissed, Oct., 1839. Installed in Abington, 8 April, 1840, and dismissed in feeble health 1 May, 1850. He still resides in Abington.

Mr. Pierce married Miss Eleanor Ware, daughter of Metcalf and Fanny Everett of Foxboro', and has several children.

His publications are,

1. Funeral Sermon of Dr. Carpenter of Seekonk, 1825.

2. A Century Sermon on the day Widow Hannah Sumner of Foxboro' completed her hundredth year, 1828.

3. Sermon on Slavery, 1835.

4. Sermon before the Norfolk Ed. Society, 1836.

5. Sermon on the Mutual Duties of Parents and Children, 1837.

6. Sermon before the Palestine Missionary Society, 1842.

7. Sermon at Dedication of the Meeting-house, E. Bridgewater, 1845.

46. REV. CHARLES FITCH

Was born in Williamstown. He was the youngest son of Rev. Ebenezer Fitch, D. D., the first president of Williams College, afterwards pastor of the church in West Bloomfield, N. Y., and was the sixth in descent from Rev. James Fitch, (or Fytche,) from Bocking, Essex, England, and of Norwich, Ct.* He graduated at Williams College 1818, studied theology at Princeton, N. J., and was ordained first in Cherry Valley, N. Y., and then in Holliston, 4 Jan., 1826. He was dismissed 1 May, 1832, and migrated westwards. In 1836, he was in Buffalo. In 1843, he was in Ohio, where he occupied a chaplaincy in some of the State institutions. He is believed to be now in Indiana, acting as an agent of the American Bible Society. Another Rev. Charles Fitch, settled once over a free church in Boston, has been confounded with the subject of the present sketch.

---

* Rev. James Fytche, born in Bocking, Essex, England, 1622, and had by two wives 14 children. The eldest, James, Esq., and maj., of Canterbury, Ct., had by two wives 13 children. The youngest of these was Jabez, Col., had 8 children, of whom was Jabez, jr., Doct., and father of Rev. Ebenezer Fitch, D. D. He married Widow Mary Cogswell, formerly Miss Backus, and had 11 children, of whom was Rev. Charles Fitch, above. *See Sketch of Dr. Fitch, Quar. Register.*

16

Mr. Fitch married Miss Sarah Hamilton, and has three children.

47. REV. CHARLES JARVIS WARREN

Was born in Boston, 3 Aug., 1796. His father and grandfather were natives of Waltham. He spent his early life in Sutton; at about 21 years of age, removed to Taunton, where, in 1820, he joined the church under Rev. A. Cobb, with whom he commenced his classical studies. He completed his academic course at Castleton Academy, Vt., and grad. at Brown University, 1826. He studied theology with Rev. Alvan Cobb, of Taunton, and was ordained pastor of the first Congregational church in Attleboro', 28 February, 1828. He was dismissed 8 July, 1730. He next supplied the newly-formed Robinson Church, Plymouth, until his settlement over the first church in South Weymouth, 1 Jan., 1833. In the following year, Aug. 13, he was dismissed, and opened a classical school in Brooklyn, N. Y. Installed 1 July, 1835, at Weathersfield, as colleague with Rev. Caleb J. Tenney, D. D.; dismissed 1 February, 1837. Next settled in Canterbury, Ct., 13 September, 1837, and dismissed 1 April, 1840, to become agent of the American Temperance Union, in some department of whose operations he has since been employed. Much of his labor has been given to the enrolment and instruction of children and youth in the temperance cause. He is now Corresponding Secretary and General Agent of the New York City Temperance Alliance, and resides at New York.

His publications have been, a Dedicatory Sermon of the Meeting-house of the Robinson Church, Plymouth; a Bible Manual and Temperance Catechism, for Youth; besides small tractates upon Free Masonry and Temperance generally.

Mr. Warren is married, and has several children.

48. REV. PRESTON CUMMINGS

Was born in Seekonk, 1 May, 1800, the son of David and Hipsey Cummings; but spent his early days in Attleboro', where he prepared for college, under the tuition of Rev. N. Holman, then and there pastor, and where he also made profession of religion in 1816. He graduated at Brown University, 1822, and studied theology under Rev. C. Park, D. D., then Professor in the University. Was ordained at Lebanon, N. Y., 22 August, 1825; and dismissed Feb. 1827, "on account of a serious injury, then supposed to be fatal to his ability to be useful." Installed at Dighton 26 December, 1827, and dismissed 5 Oct., 1835. Installed at Wrentham, North Church, 6 July, 1836, and dismissed 1 Jan., 1838. Installed at Buckland 1 Jan., 1840, and dismissed 1 January 1848, on account of a return of the malady which occasioned his first dismission. Subsequently he has preached frequently, and supplied his former charge in Dighton a year and a half; but has been chiefly occupied in compiling a "Dictionary of Congregational Usages and Principles;" containing the language of the various writers on the subjects treated, with copious references to authorities. Several years have been spent in consulting and comparing the works of the fathers of Old and New England, and the result is an invaluable key to the various opinions of prominent writers on our church polity.

Mr. Cummings has been permitted to rejoice in several interesting seasons of blessing upon his labors. One very marked revival occurred in Buckland in 1842.

Mr. Cummings married Miss Alona Davis, of Holden, sister of Rev. Elnathan Davis, and has had two children,— one of whom survives. James P. Chaplin graduated in the medical class at Cambridge, 1850, and is now a practising physician at Leicester. He married Miss Harriet V. Mann, of Holden.

Mr. Cummings's present residence is at Leicester.

49. REV. ELAM SMALLEY, D. D.

Is a native of Dartmouth; graduated at Brown University, 1827, and A. M.; and also S. T. D., 1849. He studied theology with Rev. Otis Thompson, of Rehoboth. He was ordained at Franklin, 17 June, 1829, and was, at his own request, dismissed 5 July, 1838. He was installed over the Union Church, Worcester, 19 Sept., 1838, where he still labors.

Dr. Smalley married Miss Louisa J. Washburn, daughter of Gen. Abiel and Mrs. Elizabeth Washburn, of Middleboro', and has two children.

Dr. Smalley has published a Sermon on "the Piety which the present Age demands," Franklin, 1835; A Centennial Discourse, Franklin, 1838; A Volume upon the Sacrament, 1841; "The Worcester Pulpit," 1851; Pastors' Counsels; and Funeral Sermon of Hon. D. D. Foster, 1852; besides some articles in the Quarterlies.

50. REV. AMOS AUGUSTUS PHELPS

Was the son of humble but pious parents, and was born in Simsbury, Ct., 11 November, 1804. His mother's name, previous to marriage, was Clarissa Bodwell.

He early exhibited strong traits of character; and his mother, on whom entirely devolved the care of rearing him from childhood, furnished him with the best facilities for gaining an education within her reach. He spent his early years with his uncle, Mr. Augustus Bodwell, of Farmington, Ct. When about sixteen years of age, his mother was married to Mr. William Tryon, and he was placed in a store in Farmington.

While thus employed, he became, in 1821, a subject of Divine grace, and immediately turned his desires and plans toward the Gospel ministry. His mother had, meanwhile, become again a widow, and the little property accumulated by her careful toil was involved in the insolvent estate of her deceased husband. Her only possible way of rescuing anything was by assuming all the debts, which the heroic woman actually did, and eventually paid them.

It was in this time of embarrassment and perplexity that she was called also to decide upon giving her son a liberal education. She resolved it should be done, and was enabled to accomplish it. Such energy was worthy of such a son as Mr. Phelps.

Mr. Phelps graduated at Yale College 1826, and A. M., and studied theology at New Haven. He was ordained at Hopkinton, 14 Sept., 1830, as colleague pastor with Rev. Nathanael Howe. His cordial enlistment in the cause of Temperance so displeased many in the town, as to lead to his dismission, 1 May, 1832.

Mr. Phelps then removed to Boston, and supplied the pulpit of the Old South Church, and afterwards of the Pine Street Church, where he received a call and was settled, 13 Sept., 1832. Induced chiefly by the failing health of his wife, he obtained a dismission, 26 March, 1834.

It was during his settlement at Pine street that he became an Abolitionist. In 1833, he was invited to deliver a Fourth of July Address upon the subject of Slavery. With his natural earnestness and thoroughness, he collected and studied all the documents upon the subject, and upon all sides of it, to which he could gain access. The result of his examination was, his clear, cordial, and life-long conviction of the right of *immediate emancipation.* His address was written accordingly. He subsequently enlarged it to four lectures, which were published, and became a text-book on the subject.

Immediately after his dismission from the Pine St. church, Mr. Phelps entered, April 1, upon an agency for the American Anti-Slavery Society, — in whose organization in Philadelphia, Dec. 30, he had been a prominent agent, — and visited New York, Washington, and, during the summer, the State of Maine. On the arrival of George Thompson from England, Sept., 1834, Mr. Phelps joined him, and accompanied him through New England and New York. April, 1836, he accepted the Editorship of the Emancipator, and conducted it until May of the following year; when he removed to Boston and became General Agent of the Mass. Anti-Slavery Society, in whose service he continued until the division in 1839. In 1838, he declined an invitation to the pastoral office of the Third Presb. church in New York, on account of his Congregational attachments. But he accepted a call from the Marlboro' Chapel Free church, and was installed 24 July, 1839. In 1841, March 1, he entered upon the Agency for City Missions; and the year following, March 2, he was settled over the Maverick church, East Boston, still holding a nominal connection with his missionary agency.

His health, never robust, was at this time enfeebled by his multiplied labors; and, as a respite, he sailed for England, 1 June, 1843, to attend the Anti-Slavery Convention to be holden at London, June 12, to which he had been elected delegate by the Mass. Abolition Society. He was a prominent and active member of that Convention.

The prevalent east winds at Boston induced him to resign his pastorate at East Boston, and accept the office of Corresponding Secretary of the Am. and Foreign Anti-Slavery Society, at New York, whither he removed in April, 1845. But the symptoms of Consumption so increased upon him, that he was advised to seek a milder clime. He sailed for

Hayti, 20 Oct., 1846, and reëmbarked for Jamaica in December, where he spent the winter, but without any marked benefit.

In April, 1847, he left for the United States, reached New Orleans on the 18th, and proceeded up the river to Cincinnati, and thence to New York. After a brief rest, he continued on to Castine, Me., where his family had remained. But the season was most unfavorable to him, and he journied, once more, to Roxbury, to the house of his brother-in-law, Rev. E. D. Moore. In the quiet of his family, he arranged the valuable information which he had collected respecting slavery in the West Indies, prepared his Letters to Drs. Stowe and Bacon for the press, and set his house in order to die. The anticipated event came suddenly at last. He died at little past midnight, on the morning of the 30th of July, 1847, aged 43 years; and, Aug. 2d, his remains were committed to rest in Mount Auburn.

Mr. Phelps married, Nov., 1830, Charlotte Brown, daughter of William and Margaret (Shepherd) Brown, of Wrentham. Her father died in her childhood, and her mother had become the second wife of Rev. Elisha Fisk, of Wrentham. Mrs. Phelps was born 1 Sept., 1803, and died 31 Aug., 1838, and was buried in Wrentham. She was an amiable, devoted, and exemplary Christian, and exhibited the beauty of the Gospel in her long and painful sickness, consumption. She left one child.

Mr. Phelps married, 3 Oct., 1839, Caroline G. Little, daughter of Mr. Doty Little of Castine, Me. She died in a short time, leaving one of two children to survive her. Mr. Phelps married her sister, Lucy T. Little, 9 Oct., 1844, by whom he had two children. She is still living in Ellsworth, Me. Of Mr. Phelps's children:

1. Edward Augustus, b. 21 June, 1832, lives in East Abington.

2. Lucy Little, b. 11 Jan., 1841; 4. Caroline Little, b. 18

Nov., 1845; and 5. Clara Bodwell, b. 23 July, 1847; are with Mrs. P. in Ellsworth.

Mr. Phelps's writings were voluminous, but mostly occasional pamphlets, etc., connected with his agencies. He published, however, the following volumes: 1. Lectures on Slavery, 1834. 2. Book of the Sabbath, 1841. 3. Letters to Drs. Bacon and Stowe, 1848. He also left, unfinished, a volume on the Bible View of Slavery, and materials collected for many other works, of which his early death prevented a completion.

Here is not space to give more than the most sketchy outline of his character and labors. His whole life showed him to be indefatigable in perseverance, cool and thorough in his examination of all doctrines and duties, and explicit and bold in making his conclusions fully known. Whatever he considered to be wrong in principle or practice, he fearlessly and uncompromisingly attacked; and strong had to be the entrenchments which could stand before the fire of his well-directed assaults. He was as determined an enemy to ultraism as he was to timid conservatism. In all his attacks upon slavery, he used none but what he believed to be Christian weapons, and sternly rebuked the use of any others by his casual associates.

As a preacher and pastor, he was regarded as instructive and faithful. His ministry, both in Hopkinton and Boston, was crowned with success. In the former place, he enjoyed an extensive revival, in which some 150 were hopefully converted. His labors in Pine Street church were attended with a similar, though less extensive, work of grace.

As a public lecturer and extempore speaker, he was remarkable for his systematic clearness, logical accuracy, and argumentative cogency. However entangled a subject might have become by rambling debate, under his lucid exposition the crooked became straight, light broke through the obscurity, and the point at issue was revealed in vivid distinctness.

As an advocate of emancipation, he stood unrivalled amongst his coadjutors. The progress of the cause was greatly indebted to his enlightened and fervid zeal. He was regarded as a leader, not only at the North and in England, but also at the South. The *high value* which was put upon his labors by the slaveholders, is indicated by the offer, in the Milledgeville (Ga.) "Federal Union," of Feb. 1, 1836, of $10,000 for his head!

He was a man of unblemished morals. He was a warm friend, cherishing all the domestic affections, and loved the cause of the slave, not merely as a principle of duty, but from the impulses of the heart. His characteristic calmness, collectedness, and freedom from excitement marked his closing hours. "All is right, all is right," were his last exclamations.*

51. REV. HARRISON GREENOUGH PARK

Is the eldest son of Rev. Calvin Park, D. D., and was born in Providence, R. I., 1806. He graduated at Brown University, 1824, and studied theology at Princeton, N. J., and with Rev. Dr. Wisner, of Boston. He also read law three years with Bradford Sumner, Esq., of Boston, and with Hon. J. Fisk, of Wrentham. He was ordained pastor of the church in South Dedham, 16 Dec., 1829, and dismissed in 1835; settled a short time over the second church in Danvers, and was installed over the church in Burlington 15 Nov., 1849, and dismissed in 1851. In the interim of his last two settlements, he was employed, part of the time, as travelling agent for the Mother's Magazine, and in the publication and editorship of the Father's and Mother's Manual.

Mr. Park married Miss Julia Bird, daughter of Mr. George

* Condensed from Boston Reporter, Emancipator, National Era, and Letters of Messrs. L. Tappan, A. Bodwell, and E. A. Phelps.

Bird of Dedham. Subsequently to her death, he married her sister, Miss Elizabeth Bird. He has several children.

Mr. Park published a Funeral Sermon of Rev. George Cowles, and his wife Mrs. Elizabeth Cowles, who were lost in the steam Packet, Home, 9 Oct., 1837. Preached at Danvers 12 Nov., 1837.

52. REV. ASAHEL BIGELOW

Was born in Boylston; the son of Andrew and Sarah Bigelow, and brother of Rev. Jonathan Bigelow of Rochester, and of Rev. Andrew Bigelow of Needham, and descendant of John Bigelow, Watertown, 1841. He graduated at Harvard Univ., 1823, and at Andover, 1826: ordained at Walpole, 12 March, 1828, and dismissed 1 Jan., 1849. Installed in Hancock, N. H., 15 May, 1850, where he now labors. Has published: 1. Sermon before Norfolk Co. Ed. Soc'y, 1833; 2. Sermon at ordination of Mr. Andrew Bigelow, So. Dartmouth, 15 Aug., 1841.

Mr. Bigelow married Miss Dorcas F. Homes, daughter of the late Henry Homes of Boston, and has several children.

53. REV. DAVID SANFORD

Is a native of Medway. His father was Mr. Philo Sanford, a son of Rev. David Sanford, pastor of the church in West Medway.

He graduated at Brown University, 1825, and A. M., and studied theology with Rev. Dr. Ide, and at Andover Seminary. He preached a short time in the city of Lowell, and in Somersworth, N. H.; and was ordained at New Market, N. H., 22 May, 1828. He was dismissed June, 1830, to take charge of a new church in Dorchester, over which he was installed as pastor, 14 July, 1830. He was again dismissed, Sept., 1838, to take the pastoral charge of a new church in his native place, Medway Village. He was installed there 3 Oct., 1838, and continues to labor 'amongst his own people.'

Mr. Sanford married Miss Sarah P. Daniels, daughter of Mr. Obed Daniels of Hopkinton, and has several children.

Mr. S. has published a sermon before the Norfolk Co. Education Soc'y, 1840; Sermon to Young Men, 1848; Sermon to Young Ladies, 1849; Funeral Sermon of Mrs. James B. Wilson, 1850.

54. REV. TERTIUS DUNNING SOUTHWORTH

Is a native of Rome, N. Y., and son of Rev. James Southworth, pastor of the Presbyterian church in Bridgewater, N. Y.* His mother's name, before marriage, was Mary Dennison, of Saybrook, Ct.

He studied with W. R. Weeks, D. D., of Paris Hill, and also at the academy in Whitesboro', and graduated at Hamilton College, Clinton, N. Y., and A. M. 1825 (?); attended Theological Seminary at Auburn one year, and at Andover nearly three years, and graduated at Andover, 1829.

He was ordained in Claremont, N. H., 18 June, 1834, and dismissed July, 1838. Installed at Franklin 23 Jan., 1839, and dismissed 25 April, 1850. He afterwards supplied temporarily at Bridgewater, N. Y., at Sasquoit, in the adjoining town, at Hebron, Ct., and Andover Theological Seminary. His present place of labor is Lyndon, Vt.

Mr. Southworth married Miss Martha Warren, daughter of Luther and Martha (Niles) Warren. She is a native of

* His paternal ancestry is directly traceable to Sir Richard Southworth, who was knighted by James I. of England, and whose widow Alice, migrated to Plymouth, and became the wife of Gov. William Bradford. She brought two sons with her, Constant and Thomas Southworth, prominent personages in the Plymouth Colony, from the former of whom Mr. S. (above) is descended.

Haverhill, N. H., was educated at Mr. Brace's Female Seminary, Hartford, and, at the time of her marriage, resided at Weathersfield, Vt. They have no children.

Mr. Southworth's publications are: 1. A Sermon, "Civil Government ordained of God," 1840. 2. Funeral Sermon of Rev. N. Emmons, D. D., 1840. 3. Dedication Sermon at Franklin, 1842. 4. "Memorial of Unassuming Piety," 1844. 5. Sermon before Norfolk Co. Education Society. 6. Man's Hopes destroyed. Besides pamphlets.

55. REV. DANIEL J. POOR

Was born in Woburn, and was the son of Lemuel and Elizabeth (Richardson) Poor.

He graduated at Amherst College, 1837; studied theology with Rev. Dr. Ide, and was ordained in Foxboro', 11 March, 1840. He was dismissed, at his own request, 12 May, 1847. Since this date, he has been the preceptor of an academy in Hopkinton, where he now resides.

Mr. Poor married Miss Susan Thompson, daughter of Mr. Alpha and Mary (Scottow) Thompson, and has several children.

56. REV. MORTIMER BLAKE,

The eldest son of Ira and Laura (Mowry) Blake, was born in Pittston, Me., but early removed to Franklin, with his parents.* He fitted for college, partly in private, and partly

* His earliest discovered paternal ancestor was Robert Blake of Wrentham, 1676; who married Sarah, daughter of John and Sarah Guild, of W., and had 10 children. Three of them were the first settlers of Keene, N. H.; namely, Nathan, who built the first house in Keene, Elijah, and Doct. Obadiah, the first physician in that town. — *Annals of Keene.* Josiah, son of Robert, lived in Wrentham, and had 7 children, of whom was Dea. Philip, father of Ira Blake, and grandfather of Rev. Mortimer, above.

at the Medway Classical Institute, and graduated at Amherst College, 1835. He next taught an academy three years at Franklin, during which time he studied theology under the direction of Rev. E. Smalley, D. D., then pastor. He was employed one year as preceptor of Hopkins Academy, Hadley. He then resigned school-teaching, and was ordained at Mansfield, 4 December, 1839, where he still continues.

Mr. Blake married Harriet Louisa, daughter of Mr. Joseph and Susa (Fisher) Daniels, of Franklin, and has two children.

His publications are: 1. A Funeral Sermon, 1844. 2. A Funeral Sermon, 1845. 3. Address on the erection of a Monument to Rev. Dr. Emmons, at Franklin, 1846. 4. Two Sermons, on the Import of the Church Covenant, and on the Duty of Mutual Forbearance, 1846. 5. Gethsemane and Calvary, 12mo, 1844, two editions. 6. Fast-day Sermon on the "Maine Preventive," 1852, three editions.

57. REV. MOSES GILL GROSVENOR

Is the youngest son and child of Rev. Daniel and Deborah (Hall) Grosvenor, and was born in Paxton, 23 Sept., 1796, where his father was then settled.*

---

* His grand-parents were Ebenezer and Lucy Grosvenor, natives and residents of Pomfret, Ct. They had ten children. Three were Orthodox ministers.

Rev. Daniel, one of the three, and father of Rev. Moses G., was born in Pomfret, 20 April, 1750; Yale College, 1769, chum of Prest. Dwight. Studied theology with Rev. Dr. Hall of Sutton, whose daughter, Deborah, afterwards became his wife; and was ordained at Grafton, 19 Oct., 1774. He lost his voice, and was dismissed, in 1787. He afterwards settled in Paxton, 5 November, 1794; resigned 17 Nov. 1802, and died in Petersham, 22 July, 1834, aged 84 years. He had ten children, of whom Rev. Moses G. (above) was the last.

Ebenezer, an older brother of Rev. Daniel, was born 1739; graduated

He fitted for college at Amherst; graduated at Dartmouth College, 1822, and at Andover, 1825.

He was ordained at West Haverhill, 27 December, 1826, dismissed in 1829, and installed in Ackworth, N. H., 14 Oct., 1829. He was dismissed 25 April, 1832, and was installed over the Orthodox Church in Barre, 14 November of the same year, where he continued until May, 1834. He was next settled, 30 May, 1835, at Marlboro', N. H., where he staid six years. He afterwards supplied the pulpit at Medfield a year, and at Marshall, N. Y., for six months, at each of which places he declined a settlement; also at Gardner, during six months of the year 1837.

His present abode is Petersham, in whose vicinity he occasionally preaches, as a diseased throat will permit.

Mr. Grosvenor married Miss Sophia W. Grout, daughter of John, and grand-daughter of Hon. Jonathan Grout, of Petersham. They have no children.

Mr. Grosvenor has published an Address on Church Music, delivered at West Alstead, N. H.

58. REV. THOMAS T. RICHMOND

Is a native of Mettapoiset, (Rochester,) but spent his early life in Taunton. He pursued a course of study with Rev. A. Cobb, of West Taunton, but did not graduate, and was approbated by Taunton Association.

He was ordained at Dartmouth, 17 July, 1832. During his ministry, religion was revived, and the church built up and strengthened; but he was compelled to leave, in poor

---

Yale College, 1759; ordained at Scituate, April, 1763, and dismissed April, 1780; afterwards settled in Harvard, 1782, where he died, 28 May, 1788. He married Elizabeth, daughter of Rev. Mr. Clarke, of Danvers, and had six children.

health, 23 April, 1837. He next spent four years in Newmarket, N. H., where he declined a call to settle, on account of his health. He was afterwards so far restored as to consent to a settlement in Medfield, where he was installed 26 November, 1842, and where he still continues.

Mr. Richmond married Miss Relief H. Smith, daughter of Mr. Jesse Smith, of Taunton.

He published a Sermon before the Norfolk Co. Education Society, 1849.

59. REV. TIMOTHY D. P. STONE

Graduated at Amherst College, 1834, and A. M., and studied theology at Andover. He afterwards was Teacher of Elocution in the Teachers' Seminary, in the same town. He was ordained pastor of the church in Holliston, 1 March, 1843, and dismissed 2 March, 1849, to take the chaplaincy of the State Reform School, at Westboro'. He is now Principal of the State Normal School of Connecticut, located at New Britain.

Mr. Stone is the author of several small volumes for the young.

60. REV. DAVID R. BARNES

Was employed as stated supply by the church in North Wrentham, during which time he became of member of Mendon Association. On the expiration of his engagement to that church, he returned to the State of New York, from which he came. No farther sketch of him has been obtained. He is supposed to be a native of Rome, N. Y., or its vicinity.

61. REV. SEWALL HARDING

Is a native of Medway, the son of Capt. John Harding and his wife Beulah, daughter of Judge Stephen Metcalf of Bellingham. He is a descendant of John Harding of Medfield, freeman 1640.

He graduated at Union College, Schenectady, N. Y., 1818; studied theology with Rev. Drs. Emmons and Ide, and was ordained over the second Congregational Church in Waltham, 17 Jan., 1821. He was dismissed November, 1837, to take the pastoral care of the church in East Medway, where he was installed 1 Nov., 1837. He was dismissed thence, 3 Dec., 1851, to become the Secretary of the American Doctrinal Tract and Book Society. He resides in Auburndale, Newton.

Mr. Harding married Miss Eliza Wheeler, daughter of Capt. Lewis and Betsey Wheeler, of Medway, and has four children.

His oldest son is Rev. John W. Harding. [See Licentiates, No. 118.]

His oldest daughter, Eliza, was married, 13 Oct. 1852, to Rev. Augustus Walker, of Medway, who sailed as Foreign Missionary to Syria, January, 1853.

Mr. Harding has published a Sermon before the Norfolk Co. Education Society, 1841; besides various documents connected with his present duties.

62. REV. ANDREW H. REED

Was born in Oakham, and is the son of Mr. Silas Reed, a native of Rutland. His mother's name was Elinor Hunter, of New Braintree.

He graduated at Amherst College, 1826, and at Andover, 1829. He was first settled at Raymond, N. H., 1834, and dismissed in 1837. He was installed the same year at Mason, N. H.; dismissed in 1841. He was invited to settle the same year in Mendon, but declined, and preached as stated supply until 1848. He still resides in Mendon, and preaches occasionally in the vicinity.

Mr. Reed married Miss Sarah Lawrence, daughter of Mr. John and Abigail (Reed) Lawrence, of Concord. He has two children living. Has published several articles upon electricity and cognate subjects.

63. REV. HORACE JAMES

Is the son of Dea. Galen James,* of Medford, of which town he is a native. He graduated at Yale College, 1840, studied theology at New Haven and Andover, and graduated at the latter Seminary, 1843. He settled in Wrentham, as colleague with Rev. E. Fisk, 1 Nov., 1843, and is now sole pastor of that church.

Mr. James married Miss Helen Leavitt, daughter of Gen. David and Corinna (Aldrich) Leavitt, and grand-daughter of Rev. Jonathan Leavitt, of Walpole, N. H.†

Mr. James has published, A Thanksgiving Sermon, 1846; Wrentham Jubilee, 1850; and several Reports and Lectures on Education.

---

* John James, his paternal ancestor, freeman, Scituate, 1668, died by a wound from the Indians, leaving one son, John, who was Deacon, as was also his son John, and grandson John. The fifth generation was also John, Major, who removed from Scituate to Medford, and was the father of Capt. Galen James, above. *See Deane's Scituate*, p. 293.

† Rev. J. Leavitt was born in Suffield, Ct., 22 Jan., 1731; Yale Coll., 1758; ordained, Walpole, N. H., 27 May, 1761; dismissed, May, 1765. Installed at Charlemont, Oct. 1768, and d. at Heath, set off from Charlemont, 9 Sept., 1802. He married Sarah Hooker, of Farrington, and had eleven sons and one daughter.

64. REV. TYLER THACHER

Was born at Princeton, 11 September, 1801, and is the son of Obadiah and Elizabeth (Richardson) Thacher, and brother of Rev. Moses Thacher, (Member of Association, No. 43).* He pursued his preparatory studies in part at Harford, Pa., graduated at Brown University, 1824, and studied theology with Rev. O. Thompson, of Rehoboth. He was ordained by Mendon Association as Evangelist, at North Wrentham, 4 December, 1827.

After preaching some years under appointment of the Home Missionary Society, he was installed at East Hawley, 14 May, 1834, and dismissed 31 Jan., 1843. He was afterwards employed as stated supply at North Wrentham, until he departed, in 1851, for California, with his family. He is now employed at Maysville in that State, teaching school, and preaching in the mining districts upon the Sabbath.

Mr. Thacher married, first, Miss Fidelia Thompson, daughter of Rev. Otis Thompson, of Rehoboth, by whom he had three children, two of whom (sons) survive. The eldest, a promising youth, was drowned. On the death of his wife, he married Miss Nancy Newton, of Hawley.

Mr. Thacher has published several volumes, besides numerous theological essays in periodicals. His chief works are: Taylorism Examined, 1834; Arminianism Examined, 1833. They indicate an uncommonly acute and discriminating thinker.

A California paper, announcing his arrival in that region, says, and justly: "His thorough scholarship and unfeigned piety will render him a valuable acquisition to the New State."

---

* See his ancestry in a note, under Rev. Moses Thacher, Members, etc., No. 43.

65. REV. SMITH B. GOODENOW

Was born in Damariscotta, Lincoln Co., Me. At four years of age he was left fatherless, and was taken by his friends to Providence, R. I., where he commenced learning the watch-maker's trade. In his fifteenth year he was hopefully converted, and joined the Beneficent Congregational Church, May, 1832, by the ladies of which church he was sent to Waterville Academy. He entered the College in 1834, but removed to Bowdoin College, and graduated, 1838. He was Principal of the Academic High School at Bath three years.

He was approbated to preach the Gospel, 1843, by the Lincoln Association, and engaged as missionary at Westerly, R. I., 1 April, 1843. He was ordained as Evangelist, at Providence, 17 Aug., 1843; and installed pastor of the church in Milford, 20 Oct., 1844, whence he was dismissed 1 Jan., 1846. After preaching a while in Warwick, R. I., he was settled at Edgartown, Martha's Vineyard, 30 June, 1847. He left in January, 1851, on invitation of the Presb. Board of City Missions in Newark, N. J., and commenced labor as preacher as large, Feb. 8, in that city, where he still is. He was subsequently dismissed from the pastoral office in Edgartown, Oct., 1851.

Mr. Goodenow has published a "New England Grammar," three editions. "Book of Elements," 1850. Premium Tract on the Sabbath, published by the Philadelphia Sab. Association. The wife of Mr. Goodenow died in the summer of 1852.

66. REV. CHARLES SIMMONS

Is a native of Paris Hill, Oneida Co., N. Y., and the son of Aaron Simmons, Jr., whose father belonged to Little

Compton, R. I.* His mother was Lydia Wilbor, daughter of Charles Wilbor, of Little Compton, and sister of the late Gov. Wilbor, of the same place.

He spent his early life in the family of Rev. W. R. Weeks, D. D., of Paris Hill, N. Y., and in travelling as general agent for the Utica Christian Repository, which Dr. Weeks then conducted, and for similar publications. He also served an apprenticeship as blacksmith, and carried on the business as partner a year, during which time, he engaged to go, in this capacity, under the patronage of the Am. Board, to one of the Indian tribes near Green Bay. But they abandoned the enterprize, and he was released. He then engaged in study, for college, with Dr. Weeks; but on his advice, he relinquished the idea of graduating, studied theology, and was approbated by the Oneida Association, 24 May, 1832.

Mr. Simmons commenced preaching in Hebronville, South Attleboro', in July, and was ordained there, 26 Dec., 1832, and dismissed 21 Oct., 1838. He spent the winter following in Middleboro', assisting Rev. Mr. Putnam, in that extensive town. He was stated supply at North Scituate, 1839, and also at Wareham the year and a half following. Since this latter date, he has resided in North Wrentham, preaching occasionally, but employed chiefly in the distribution of Dr. Emmons's Works, and upon his own publications.

Mr. Simmons married Miss Eliza Perrigo, daughter of Mr. John Perrigo, of North Wrentham, and has two children.

Publications. Besides many articles in the Utica Repository, Hopkinsian Magazine, N. E. Telegraph, etc., he has issued, 1. Tract on U. S. Slavery, 24 pp. 1841. 2. Scripture Manual, 1st edition, at Wareham, 1841; 2d, in 1844.

---

* The first Simmons of his family, Moses, settled at Duxbury, of whose sons, one went to Vt., another to R. I. Aaron migrated to Paris Hill, when a wilderness, about 1790. He was grandfather to Rev. C. Simmons, above.

Stereotyped, 1845. Over 40,000 copies of this valuable work have been sold in this country, and it has been translated into other languages at some of the Mission Stations. 3. A tract on Human Ability and Dependence, 1850. 4. A Manual of Maxims, 1852.

67. REV. CALVIN WHITE

Is the son of Israel and Margaret (Tubbs) White, of Raynham, in which town he was born 12 Sept., 1799.* In 1819, while living in Dorchester, he became a subject of renewing grace, and united with the church under Rev. Dr. Codman. He commenced study for college, and, after two years, entered Bangor Seminary, whence he graduated, 1827.

He preached as missionary about two years, and was agent of Lincoln Co. Bible Society, three months of the time. He was ordained, 28 Oct., 1829, in Robbinston, Me. The church consisted of 7 females and *one* male, and he was a *rum-seller!* Mr. White's labors were blessed with a revival, and the addition of 21 members to the church, out of a congregation of less than 100. The church was too feeble to support him, and he was dismissed 19 July, 1831. He left a total-abstinence temperance society in the town, of over 100 members. He next preached several months in East Machias, and was installed in Gray, Me., 7 Aug., 1833. He received a dismission in June, 1837, and removed, with his

* His ancestry is traceable to John White, of Raynham, m. Hannah Smith, 24 Feb., 1679. Had 10 ch. II John, Jr., eldest son, born 16 Aug., 1681, had 5 ch. certainly, of whom was George. III. George m. Hannah Briant, 4 June, 1745, and had 9 ch. Israel was the 7th. IV. Israel, b. 20 Aug., 1757, m. Margaret Tubbs, 12 Sept., 1782, had 12 ch., of whom Calvin, above, was the 9th. His wife, Margaret Tubbs, was born in Berkley, 1762. Her father was Maj. Samuel Tubbs, of the Revolution, and Deacon of the church in Berkley, and afterwards in Dresden, Me., where he died.—*Rev. C. White, Gardiner, Me.*

family, to Amherst in this state. From April, 1839 to Jan., 1841, he resided in Loudon Village, N. H., where he declined a settlement. A year was next spent in Provincetown, Cape Cod. In April, 1844, he commenced preaching in Dover, where he remained three years. In 1849, he removed to Gardiner, Me., where he now resides, and in whose vicinity he has 'abundant opportunities of preaching the Gospel to the poor, without money and without price.'

Mr. White married, first, Mary N. Dickinson, daughter of John and Rebecca Dickinson. Her father was a native of Amherst, but spent 25 years in East Machias, Me., as a lawyer and Judge of Probate, and where Mr. W. married her, 2 Feb., 1830. She died at her father's, in Amherst, 2d May, 1841. His second, and present wife was Ellen Maria, daughter of Ebenezer Nickerson, of Boston, whom he married 8 Jan., 1845. Mr. White had, by his first wife, 5 children, and 4 by his present wife, two of whom are dead.

Mr. White has issued no publications.

68. REV. ORAMEL W. COOLEY

Was born in Hawley, and is the son of Calvin and Rosamond (Field) Cooley.

He studied Theology at the Seminary in Bangor, and was ordained at Dover, 4 May, 1848. He was dismissed in 1850, and migrated, with his family, to Illinois, in which state he is now laboring, in Grandville or vicinity.

Mr. Cooley married Miss Sarah Adams, of Hopkinton.

69. REV. HENRY L. BULLEN

Is a native of Medway. His parents' names are Lewis and Esther (Grout) Bullen.* He commenced his classical

* His grandfather was Jeduthun, son of John Bullen, a descendant of Samuel, of Dedham, freeman, 1641.

studies at Franklin Academy, and entered Western Reserve college, but graduated at Dartmouth Coll., 1842. He afterwards taught school three years in Savannah, Ga., where he was approbated to preach, by the Hopewell Presbytery, at Madison, Ga. He returned to Mass., and taught school in Sherborn and Holliston; from which town he removed to the West.

He was ordained as Home Missionary, 7 May, 1850, and labored at Port Byron, Ill., and in Lee and Clair counties, Iowa.

He is now acting as professor of Mathematics and Natural Philosophy, in Iowa College, at Davenport, Iowa.

70. REV. WILLIAM BARNES

Was born at Portsmouth, Ohio, and is the youngest son of Thomas and Sarah (Evans) Barnes, who migrated from Sussex Co., Del., in 1809. He was baptized, in infancy, by a Methodist minister, in a log cabin, upon the banks of the Ohio. To this denomination, of Methodists, all his family belong, and in their faith he was educated. From 1823 to 1833, he resided with his parents in Marion Co., O., and attended, meanwhile, at Worthington Academy six months, and taught school six months. While studying for the legal profession, at the Huron Institute, in Milan, in 1833, he became converted, and joined the Presb. church in that town. He graduated at Yale Col., 1839, and taught an Academy at Southold, L. I., the following year. He graduated at East Windsor, and was approbated by the New London Association, 1 Sept., 1841. Ordained at Hampton, Ct., 21 Sept., 1842, dismissed in 1847, and installed at Foxboro', 15 Dec., 1847. He has recently asked a dismission from his charge on account of ill health, and has returned to his former residence. Mr. Barnes married, 18 Aug., 1842, Miss Eunice Alvard

Taylor, daughter of Nathaniel and Betsey Taylor, of Manchester, Ct., and has three children.

71. REV. JOSHUA THOMAS TUCKER

Is the son of Joshua Tucker, and is a native of Milton.* He prepared for college at Phillips Academy, Andover, and graduated at Yale, 1833, pursued his theological studies at Lane Seminary, Cincinnati, O., and was approbated to preach the Gospel, April, 1837, by the Presbytery of St. Louis, Mo.

He was ordained by the Presbytery of Alton, Ill., Oct., 1837, and preached as a missionary until 1840 at Chester and Rushville, Ill. From 1840 to 1846, he had the pastoral charge of the Pres. church, in Hannibal, Missouri; From 1846 to 1848, he was minister of the North Pres. Church, St. Louis, Mo., and joint editor of the "St. Louis Herald of Religious Liberty," a weekly paper. At this last date he was compelled, on account of broken health, both of himself and his family, to leave the western missionary service and return to the region of his nativity.

Mr. Tucker commenced ministering to the church in Holliston, 1 April, 1849, and was installed in the pastoral office, 6 June, following. He is still in Holliston.

Mr. Tucker married, first, Mary Oland Stibbs, daughter of Christopher and Elizabeth Stibbs, of London, Eng.; she died in 1844.

His present wife was Miss Anne D. Shackford, daughter of

---

* His immigrant ancestor was *Robert*, of Weymouth, 1639; who had two sons, Ephraim and Manasseh, and probablya third, Robert, Rep. for Milton, 1680. *Manasseh*, was Deacon of 1st church in Milton, and had four sons: one of whom was *Samuel.* He had two sons, Samuel and Nathaniel. (Nathaniel grad. H. U., 1744, and Rev., settled in N. Y. State.) *Samuel* had a son Samuel, whose son Joshua was father of Rev. Joshua Thomas Tucker above.

John and Jane Shackford, of Portsmouth, N. H. Of his five children, two only survive.

Mr. Tucker has published:

1. Dying Scenes — A Memorial of Mrs. Mary O. Tucker, 1844.

2. Thanksgiving Discourse, Hannibal, Missouri, 1845.

3. Discourse, Historical, of first Pres. Church, Hannibal, Missouri, 1845.

4. God's Ministry of Judgment — Sermon on the Day of National Fast, Holliston, Mass., 1849.

5. Life's Lessons of Wisdom — a Funeral Sermon on Mr. Harding Daniels, Holliston, Mass., 1849.

6. The Citizen and the Commonwealth — Sermon on State Fast Day, Holliston, Mass., 1851.

7. The Maine Temperance Law — a Thanksgiving Sermon, Holliston, 1851.

72. REV. PRESTON POND

Was born in Wrentham, and is the son of Gen. Preston and Abial (Blake) Pond.*

He commenced his course of liberal studies at Bangor, Me., graduated at Bowdoin Coll., 1840, and at the Bangor Theol. Seminary, 1843.

He was ordained at Eastport, 8 Oct., 1843, and dismissed April, 1845. He next labored a year in South Newmarket, N. H., and commenced preaching as stated supply at Milford in Sept., 1846. He was installed as pastor 24 May, 1849, and dismissed 16 Feb., 1852, to take the pastoral charge of the Edwards Church, Boston; over which he was installed, 25 Feb.

---

* Gen. P. Pond is brother of Rev. E. Pond, D. D. (Lic. No. 58.) For the ancestry of the Pond Family, see Enoch Pond, Lic. No 17.

Mr. Pond married Miss Elizabeth S., daughter of Deacon John and Sarah Thompson, of Durham, N. H.

73. REV. GEORGE H. NEWHALL

Is the son of George and Mary (Woods) Newhall, and was born in Athol. He graduated at Amherst College, 1845, and at Andover Theological Seminary, 1848.

He was ordained over the church in Walpole, 18 Sept., 1850.

Mr. Newhall married Miss Harriet F. Lindsey, daughter of Stacey Lindsey, Esq., of Prescott.

74. REV. CHARLES CHAMBERLAIN

Is a native of Holliston, and the son of Enoch jr. and Lucy (Holbrook) Chamberlain. He prepared for College at Leicester Academy, graduated at Brown Univ., 1836, and officiated as Tutor, during the years 1837 and 8. He studied theology in part, at Andover Seminary, and with Rev. Dr. Ide, and completed the usual course at Union Theol. Seminary.

After laboring two years at the West as missionary, he returned to Massachusetts, and was ordained over the church in Berkley, 8 July, 1842. He was dismissed in 1844, and afterwards preached in New York, Freetown, and Mendon. He was installed at Auburn, in this state, 9 July, 1851, and there now continues.

Mr. Chamberlain married a daughter of Moses and Chloe (Hodges) Bassett, natives of Norton, but residents, after marriage, at Providence, R. I.

75. REV. SAMUEL HUNT

Is the son of Dea. Richard and Ann (Humphrey) Hunt, of Attleboro', in which town he was born. He graduated at Amherst College, 1833, and studied theology with Rev. J. Ide, D. D.

He was ordained at Natick, 17 July, 1839, and dismissed May, 1850. He was installed pastor of the church in Franklin, 4 December, 1850, which office he fills at this date.

Mr. Hunt has published "Letters to the Avowed Friends of Missions," 1844; "Political Duties of Christians," 1848.

Mr. Hunt married Miss Mary Foster, daughter of Maj. Josiah Foster, of Southampton, L. I. She died Dec., 1849, leaving three children.

76. REV. JOHN HASKELL

Is a native of New Glocester, Me., and son of Caleb and Judith (Collins) Haskell. He graduated at Bowdoin College, 1846, and at Bangor Theological Seminary, 1850. He was ordained pastor of the church in Dover, 25 December, 1851.

Mr. Haskell married Miss Lucy J. Dickey, daughter of Mr. George and Lucy L. (Patch) Dickey, of Bangor.

77. REV. ASA HIXON

Is the son of Mr. Asa Hixon, of Medway. He graduated at Brown University, 1825, pursued his theological course at Auburn Seminary, N. Y., and was ordained at Oakham, 7 Oct., 1829, as colleague with Rev. Daniel Tomlinson. He was compelled to resign his charge, 25 Dec., 1832, on account of ill health, which continued, with increasing debility, until he was, and continues to be, entirely disabled from public speaking. He now resides in Franklin.

Mr. Hixon married Miss Charlotte Baker, daughter of Capt. David and Jemima (Richardson) Baker, of Franklin, and sister of Rev. Abijah R. Baker, of Lynn, and has one child, a son.

BIOGRAPHICAL SKETCHES

OF THE

LICENTIATES OF MENDON ASSOCIATION.

---

1. REV. DAVID THURSTON.

[See Sketches of Members, No. 5.]

2. REV. MOSES TAFT

Was born in Mendon, 20 July, 1722; graduated at Harvard University, 1751, and received A. M. in course. He was ordained second minister of the new south precinct, in Braintree, now first church in Randolph, 26 Aug., 1752. Rev. John Shaw, of Bridgewater, preached the sermon. The written parts of the ordination, with Mr. Taft's confession of faith, were published; the only known copy of which is in the Mass. Hist. Library.

In 1789, Rev. Jonathan Strong, D. D., was settled as his colleague. He died 12 November, 1791, aged 69, having been settled 39 years.

Mr. Taft married, 15 Aug., 1753, Mary Dorr, oldest child of Rev. Joseph Dorr, of Mendon. She died 10 Jan., 1796. Their children were,

1. Moses, born 10 June, 1754; graduated Harvard University, 1774; physician in Sudbury; died, 1799.

2. Eleazer, born 11 Oct., 1755; H. U., 1783; resided in Exeter, N. H., and died there in 1834.

3. Joseph, born 15 Aug., 1756; H. U., 1783.

4. Phinehas, b. 11 Aug., 1762; H. U., 1789. He studied theology with Dr. Strong and Dr. Emmons, was a promising young man, and thoroughly orthodox, after the Hopkinsian model, but he died in 1798, having never actively entered upon the ministry. Mr. Taft had also four daughters, married respectively to an Allen, a French, a Henshaw, and Samuel Stetson, of Boston.

"Mr. Taft's doctrinal views were evangelical, though some supposed, with little reason, that, towards the close of his ministry, he inclined somewhat to Arminianism. As a preacher, he was not especially distinguished. His ministrations at last were exceedingly dull. His health became very infirm, and his excessive use of tobacco and opium impaired his usefulness, and induced a premature old age. He became, as a consequence, quite indolent and inefficient in his habits, and finally a paralytic.

"His character resembled that of Eli more than that of Nehemiah.

"It is not known that he ever published anything, other than the confession of faith already mentioned. A manuscript sermon of his, dated 1771, still in being, although in nearly illegible cacography, shows him to have been naturally capable, and, at that date, doctrinally evangelical."*

3. REV. CORNELIUS JONES

Is recorded as a native of Bellingham. He graduated at Harvard University in 1752, and received A. M. He was ordained as first pastor of the church in Sandisfield in 1756, on the same day in which the church was organized. Prest. Edwards, then in Stockbridge, preached the ordination

* Letter of Doct. E. Alden, Randolph.

sermon, which, through the lack of a meeting-house, was delivered in a *barn*.

Mr. Jones was dismissed in 1761. Rev. D. D. Field says,* "He never resettled, but preached occasionally. He resided for a number of years in Rowe; then removed to Skeenesborough, now White Hall, N. Y., where he died at an advanced age." The Harvard Catalogue says in 1783, the name of his wife was Sarah, and he was married while at Sandisfield. Nothing more is known of him. And even at White Hall, the oldest citizen can give no information *whatever* in relation to him.†

4. REV. NATHANAEL POTTER

Is supposed to have been a native of Elizabethtown, N. J. He graduated at Princeton, N. J., 1753, and A. M.; also at Harvard, 1758. He was settled in Brookline, 19 Nov., 1755, and dismissed, 17 June, 1759. He is said to have died at sea. At what date, is unknown.

Mr. Potter published, in 1758, "A Discourse on Jeremiah 8: 20, preached on the Lord's Day morning, Jan. 1, 1758, at Brookline; wherein is briefly attempted A Discovery of the Causes of our late National Calamities, Disappointments, and Losses, — that they are owing to our Sins," etc. 8vo. 27 pp.‡

5. HON. JOSEPH DORR, JR.

Was born in Mendon, 24 May, 1730. He was the only son of Rev. Joseph Dorr, of Mendon. He graduated at Harvard, 1752, and A. M., and preached occasionally for several years, but was never ordained. He early turned his

* Quarterly Reg., Vol. VII., p. 35.
† Letter of W. G. Wolcott, P. M., White Hall, N. Y.
‡ Copy in Mass. Hist. Soc. Library, shelf 74, bk. 21.

attention and energies to the political affairs of the times, and became an earnest, unceasing, and vigorous co-laborer with the earliest patriots of the Revolution. Worcester, in his immediate neighborhood, was the central point of the first movements of the Revolution; and none were behind Mr. Dorr in hastening it onwards, and directing its course. It is said that three hundred days of each year from 1773 to 1780, were devoted by him to the public service without compensation.

Mr. Dorr filled many important civil offices. He was town-clerk, justice of the peace, member of the secret committee, of the committee of safety, and of the committee of correspondence. He was one of the commissioners chosen to wait upon the Mandamus Councillors of the county of Worcester, and to demand the surrender of their charter. He was also member of the Legislature, and, after the Revolution, was appointed Justice of the Court of Common Pleas, and Judge of Probate; which last offices were held by him till near the close of life. Judge Dorr died 31 Oct., 1808, aged 78. He married Catharine Bucknam, 6 Dec., 1768, and had eight children. Two oldest died young. The others were,

3. Joseph Hawley, born 20 July, 1772, a merchant of Boston. He married Lucy Penniman of New Braintree, and is still living. He is the father of Joseph H. Dorr, M. D., of Philadelphia.

4. Samuel, born 23 June, 1774. President of "New England Bank," and Representative and Senator for Boston, where he died Dec., 1844. He married, 1st, Lucy, daughter of Joseph Fox, Esq., of Fitchburg, and 2d, a Miss Brown, and had seven children. Among them is James A. Dorr, Esq., H. U., 1813, lawyer in New York.

5. Sarah, b. 10 Aug., 1776, and married to Jonas Newell, of New Braintree.

6. Thomas Shepherd, born 11 Nov., 1778; died October, 1816.

7. Mary, born 7 January, 1784, and married to Oliver Fox, Esq., of Fitchburg.

8. Edward, born 10 Oct., 1786, and settled in Nova Iberia, La. He owned Dorr's Island at the mouth of Trinity River, Texas, and became celebrated for his droves of horses and cattle. He died in April, 1847.*

6. REV. ASAPH RICE

Was born in Hardwick, in 1733, and graduated at Harvard, 1752, and A. M.

The early Indian wars awakened an interest in the spiritual condition of the Western Aborigines. After the close of the second war, Rev. Eli Fobes, afterwards Dr. Fobes, of Northfield, who had served as chaplain to the colonial troops of 1758, visited the Six Nations as a missionary; Mr. Rice accompanied him on his return to them, in 1762. They were to be supported by a society in Scotland, and were to labor among the Oneidas. Rev. Dr. Chauncey, in his ordination sermon of Mr. Bowman, as the *third* missionary, at Boston, 31 Aug., 1762, calls Mr. Rice, "a promising young man, who went out to spend his life in the service."

On the arrival of Rev. Messrs. Fobes and Rice at Ohonoquagie, they assembled the chief men of the tribe, who gave thanks for their arrival, and only waited for the return of three sachems, then absent, to accept formally the services of the missionaries. A Rev. Mr. Hawley had spent some time with them previous to the war, and prepared them to favor the introduction of the Gospel. Mr. Fobes writes: 'we have set up a school here. Have had a dozen a day for twenty days.' Two white boys were members.

* Hist. and Geneal. Register, Vol. III., p. 312.

Mr. Fobes returned 29 Oct., 1762, leaving Mr. Rice, who was now, or soon after, joined by Mr. Bowman. An Indian church was gathered by them at Ohonoquagie, on the banks of the Susquehanna. It embraced at first ten members, five males, and five females; to which three were added before Mr. Rice returned. This church and school were the first amongst the Six Nations, and furnished some of the earliest Indian pupils of Dr. Wheelock, afterwards President of Dartmouth College.*

Mr. Rice returned in 1765, and was ordained pastor of the church in Westminster, 16 Oct., 1765, where he continued until his death, 20 March, 1816, at the age of 83.

He married Mary, daughter of Rev. Ebenezer Morse, of Shrewsbury. She was born 24 Dec., 1747, and died on the birth of her first child. Her father, afterwards of Boylston, was also a physician, and had, besides, many private pupils; among whom was Dr. T. Harris, of Dorchester. Of Mr. R's family history, no further account has been obtained.

Little of Mr. Rice's further history is known. No records of the church during his fifty years' ministry, exist. The church numbered ninety members at his decease.

"Mr. Rice is said to have been a man of great dignity, and very commanding in his personal appearance. He had many excellent qualities. The children and youth both respected him, and also stood in great awe of him, by reason of his dignified person. He was a man of some talent, and considerable influence in his region. He was reputed to have been an Arminian in his doctrinal affinities."†

7. REV. BENJAMIN CARYL

Was the son of Benjamin, and grandson of Benjamin and Mary "Carril," and was born in Hopkinton, 1732. He grad-

* See Indian Documents, Miss'y Rooms, Boston.

† Letters of Rev. O. A. White, Westminster.

uated at Harvard, 1761, and A. M.; and was settled in Dover, 10 Nov., 1762, — the first minister of that church, — where he died 14 Nov., 1811, after a ministry of fifty years, and in the 80th year of his age.

Mr. Caryl married, 9 Dec., 1762, Mrs. Sarah Colick, widow of Dr. Colick, of Wrentham. She was a daughter of Rev. Henry Messinger, of Wrentham. She had had one son, Cornelius Colick, by her former husband, and had two sons by Mr. Caryl, viz.:

1. Benjamin, b. 6 Dec., 1764, and died 12 Sept., 1775, aged 11 years.

2. George, b. 1 Apl., 1767, grad. Harvard, 1788, m. Miss Pamela Martin, and settled in Dover as physician. Was very successful, and highly esteemed. He died 9 Aug., 1829, leaving a son and two daughters, who, with his widow, still live.

No obituary of Mr. Caryl was ever published. But his report is of a goodly savor. "He was greatly beloved by all, and his memory is cherished with affection and respect. All are uniform in testifying that he was a good man and thoroughly orthodox. He was remarkably gifted in prayer. When he delivered his message, the tears were often seen to roll down his cheeks. He kept himself very much at home, seldom attending public meetings abroad. He drew as little from books as any man of his time. A lawyer of some eminence remarked of his library, that "it consisted of a Bible, a concordance, and an old jacknife." His sermons are written in a very legible hand, and the style is quite perspicuous. But one of them — a Thanksgiving Sermon — was published. His funeral sermon was preached by Rev. Mr. Palmer of Needham.

His epitaph is as follows: —

IN MEMORY OF

REV. BENJAMIN CARYL,

WHO DIED NOV. 14, 1811, Æ. 80 YEARS, AND IN THE 50TH YEAR OF HIS MINISTRY.

"The fathers, where are they?
And the prophets, do they live forever?"

ERECTED BY THE REQUEST AND AT THE EXPENSE OF HIS SOCIETY.*

8. REV. EBENEZER CHAPLIN.

[See Sketches of Members, No. 9.]

9. REV. EZEKIEL EMERSON

Was the son of John and Mary Emerson, of Uxbridge. He was born in Uxbridge, 14 Feb., 1735. He graduated at the college of New Jersey, 1763, and during the following summer of 1764, commenced preaching in Phipsburg, formerly part of Georgetown, Lincoln Co., Me.

Here was one of the earliest colonies in this province, and the Gospel had been statedly enjoyed in the town from 1738, but no church was organized until two days before the ordination of Mr. Emerson, which ordination took place, 3 July, 1765.

"He remained, happily and peaceably, with the people for about fourteen years. At that period, the Revolutionary war rendered his situation unpleasant. The settlements on the coast, and especially at the mouth of large rivers, were considered unsafe, the expenses of the war lay heavy on the people, and the depreciation of the paper currency of the country made Mr. Emerson's nominal salary to be of little value. All these circumstances induced him to remove for a season. He accordingly suspended his ministrations at Georgetown, and, taking his family, removed up the river to Norridgewock, where he remained until 1 May, 1783.

* Letter of Rev. J. Haskell, Dover.

The country was then at peace ; and, taking the advice of a Council, he returned, resumed his ministerial labors in Georgetown, (now Phipsburg,) and continued to discharge them steadily and faithfully until 1810. At this time, his mental powers became impaired to a considerable degree, and he found it necessary to retire from the ministry. He died 9 Nov., 1815, at the age of 80 years. He is spoken of with marked respect, as an "excellent man." *

Mr. Emerson married Catharine Dorr, second daughter of Rev. Joseph Dorr, of Mendon, 27 March, 1760. He had nine children, and all but one reached maturity and became heads of families. The two eldest, Phebe and Ezekiel, were born in Mendon, and settled in Norridgewock. The third, Hawley, settled in Georgetown. Calvin settled in Fairfield.

Luther, b. 26 Sept., 1772, grad. Dartmouth, 1799. Lawyer in Sedgwick, and then in Ohio. The remaining children were, Eusebius, Susannah, Mary, and Elizabeth. Elizabeth died in early childhood ; the others left families in Norridgewock and Fairfield, Me.

10. REV. SILAS BIGLOW.

Was the son of Samuel and Jedidah (Hathorn) Biglow, Jr., of Westboro', whose father and wife were of Marlboro'. He was born in Shrewsbury, 10 Oct., 1739, and graduated at Harvard, 1765, and A. M. He was ordained at Paxton, 21 Oct., 1767, and died shortly after, 16 Nov., 1769, at the age of 30 years.

Mr. B. was engaged to Sarah, daughter of Rev. Dr. Hall, of Sutton ; but his sudden death prevented the union. She afterwards married Gen. Chase, of Cornish, N. H.

"Mr. Biglow was very highly esteemed for his intellectual

* Greenleaf's Eccl. History of Maine, and Williamson's History of Maine, as quoted in Hist. and Geneal. Register, Vol. III, p. 312.

and moral worth, and his ministry was very satisfactory to the people of his charge."*

11. REV. ALEXANDER THAYER

Was the son of William and Abigail (Sumner) Thayer,† and was born in Mendon, 25 Jan., 1744. He graduated at the college of New Jersey, 1765. He was ordained at Paxton,—the successor of Rev. Mr. Biglow above — 28 Nov., 1770. His political affinities did not at all harmonize with those of the staunch freedom-loving people of Paxton.

He was dismissed on account of his strong Loyalist opinions, 14 Aug., 1782. After his dismission, he removed to Holliston, and there spent his days as a private citizen. He died 25 Sept., 1807, aged 64 years. The stone marking the place of his sepulture, has the following:—

Beneath this stone his body lies,
And mingles with its native earth;
The immortal spirit to the skies
Is gone to God who gave it birth.

Mr. Thayer married Miss Abigail Goulding, and had seven children: Patty, Nabby, Polly, Ursula, Sarah, John, and Alexander.

12. MR. JOSIAH READ

Was the son of John and Lucy Read, of Uxbridge, in which town he was born, 23 July, 1753. He graduated at Brown

* Letter of Rev. W. Phipps, Paxton.

† Rev. Mr. Thayer's ancestral line is as follows: Alexander, the son of William and Abigail (Sumner) Thayer, who was the son of Thomas and Mary Thayer, of Mendon, who was the son of Ferdinando and Huldah (Hayward) Thayer, of Braintree, who was the son of Thomas and Margary Thayer, who came to New England with three children: Thomas, Ferdinando, and Shadrach, and was admitted freeman, 1647, and died 1665.

University, 1775, and A. M. He also received the honorary degree of A. M. from Yale, 1781, and from Harvard, 1785. He did not enter the ministry. But what became of him, and what was his history, has not been ascertained.

13. REV. ELISHA FISH, JR.

Was born in Upton, 31 March, 1756. He was the son of Rev. Elisha Fish of the same place, and grandson of Moses Fish, a respectable and enterprising farmer in Groton, Ct. His mother was Hannah, daughter of Dea. Fobes, of Westborough. He was brother to Rev. Holloway Fish, (Licentiate No. 24).

He graduated at Harvard, 1779, and A. M., studied theology with his father, and was settled in Windsor, 16 June, 1785. He was dismissed 5 July, 1792, and settled in Gilsum, N. H., 29 May, 1794, as the first pastor of the church, and where he continued until his death, 28 March, 1807, in his 51st year.

Mr. Fish married Abigail Snell, daughter of Ebenezer and Sarah (Packard) Snell, of Cummington, formerly of North Bridgewater. She was sister of Rev. Thomas Snell, D. D., of North Brookfield, and of Mrs. Doct. Peter Bryant, mother of William Cullen Bryant, the Poet. They had six children; five of whom, two sons and three daughters, still reside in Gilsum, unwavering friends of the Gospel and the distinguishing doctrines which their father taught. Mrs. Fish, after living a widow 42 years, died in Gilsum, 1 Nov., 1841, at the age of 85.

While at Windsor, Mr. Fish received an injury in his right ancle, which resulted in the loss of the limb, the embarrassment of his energies, and probably the impairing of his health, and the shortening of his life. The church was small, but sound in doctrine, and united in their pastor. But Antinomianism prevailed in the parish to such an extent as before long rendered his support so precarious, his situation so unpleasant and his prospect of continued usefulness so dubious, that he asked and received a dismission. His labors, however, were not in vain. Besides witnessing a season of unusual ingathering into the church, he prepared the way for a successor of like sentiments — Rev. Gordon Dorrance, — who remarked that he could never have been sustained there, had not Mr. Fish by his previous labors, broken up the hard and difficult field.

His interest in the spiritual welfare of his people at Gilsum, N. H., was great, as both his labors and prayers testified. But he was apparently less successful in the ministry here, than many of his brethren. Still God did not leave him wholly without witness, even in Gilsum, but granted him what might be termed "a season of revival."

"In disposition Mr. Fish was friendly and affectionate; in manners easy; in conversation frank and sincere, yet winning and conciliatory. He was styled a Hopkinsian, of which appellation he was not ashamed. Nor did he hesitate to acknowledge and defend on all suitable occasions, what he esteemed to be the peculiar doctrines of the Gospel. In his ministry, he urged them with exemplary fidelity, whether men would hear or forbear. The duties too, which flow from these doctrines, he fearlessly expressed and conscientiously exemplified."

An illustrative anecdote may be given. About the time of his settlement in Gilsum, he was called to a council in a neighboring town, to ordain a candidate of that class, whose creed, as one of the number remarked, 'rather consisted in *not* believing.' Only one other Evangelical minister was invited on the council, and he found it necessary or convenient to be absent on a journey. Thus Mr. Fish was without a single sympathizing clerical friend. When he found the council disposed to proceed without examination or inquiry, he insisted upon a confession of faith from the candidate. The answer of the candidate, that 'the Bible was his confession of faith,' was received by the council with applause. But Mr. Fish was not so easily satisfied, nor would he be silenced; but continued his interrogatories, till the candidate stood confessed before the council as an Arian, and a favorer, if not an advocate of Universalism. He now felt that the path of duty was plain, and after a manly defence of the truth in face of violent opposition, he entered his protest, in which five lay-members united, against a man who entertained views so subversive of the Gospel. For this he met with severe rebuke from some of the members of the council. But his conscience approved his course; and one of his most violent assailants on that council, subsequently became a friend to the same system of truth, and advocated the very faith he before had endeavored so vigorously to destroy.*

14. REV. MOSES WARREN

Was the son of Dea. Jonas and Lydia Warren, was born in Upton, 31 Oct., 1758. He graduated at Harvard college, 1784, A. M., 1788, and was ordained over the church in South Wilbraham, 3 Sept., 1788. Rev. E. Fish, Jr., of Windsor, preached the sermon from Mal. 2: 7. He continued in the pastorate here forty years, until his death, 19 Feb., 1829, in his 71st year.

Mr. Warren married the daughter of Hon. John Bliss, Esq., of his own parish,—a man of great worth, of ardent piety, and who was one of the Judges of the court in the county of Hampshire, for many years. He had four children, who lived to adult age,—three sons and a daughter.

* Letter of Rev. E. Adams, Gilsum, N. H.

Two of the sons received a classical education at Williams College; one of whom entered the ministry and spent his days principally at the South; and was highly esteemed, as a sound orthodox divine and an interesting preacher. He has been dead for some years, as are both the other sons. The youngest died May, 1851, in South Wilbraham, having occupied the same house as his father during his forty years' ministry. The daughter of Rev. Mr. Warren was married to Rev. Levi Smith, and is still living with him at East Windsor Hill, Ct.

"Mr. Warren sustained a respectable standing in his class as a classical scholar. He was uncommonly amiable in his disposition and circumspect in his deportment, so that he was highly esteemed by his instructors and beloved by his acquaintance.

"As a preacher of the Gospel, Mr. Warren was considerably above mediocrity. His sermons were written in a simple but chaste style, were remarkable for the appropriate introduction of Scripture language, which ever rendered them edifying to pious hearers. They were delivered with a solemnity which indicated the responsibility which he felt to the Master whom he served, and the anxious desire he had to be useful to his hearers.

"His demeanor was marked by a diffidence which prevented his intellectual worth from being readily appreciated by strangers, or by those who were slightly acquainted with him. But his remarks on the performances of others, at the Associational meetings, on Councils, and at other times, were always discriminating and instructive. And they were ever given with a spirit which made them highly respected.

"Mr. Warren was always tender of the feelings of those who differed from him, and carefully avoided all severe reflection, while he defended his own views with firmness. He never made an enemy. He was greatly beloved by his parishioners, and lived in peace with Christians of other denominations in his own town, and was highly esteemed by them.

"He was a man of prayer. It was his uniform practice, when he visited any of his ministerial brethren, or was visited by any one of them, to propose uniting in a short season of devotion before they separated. This practice arose from the overflowings of a pious heart; for no man could suspect him of having a wish for self-exaltation.

"Mr. Warren lived in quietness and harmony with the people over whom he was first ordained. And although individuals, from time to time, left his ministry to join other denominations, it was not from disaffection to him; for all esteemed him as "a good man, and full of the Holy Ghost and of faith." His salary was always small, but he was contented with it. His people cheerfully paid it, and never manifested any desire of a change in their relations.

"The Hampden Association, to which Mr. Warren belonged, assembled at his house two or three days before his death. He had looked forward to this meeting, as he told them, with much interest, for he always enjoyed the society of his brethren. But he was too unwell to attend to the exercises. No one, however, supposed that he was sick unto death; and when they took leave of him, on his bed, they did not sorrow because they expected "to see his face no more." All were surprised, when they were so soon called to follow their revered and beloved brother to the house appointed for all living." *

15. REV. JACOB CRAM

Was the son of Col. Jonathan Cram, of Hampton Falls, N. H., and a descendant of John Cram, one of the first set-

* Letter of Rev. S. Osgood, D. D., Springfield.

tlers of Exeter, N. H., 1639.* He was born 12 Oct., 1762, fitted for college at Dummer Academy, Byfield, and graduated at Dartmouth Coll., 1782, and A. M. in course. He studied Theology with N. Emmons, D. D. His college class embraced four members, one of whom was Caleb Bingham, known as compiler of the "American Preceptor."

In 1788, June 2, he received an invitation to settle over the church in Hampstead, N. H.; but, on the strength of an invitation from Hopkinton, N. H., he left, without returning any formal answer to the call from the former place, and on the 25th Feb., 1789, was ordained at Hopkinton. He was dismissed, 5 Jan., 1792, apparently on account of difficulties connected with his pecuniary transactions amongst his people. He next labored as a missionary amongst the Stockbridge Indians in Western New York. He, together with Rev. David Avery, were the *first missionaries* appointed by the Massachusetts Home Missionary Society. Mr. Cram's commission is dated 3 July, 1800, and specifies as a field "the region between Whitestown and Genesee river, Western New York."†

After laboring a while, he left that region, 15 May, 1801, and came to Exeter, N. H., where he spent the rest of his days. His ruling feature of character, parsimony, which had from the beginning obstructed his usefulness, rapidly settled into a species of monomania, and prevented his employment almost entirely as a preacher, during the rest of his life. He died at Exeter, 21 December, 1833, aged 71 years.

---

* Col. J. Cram married Miss Mary Cram. They had seven children: 1. Rev. Jacob, the present subject. 2. Jonathan, of Marietta, O. 3. Benjamin, of Pittsfield, N. H. 4. Lois, married to Rev. John Webber, of Sandown, N. H., who afterwards went to the West. 5. Mary, married to Joseph Ware. 6. Eunice, and 7. Martha, also married.

† Letter of Rev. J. S. Clark, D. D., Sec. M. H. M. S.

Mr. Cram married Miss Mary Poor of Exeter, daughter of General Poor, of Revolutionary fame, a truly excellent and pious man; but who was drawn into a duel with a French officer, and was killed. Her mother's name was Osgood, of Andover, where General Poor also belonged. Mrs. Poor was opposed to the union, on account of Mr. Cram's eccentricities; but the daughter, like her mother before her, had her own way, and was privately married at the house of a neighbor, 13 Sept., 1804. She died 19 July, 1848, aged 79, having been born in 1769, and married at the age of 35, when Mr. Cram was 41. Their only child was Martha, who, at 18, became the third wife of a Col. Rogers, and was the mother of two sons, Jacob and Charles, still living. She died at an early age.

Mrs. Cram was a woman of distinguished excellence. Her piety was profound, vital, strict. She had some peculiarities. It was because of her strict injunctions, that no tombstones mark the grave of either her husband, her mother, or herself. They all lie buried together undistinguished and undistinguishable, in an old cemetery near the railway station at Exeter.

Rev. Mr. Cram appears, by current traditions, to have been an *original* in very earnest. His besetting sin, or infirmity, as you please, has been alluded to. It obtained, in the course of his life, to some very instructive developments. If his history could be fully written, it would prove a curious episode in the common run of these brief and barren sketches.

He was naturally and from the beginning very eccentric, and of strong passions; and his ruling propensity, penuriousness, early gained a decided visibility. His patrimony, by most solicitous protection and increase, rose at one time to about ten thousand dollars. But it proved to be another illustration of Solomon's class of riches, "kept for the owners thereof to their hurt," developing miserly habits and questionable deeds. He took great pains to conceal his property, to avoid paying taxes. He once owned the tract of land on which the city of Utica, N. Y., now stands. But it was sold at auction, under execution, to pay the taxes which he begrudged.

His ruling feature, so carefully cultivated and indulged, very early shaded off into a downright but very subtle and peculiar derangement, involving the stability of his other mental attributes. Yet so peculiar and subtile was it, as to leave a wide debatable space for locating the line of responsibility.

He had, in his later days, frequent paroxysms of the missionary spirit, when he would visit the towns in the vicinage, carrying books, and preaching as he could get an audience. He then insisted upon the utmost deference to his ministerial office, and was most sensitive to any the least apparent slights. Wherever he tarried, he insisted upon conducting family prayers, saying grace at the table, and would often awake early in the morning and lie in bed, singing most lustily, Old Windham, and similar tunes, to the annoyance or diversion of the aroused inmates of the house.

Anon, this impulse would pass away, and he would oscillate to the laical extreme, and dressed in leather apron and cast-off garments, teach contempt for appearances, after the manner of Socrates. Again, a passion for military display ruled the hour. Through the influence of his son-in-law, Col. Rogers, he had been appointed chaplain of the militia regiment. He appeared regularly upon the muster-field for many years, with three-cornered hat and flowing sash, and often paraded in the streets, at other times, clothed in regimentals, and unabashed by the public gaze.

The erection of a Universalist meeting-house in Exeter grievously annoyed him. As the only available off-set, he determined to anticipate its owners, and stamp an orthodox dedication upon it. Watching his opportunity, when the house was nearly completed and the workmen were at dinner, he gathered in a few boys, and, with their help in singing, though with many drawbacks in the way of noise and giggling on their part, he performed a species of dedicatory service, which he boasted of for weeks afterwards, as a most shrewd triumph. But, whether through the influence of the dedication, or the subsequent preaching, or from some other cause, the building is now used as a *billiard-room!*

Mr. Cram's habit was to dress very slightly in winter. In this way he contracted a cold which terminated his days.

Although he was not an attractive preacher, he was much of a scholar, and exhibited in his selection of a library, which was sold after his widow's death, an uncommon appreciation of sterling works. His own manuscripts were all committed to the flames. No printed work of his is known, other than a fragment, somewhere existent, entitled, "Conference with Red-Jacket," in which the white man is Mr. Cram.*

16. REV. SOLOMON AIKEN

Was born in Hardwick, 15 July, 1758. He was the second son of John and Jerusha Aiken, whose parents migrated from Scotland. At the age of 18, he enlisted in the Revolutionary army, served two years, and was honorably discharged. During this time, he indulged a hope of conversion, and immediately after his discharge commenced his studies. He graduated at Dartmouth College, 1786, and A. M.; studied theology with Rev. E. Fish, of Upton.

He was settled in Dracut, 4 June, 1788, dismissed 4 June, 1812, and entered the U. S. Army, as chaplain. He was stationed on Fort Independence in Boston harbor. At the end of the war, he returned to Dracut, and resided there, preaching occasionally until 1818, when he removed with his

* Letter of Rev. R. D. Hitchcock, Exeter, N. H.

family to Hardwick, Vt., where he died, 1 June, 1833, aged 75 years.

His stone bears the following inscription: —

THE GRAVE

OF

REV. SOLOMON AIKEN.

BORN JULY 15, 1758.

DIED JUNE 1, 1833.

In youth, a Soldier of the Revolution; in age, the Christian Pastor;

And through life, the firm and inflexible Friend of

CIVIL AND RELIGIOUS LIBERTY.

Mr. Aiken married Mary, daughter of Capt. Daniel Warner, of Hardwick, Mass. She died at Hardwick, Vt., Oct., 1820, deeply lamented as a devoted Christian. They left 9 children, — 4 sons and 5 daughters, viz: Solomon, Justus Warner, Daniel, and Samuel Adams, all living. The latter, S. A. Aiken, is well known as Professor of Penmanship. The eldest daughter, Mrs. Sophia Spalding, died in 1849. The youngest, Selina, wife of Dea. G. H. Cook, died in Portland, in 1850. Alma, the second daughter, is in Boston. The other daughters, with the sons above mentioned, reside in Hardwick, Vt.

Mr. Aiken enjoyed uncommon health and vigor. He never took a particle of medicine, or lost a relish for food, until his final and brief sickness, — a pleurisy fever.

He possessed peculiar power as a logician, and was very popular as a preacher. He was kind-hearted and benevolent, almost to a fault.

But it is chiefly as a political writer that Mr. Aiken is remembered. He was sent as representative two years, by the town of Dracut. He published several sermons and pamphlets, chiefly upon political themes, which excited much attention in their season. Among them are, 2 Sermons at Dracut, 1809; Letter to Dr. Samuel Spring, of Newburyport, in Answer to a Review of the Sermon; Fast Sermon, 1812; Sermon on the Rise and Progress of Religious Dissention in the United States; Ordination Sermon of Rev. S. T. Barton, Tewksbury, 1792.

17. REV. ENOCH POND

Was the eldest son of Dea. Jacob Pond,* of Wrentham, where he was born, 27 April, 1756. He graduated at Brown University in 1777, and A. M.; and entered the American Army for one year. He served as Ensign in Col. William R. Lee's regiment, to which office he was appointed 4 June, 1777. On the expiration of his time of enlistment, he was employed for some years as school-teacher in Boston, where he was much admired. He studied theology with Rev. Dr. Emmons, and in 1789 was ordained over the church in Ashford, Ct., where he continued until his death, 6 Aug., 1807, in the 52d year of his age. His disease was consumption.

Mr. Pond married, first, Miss Margaret Smith, daughter of Col. John Smith, of Wrentham, by whom he had nine children. She died in 1800, and on the Sabbath following, while her remains awaited interment, Mr. Pond preached to his people. Dr. Welch calls her, in her funeral sermon, — "a prudent, discreet, and faithful wife, a kind and tender mother, an affectionate sister, a benevolent neighbor, a faithful friend." His second wife was Mrs. Mary Baker, of Roxbury, who survived him.

* His emigrant ancestor, Ephraim Pond, came from England, and was one of the first settlers of Wrentham. He had a son Ephraim, who was father of Dea. Jacob Pond, sen., and grand-father of Dea. Jacob Pond, jr. Dea. Pond, jr., died 1815, aged 86, and was the father of Rev. Enoch, above, — his eldest son. His youngest son was Dea. Elijah Pond, who died, 1847, aged 82, and who was the father of Rev. Enoch Pond, D. D., of Bangor, and also of Gen. Preston Pond, who is in turn the father of Rev. Preston Pond, jr., of Boston; — a clerical family!

Mr. Pond's ministry was marked by several powerful revivals of religion. One in 1798 resulted in the addition of 80 members to the church.

"He was peculiarly tender and affectionate in his family. He was never idle. He was a peacemaker in the neighboring churches, and universally beloved. He fitted many scholars for the university, and some for the Gospel ministry. As a preacher, he was plain, practical, and persuasive. He had a readiness of utterance, a force and fluency of expression, which are possessed by few. His performances during the latter part of his life were chiefly extemporaneous. The ease and pertinence with which he could express his ideas with little premeditation, led him on some occasions to neglect, perhaps to a fault, a preparation for the pulpit. He was, in short, an amiable companion, and a man of modest, unassuming worth. By means of his councils, instructions, and prayers, Ashford rose from a state of comparative rudeness to be one of the most flourishing inland towns of Connecticut."

He was particularly celebrated as a skilful singer.

The following lines, prepared by one of his neighboring brethren in the ministry, to be recorded upon his tombstone, are considered a just tribute to his memory: —

GENEROUS IN TEMPER,
Correct in Science, and Liberal in Sentiment;
The Gentleman, the Scholar, and the Minister of the Sanctuary,
APPEARED WITH ADVANTAGE IN
MR. POND.
The Church and Society in Ashford were favored with his
GOSPEL MINISTRY EIGHTEEN YEARS.

In yonder sacred house he spent his breath.
Now silent, senseless here he lies in death.
These lips again shall wake, and then declare
A loud Amen to truths they published there.*

---

* See obituary in Panoplist and Magazine, XIV., 315.

18. REV. WALTER HARRIS, D. D.

Was born in Lebanon, Ct., 8 June, 1761. His parents were Nathaniel and Grace Harris, of whose five children, — two sons and three daughters, — he was the youngest. He graduated at Dartmouth College, 1787, and A. M.; whence he also received a Doctorate in 1826. He studied theology with Rev. Dr. Emmons, and was ordained the first pastor of the church in Dunbarton, N. H., 26 Aug., 1789. After forty years' labor, his health became impaired, and he asked and received a dismission, 7 July, 1830. He died 25 Dec., 1843, aged 82.

Such are the chief statistics of Dr. Harris's life. But his whole history deserves a minute study. A condensed brevity alone is here allowable.

The father of Dr. Harris died shortly before his birth, and he was deprived of his mother before he was sixteen. The three daughters were provided for in other families, and Walter and his brother Nathaniel, two years his senior, were left, without parent or guardian, and with a mere pittance of property, to provide for themselves. They enlisted into the Continental Army in May, 1777. In the same year, Nathaniel fell in battle at Philadelphia, and Walter was frequently in jeopardy. But he served out his term of three years' enlistment, as fifer, and was honorably discharged, May, 1790, then not quite nineteen.

With his scanty wages and patrimony, he migrated to Lebanon, N. H., purchased a tract of wild land near Dartmouth College, and went alone with his axe into the forest to spend the winter. But the young pioneer was soon surrounded by the thrilling scenes of a powerful revival of religion in the town. And a sermon he heard in the neighborhood, awakened him to his own *actual* destitutions.

The struggle was long, obstinate, and characteristic of the

future man. Wearied with his anxious searchings, and crushed with his increasing convictions, and with his protracted fastings, he resolved, in despair, in the midst of winter, to cast himself down upon the snow in the bleakest place in his field, and there remain in prayer till he perished with cold or found relief. He chose a position on the north side of a stump, near an opening among the trees, where the cold winter's blasts rushed through with unendurable keenness, and fell upon his knees, determined never to leave the spot till he should hear the voice of mercy. He remained but a short time before he seemed to hear, in reality, a voice, saying in wrath, — "*What, rebel! seek to limit the Holy One of Israel! Arise! and flee for thy life, — or thou art a dead man!*" He fled to the house in horror at his guilt.

After passing through what seemed to him a foretaste of the pains of hell, he fell submissively, cordially, upon the sovereign, electing love of God in Christ for salvation. His experience imparted a peculiar thoroughness and fidelity to his subsequent preaching.

His mind was from this moment directed to the Gospel ministry, as the chosen avocation of his heart. And although without even a common school education, and encumbered with his farm, yet he resolved, after prayerfully weighing the solicitations of friends, that he would 'go to college.' With him, this was almost tantamount to execution.

He first attended a common school; then began the study of the languages with a private teacher, and finally completed his preparation in Moore's Charity School, on Dartmouth plain. At his graduation from college, his commencement exercise was delivered in Hebrew.

This testimony is given of his college career by one of his instructors: — "Rarely have I met with a man more decided and unequivocal, more upright and downright than he. He had a mind of uncommon strength, and unusually patient of labor. He was most distinguished in the solid and useful branches of study."

After his graduation, he taught a Latin school six months in Boscawen. It was here that an occasional sermon of Dr. Emmons fell into his hands. Having perused it with deep interest, he laid it down, and said, with emphasis, "I will study divinity with the author of that sermon, if I can find him." He did find him; and never fit teacher had a fitter learner.*

---

* It is his creed that was, by vote, copied into the Records, and became the theological basis, of the Mendon Association. It is here inserted: —

"I believe that there is one, and but one, true God; who created, upholds, and governs all things in the universe; and who is possessed of all natural and moral perfections. That the scriptures of the Old and New Testaments are the word of God; that they were written by men Divinely inspired; that they exhibit a perfect rule of conduct, which we are bound to follow; and that they contain all knowledge requisite to eternal salvation. That the Deity subsists in three distinct persons, the Father, the Son, and the Holy Ghost; that these three are perfectly equal in all Divine perfections and excellence. That God, from all eternity, has fore-ordained and perfectly seen through all events, which ever have, or ever will, take place, both in the natural and moral world. That God made the first man perfectly holy, and set him as a public head or representative of his posterity; and that he sinned against God, and fell from Him; and in consequence of his fall, all his descendants now come into the world sinners, totally depraved, and under Divine condemnation. That Jesus Christ, being God and man, in one person, has wrought out a complete righteousness by his obedience, sufferings, and death, and made an atonement sufficient for all the human race. That God has, from all eternity, elected some to everlasting life, whom he will, by his special and sovereign grace, bring to the acceptance of Jesus Christ, while he leaves others to neglect him, to their own eternal destruction. That it is wholly through the righteousness and atonement of Christ, that we are accepted and justified in the sight of God. That a man must be regenerated, or renewed in the disposition of his mind, in order to see the kingdom of God; and that faith and all holy exercises are wrought by the effica-

After approbation, he preached at Canterbury, Dunbarton, and Royalton, Vt., and again at Dunbarton, where he received a call to settle amongst them. He accepted conditionally, returned to Franklin and studied three months longer with Dr. Emmons, and then was ordained.

The church had been organized on the 18th of June preceding.

Arminianism and lax discipline prevailed extensively in the town; but the faithful doctrinal preaching and earnest prayers of Dr. Harris, and his near brethren, Rev. Moses Bradford of Francestown, Rev. Reed Paige of Hancock, and Dr. Wood of Boscawen, effected, under God, an entire revolution in the sentiments and practice of the churches throughout the then large county of Hillsboro'.

A powerful revival followed soon after the settlement of Dr. Harris, and brought most of the *principal* men under its power. He enjoyed four or five other seasons of refreshing during his ministry. The feeble church of his early labors in his later days became marked for its intelligent, discriminating piety, — "a city set on an hill."

The following are some of the features of his character, set forth in a discourse on occasion of his death.* "He was an instructive preacher. His words were well chosen;

---

cious power of the Holy Ghost. That the saints shall persevere in holiness, and be kept by the mighty power of God, through faith, unto eternal salvation. That it is the duty of professors to give up their infant offspring to God in baptism. That none but those who can give sufficient evidence that they are born again, and are the true friends of Christ, ought to be admitted to partake of the Lord's Supper. That God has appointed a day, in the which he will judge the world by Jesus Christ; when he will receive the righteous into life eternal, and send away the wicked into everlasting punishment."

* See Commemorative Discourse before Hopkinton Association, 14 May, 1844, by Rev. A. Burnham, Pembroke, N. H. Also, Hop. Mag., Vol. IV. p. 573. Fun. Sermon, by Rev. E. P. Bradford, New Boston, N. H., and Fun. Sermon, by Rev. J. M. Putnam, Dunbarton.

his language, remarkably plain; his method, natural and lucid. But what contributed most to make his preaching instructive, was the prominence he gave to the doctrines of grace, and, the happy connection he maintained between doctrine and practice. He followed, very closely, his theological teacher's method of sermonizing, as well as, entirely, his system of theology. He was a plain, direct, experimental, searching preacher. The Sabbath after his ordination, he specified the principal doctrines he should preach, and the course he should follow; and then added, with his peculiar emphasis: 'These doctrines I shall preach, and this course I shall pursue, if you stone me out of the pulpit.' He had the faculty and the disposition to tell the truth, in the most sincere, simple, and plain manner. The doctrines of the Gospel were preached, explained, enforced, and repeated, plainly and fully, till they were understood, not only by the church, but speculatively by the whole society. Hence converts had no difficulty in deciding what are the truths of the Bible. He has left his mark deep upon the people who enjoyed his ministrations; and so, he 'being dead, yet speaketh.' His published discourses were fourteen, all occasional sermons.

Dr. Harris's first wife was Jemima Fisher, daughter of Nathaniel Fisher, and sister of the late Lewis Fisher, Esq., of Franklin, by whom he had seven children. After her decease, he married the widow of Rev. John Cleaveland, of North Wrentham. And his third and last wife was Mrs. Jane Aiken, relict of Mr. James Aiken.

19. REV. REED PAIGE

Was born in Hardwick, 30 Aug., 1764. He was the son of Col. Timothy Paige. He was graduated at Dartmouth Coll., 1806, and A. M. in course; studied Theology with Rev. Dr. Emmons, and was ordained the first minister of the church in Hancock, N. H., 21 Sept., 1791, where he continued to labor until his death, 22 July, 1816, at the age of 52.

Mr. Paige married Miss Hannah Paige of Bedford, who survived him, and by whom he had seven children. Six of them reached maturity. Their residences are unusually separated from each other.

Of his two daughters — both married — the elder lives in Peterboro', N. H.; the younger, in Oswego, N. Y. His third child, and oldest son, David Paige, settled in La Port, Indiana. The second, Timothy, in Detroit, Mich. George Reed Paige was in Illinois, and the youngest, William, in St. Louis.

Rev. Mr. Paige was an excellent scholar. He was esteemed by his brethren in the ministry, and by his people, as a man of strong mind and a good preacher. He was highly respectable as a divine, sound in religious sentiment, and correct in moral practice. It is enough to say that he was the warm coadjutor of such men as Dr. Harris of Dunbarton, and Dr. Wood of Boscawen.

In the latter part of his life, Mr. Paige entered deeply into politics, and represented the town of Hancock, in the State legislature, for seven years, from 1809 to 1814, and again in 1816. He died while in the office of Representative.

His publications were: Ordination Sermon of Rev. Jabez P. Fisher, 1796; a 4th of July Oration; Election Sermon, 1805; Fast Sermon, 1812; and an occasional Sermon at Lyndboro', 1815.

20. REV. ELIAS DUDLEY

Was born in Saybrook, Ct., 12 Aug., 1761, but subsequently removed, with his parents, to Newport, N. H.* He

* He was the son of Daniel and Susanna Dudley, who had four children, viz.: Josiah, Daniel, *Elias*, and John. The father died at Newport, N. H., 1 Feb., 1811, aged 92. The mother d. 6 Aug., 1791, aged 67. — *Rev. H. Cummings, Newport, N. H.*

graduated at Dartmouth, 1788, and A. M., and studied Theology with Rev. Dr. Emmons. He was ordained the third pastor of the church in Oxford, 13 Apl., 1791. Dr. Emmons preached the sermon. His salary was £75, with a settlement of £150, in three annual instalments. He was dismissed at his own request, by the advice of physicians, 6 March, 1799, and removed, the same year, to Newburyport, where he went into business.

While here, he took several short voyages, in a fishing vessel, to Labrador, for the benefit of his health. About 1805, he removed, with his family, to Prospect, Me., where he died, 25 Jan., 1808, of consumption, at the early age of 47 years.

Mr. Dudley married, 22 Oct., 1793, Miss Mary Spring, daughter of John Spring of Northbridge. She returned to Uxbridge, after her husband's death, and there died. They had three children while living in Oxford, and four more subsequently — three sons and four daughters, viz.

1. Hannah, b. 19 Nov., 1794, m. Luther Bullard, of Uxbridge, and died 7 June, 1845. Their son, Charles H., is in the ministry, at Rockville, Ct.

2. Otis, b. 14 Nov., 1796, lives at Williamsburgh, O. Has 5 children.

3. John Spring, b. 19 July, 1798, and d. at Millbury, 23 Aug., 1816.

4. Daughter, died in infancy.

5. Elias, lives at Cincinnati, O.

6. Mary, died in Uxbridge, 1 Aug., 1837, aet. 32.

7. Daughter, died young.

Mr. Dudley is represented as a man of excellent character, and a faithful and efficient preacher of the Gospel. He was much interested in education and the moral culture of youth, and acted as private instructor to many of the young, who frequented his house. His talents as a teacher are still spoken of by his surviving pupils with great interest and high commendation. But he was of melancholic temperament, and subject to great depression of spirits. He suffered much under an impression that he was unfaithful and deficient in his duties as pastor and teacher of his flock. This feeling, induced by his continued feebleness of health, led him repeatedly to ask a dismission from his charge. But the real opinion of his fidelity, entertained by the church, is indicated by their repeated refusals to grant a separation.

It is related of him, that, during the last year of his ministry, he would prepare for the Sabbath, and, when the hour of service came, his depression would often weigh so heavily upon him, as to compel him to send word to his waiting people, that he could not appear before them.

Divine service was generally held but half the day, towards the close of his labors. Yet the people declined his repeated requests for a final separation; and at last, consented on the representation of physicians, to refer the subject to a mutual council. So highly was he prized as their pastor by the people of Oxford.

His communications to the church and town, are the best exponents of the state of feeling between him and them. As early as 14 Sept., 1798, he proposed to leave the desk for them to hear a candidate, and offered to deduct the expense from his own income. On a renewal of the proposition, 9 Jan., 1799, a committee of conference was chosen, who agreed to concur with the church in seeking advice about his dismission. To this committee he says:—"My health is yet extremely low, and my state, I think precarious. From the nature of my complaints, being very much upon my lungs, I must freely own, I see no probability of being able to preach. What a number of years may do for me, should I be continued in life, is unknown to us; but I think it must be several years, should I do as well as can be expected, before I can engage in public speaking."*

* Letter of Mr. G. F. Daniels, Oxford.

The council which advised his removal, express in their result, much sympathy for him in his affliction, and bear testimony to the excellence of his character as a minister of the Gospel.*

21. REV. HERMAN DAGGETT

Was born in Wrentham, 3 Oct., 1765. He was the son of Ebenezer Daggett, M. D., who was a native of Attleboro', but pursued his profession in Wrentham. His mother was daughter of Timothy Metcalf, Esq., of Wrentham.†

He graduated at Brown University, 1788, and A. M., and studied theology with Rev. Dr. Emmons. He was ordained at Southampton, Long Island, 12 April, 1792, and dismissed in 1796: when he removed to Westhampton, where he was settled in 1798, and dismissed 9 Sept., 1801. Thence he removed to Middletown, in Brookhaven, and was installed 20 Oct., 1801, and continued until 20 April, 1807, when he removed to Ridgefield, Ct., and from thence to Cornwall, where he established and became principal of the celebrated Mission School. He remained here until his death, 19 May, 1832, leaving a widow, but no children.

Mr. Daggett possessed a peculiarly even temperament. A gentleman intimately acquainted with him on Long Island,

---

* Rev. H. Bardwell, Oxford.

† Doct. Daggett was the son of Ebenezer and Mary (Blackinton) Daggett, of Attleboro', and brother of Rev. Naphtali Daggett, D. D., for 11 years Pres't of Yale College, and prof. of Divinity for 25 years.

The pilgrim ancestor of this family, was John Daggett, Watertown, 1642. He removed to Martha's Vineyard with Gov. Mayhew, 1644. His son (?) Thomas Daggett, married Hannah, eldest daughter of Gov. Mayhew. Their son John, moved from Chilmark to Attleboro', about 1709, and had 9 children; of whom Ebenezer was the second. He married Mary Blackinton, daughter of Pentecost B., of Attleboro', and from whom came in the second generation, Rev. Herman Daggett.—*Daggett's Hist. Attleboro'.*

relates, "that he was never known to laugh, although of a cheerful and happy turn of mind; to smile was all he ever did."

His style of composition was plain and direct; his manner of preaching deliberate and solemn. He was highly appreciated while in the ministry.

The Cornwall school was instituted through his agency in the autumn of 1816, and opened May, 1817. Mr. Daggett was the first appointed teacher, but being unable to engage, Mr. Edwin W. Dwight took his place for a time. Mr. Daggett commenced the supervision of the school, in May, 1819. For this enterprise he was, say the committee in one of their annual reports, "peculiarly qualified."

Mr. Daggett published a sermon on "the character and work of John the Baptist;" delivered at Patterson, N. J., 1813.

22. REV. ROYAL TYLER

Was born in Uxbridge, 24 May, 1770. He graduated at Dartmouth, 1798, and studied theology with Rev. Dr. Emmons. He was ordained at Andover, Ct., July, 1792, and dismissed May, 1817. Installed over the church in Salem, Ct., in 1818, and dismissed in 1824. He died at Salem, Ct., 10 April, 1826, aged 56.

Mr. Tyler married Miss Lydia Watson, daughter of Joseph Watson, of Thompson, Ct., by whom he had eight children, namely:

1. Samuel L., graduated Brown University, 1820; taught academy in Florence, Alabama, and died there, 5 Oct. 1822.
2. Royal W., a farmer; resides in Salem, Ct.
3. George W., physician in Providence, R. I.
4. Nathan, lawyer; died in Meadville, Pa., 5 March, 1833.
5. Abigail W., married to Dr. Alfred Riggs, Fourth St., New York.
6. Lydia, died young.

7. Benjamin S., physician in Royalton, Cuyahoga Co., Ohio.

8. Gideon W., merchant in Granger, Medina Co., Ohio.

Mrs. Tyler died August, 1835, at Ohio City, O.

Mr. Tyler's ministry was marked by several revivals of religion. But of his character, we have had access to no materials for judgment.

23. MR. JOSIAH HOLBROOK

Was born in Wrentham, 19 January, 1765. He was the third son of Daniel and Esther (Hall) Holbrook. He grad. at Brown University, 1788, and A. M.; and studied Theology with Rev. Dr. Emmons. He went to the South, and is believed to have died in Beaufort, S. C., in 1796 or 7.

It is not known that he was ever settled, nor have any further particulars of him been collected.

24. REV. HOLLOWAY FISH

Was the son of Rev. Elisha Fish of Upton, and brother of Rev. Elisha Fish, jr., of Gilsum, N. H. He graduated at Dartmouth, 1790, and was ordained at Marlboro', N. H., 25 Sept., 1793, where he died, in the pastoral office, 1 Sept., 1824, aged 62.

Mr. Fish married Miss Hannah Harrington, of Westborough. They had no children. An adopted son of theirs, Mr. Holloway Brigham, still lives in Westborough.

Mr. Fish enjoyed two seasons of revival amongst his people, and 129 were added to the church by profession, and 45 by letter, during his ministry.

He is represented as a man of sound judgment, a faithful pastor, and a decided Hopkinsian in his theological views. His influence was of great worth in withstanding and arresting the tendency towards Arminianism in his vicinity. He preached the doctrines of Divine sovereignty with great boldness and plainness. And though not a popular preacher, his voice being indistinct to strangers, he was an eminently useful minister of the Gospel.*

His epitaph is as follows:—

MEMENTO MORITURUS.

IN MEMORY OF

REV. HOLLOWAY FISH,

Who died Sept. 1, 1824, Æ. 62.

HE WAS GRADUATED FROM DARTMOUTH COLLEGE, 1790;

Ordained in Marlboro', Sept. 25, 1793;

AND THIRTY YEARS THE BELOVED PASTOR OF

The Church and Society.

HE DIED PRAYING FOR HIS PEOPLE.†

25. REV. JOHN MORSE

Was the second son of Dea. James and Hannah (Daniels) Morse, of East Medway, where he was born, 20 Nov., 1763.‡

Mr. Morse became personally interested in religion under the preaching of Rev. John Leland, of Peru. He graduated at Brown University, 1791, and studied theology with Rev. Dr. Emmons and Rev. David Sanford of West Medway. He went to the then "far West," and was soon ordained, in 1792, over the Congregational Church in Green River, N. Y. He continued the pastor of this flock for 23 years.

---

* Letter of Rev. L. Wiswall, Me.

† Letter of Rev. G. Lyman, Marlboro', N. H.

‡ Dea. James Morse, the father of Rev. John Morse, was the eighth child of Henry and Sarah Morse, who was the son of Joseph and Prudence (Adams) Morse, who was the son of Capt. Joseph, jr., the son of Joseph, who was the son of Samuel Morse, born in England, 1558, and appears in Dedham, 1635, and who died at Medfield, 5 April, 1654.—*Book of the Morses.*

In 1816, he removed to Otego, N. Y., and was installed pastor of the Presbyterian Church, where he remained for 12 years. The last sermon he preached was on the occasion of the death of President Harrison. He died 3 Jan., 1844, aged 80 years; over 50 of which he spent in the ministry.

Mr. Morse married Clarissa Sanford, daughter of Rev. D. Sanford, of Medway, 4 Feb., 1793. They had two children:

1. David Sanford, born 22 Dec., 1793; Rev. and settled in Richford, N. Y. He married Miss Margaret Vandyke.

2. Clarissa, born 4 May, 1796, and married to Isaac Fairman, of Medina, Orleans Co., N. Y.

Mrs. Morse died at Pompey Hill, N. Y., 15 March, 1850. It is said of Mr. Morse that he took a very prominent and active part in the extensive revivals in 1785, in and around his native place; holding conference meetings in Holliston, and in West Medway, in different neighborhoods. The influence of these meetings went far towards deciding the character of the churches in those two communities, especially when the popular movement was opposed to a pure Gospel. This revival also fixed his purpose to become a preacher of righteousness.

"Soon after his settlement at Green River, a powerful revival of religion followed his ministry, during the whole of which the church continued remarkably united in him.

"His theology was sound, and of the New England stamp, which enabled him, during the prevalence of the 'new measures' in central New York, to see the rock upon which the churches were driving.

"He loved and preached the distinguishing doctrines of grace which supported him in his last sickness and death. During his short illness of four days, he enjoyed his mental faculties in a remarkable degree. Not a cloud was over his mind to darken his prospects beyond the grave."*

---

* See Book of the Morses.

26. REV. SAMUEL JUDSON.

[See Sketches of Members, No. 22.]

27. REV. NATHANIEL HALL

Was born in Sutton, 9 April, 1764, and was the son of Dea. Willis Hall* and Anna (Cage) Hall. His mother was the daughter of William and Anna Cage, of Grafton and Warren, formerly of Scotland.

Mr. Hall graduated at Dartmouth, 1790, and A. M., and studied divinity with Rev. Dr. Emmons. He was ordained over the Congregational Church in Granville, N. Y., 3 Oct., 1797, and continued its pastor until his death, — by a cancerous tumor, 31 July, 1820, at the age of 56.

His gravestone bears the following inscription: —

A SPIRITUAL COMPANION,
An able Pastor, a faithful, instructive Preacher, a consistent,
PENETRATING DIVINE.
His influence in this region was precious.
The intelligent Christian who knew him best,
WILL REVERE HIM MOST.
The plan of Grace which he loved and defended,
SUPPORTED HIM IN DEATH.

Mr. Hall married, 22 Jan., 1798, Hannah Emerson, daughter of Dea. Daniel Emerson, of Hollis, N. H., and

---

* He was descended from Capt. John Hall, of Medford, formerly of Concord and of Charlestown, who married Elizabeth Green, 2 April, 1656, and who was the son of Widow Mary Hall, of Charlestown. His son, Dea. Percival Hall, born 1672, and married Jane Willis, migrated to Sutton, and was the father of Dea. Willis Hall, above mentioned. — *Rev. D. B. Hall, Cleaveland, N. Y.*

sister of Rev. Joseph Emerson. (Licentiates, No. 40.) She was born 7 Dec., 1773, and died 22 May, 1832.

They had nine children, seven of whom are still living:

1. Hannah Emerson; born 9 Nov., 1798, and married Aug., 1823, to Rev. Abijah Crane, for fifteen years Central Agent of the American Home Missionary Society. He died at Clinton, Oneida Co., N. Y., 14 May, 1847. His wife died at Clinton, 12 June, 1846.

Their son, Edwin H. Crane, graduated Hamilton College, 1844, and Auburn, 1851; married Ann Eliza Cowles, of Otisco, Onondaga Co., N. Y., and embarked, 31 May, 1852, as Missionary to Nestoria. A second son, Lewis H. de Loss Crane, graduated Hamilton College, 1845, and is now a lawyer in Selden, L. I.

2. Willis, born 1 April, 1801; graduated at Yale College, 1824, and studied law. He settled in New York City, represented the City and County of New York in the State Legislature of 1838. In 1839, appointed Attorney-General of the State. Representative for the City and County of Albany in 1842. In 1847, was Councillor to the Board of Aldermen of New York City. He married Mrs. Helen Haudley.

3. Nathanael Emmons, dentist in Middle Granville, N. Y.; married Miss Mary Fell, of Bloomington, Ill.

4. Eliza, resides in Middle Granville, N. Y.

5. Richard Baxter, was a portrait-painter; now a physician in Sacramento City, Cal.

6. Daniel Emerson, born 9 May, 1810; graduated at Yale, 1834; lawyer in Mobile, Ala. He married Delphine E. Kennedy, 13 Jan., 1840, and died 24 April, 1852.

7. David Brainerd, graduated at Union College, 1839, and at Princeton Theo. Seminary. Is now settled at Cleaveland, Oswego Co., N. Y.

8. Mary, resides at Middle Granville.

9. Edwards, graduated at Hamilton College, 1840; phy-

sician in New York City. He married Maria M. Chambers, of Trenton, N. J.*

"As a preacher, Mr. Hall was always interesting to those who hear for instruction. His discourses contained the sincere milk of the Word. His discernment of defects in the matter or method of a sermon was singularly acute. This rendered him particularly useful in ministerial circles, and to theological students. His gifts and influence in our churches as a religious instructor, an able councillor, and faithful disciplinarian, were such as we know not how to spare.

"His discernment of moral truth, and his ability to investigate and defend its principles, were distinguishing. Loose and unsystematic notions in divinity and moral science, rarely escaped his observation.

"He saw with clearness, the first leadings of error, in principle or practice, and opposed them with candor and firmness.

"It was the habitual object of his zeal and effort to instruct his hearers in the doctrines of grace, — to convince them of those self-denying truths which stain the pride of all flesh.

"His discourses were serious and practical. Practical improvement was the moral and literal end of every sermon. And God was pleased to crown his labors with many precious fruits. These consisted in the enlightening and restraining power of Gospel truth on his hearers generally, and in the conversion of many souls.

"In the course of his ministry, he enjoyed three special revivals among his people. In 1800, when the church received 45 hopeful converts. In 1814, 77 were added to the church. In 1816, 45 were added. The whole number received during his ministry was 255.

"Days of religious harvest appeared to be particular sea-

* Letter of Rev. D. B. Hall, Cleaveland, N. Y.

sons of his enjoyment; and his skill in divinity rendered him a consistent and very useful guide to inquiring souls.

"He was the warm friend of Bible, Missionary and Education Societies. He was also a companionable and interesting friend, and his house was always the mansion of unaffected hospitality."*

Mr. Hall's only publication is a sermon preached before the Evangelical Society, in Poultney, Vt., at their annual meeting, 22 Nov., 1815.

28. REV. JOHN FITCH

Was the oldest son of Rev. Elijah Fitch, of Hopkinton, where he was born in 1770. He graduated at Brown University, 1790, and studied theology with Rev. Dr. Emmons.

In 1793, July 29, he was invited to settle in Danville, Vt., where he was ordained the first pastor, 30 Oct., 1793, in a grove of maples, at the base of a circular valley. His salary was two hundred dollars, paid in produce.

After laboring twenty-three years, he was dismissed, 1 Oct., 1816, on account of feeble health, and took a journey to the West. In about two years he returned, resigned the office of the ministry, and removed to Guildhall, Vt., where he died, 18 Dec., 1827, aged 57.

The interval after his return, was partly spent as teacher at Thetford, and at Guildhall.

Mr. Fitch married, first, Miss Sally Magoon, of Danville, by whom he had one daughter: Hannah, who was married to Dea. Asa Sargent, of the same place. Mr. Fitch's second wife was Mrs. Lydia Parmer, sister to Mr. Jeduthun Loomis, of Montpelier, Vt.: by whom he also had one daughter, Nancy Jane.

---

* Obituary in Boston Recorder, by Rev. W. Jackson, D. D., Dorset, Vermont.

She became the wife of a Mr. Elkin, formerly professor in Mandaville College, but now resident in New Orleans.

Mr. Fitch wrote largely for "The Adviser," published at Middlebury, Vt., and issued several sermons; among them was an Election Sermon, before the State Legislature, at Danville, 1805.

The church of Danville at its organization, 9 Aug., 1792, embraced twenty members. During Mr. Fitch's ministry, sixty-five were added.

He stood high in the estimation of his people up to the time of his dismission, and though no marked revivals of religion occurred, he was regarded at large, as an able and faithful minister. He was a strong writer, but not an eloquent speaker; yet he possessed a considerable degree of freedom, coupled with moderation.*

29. REV. ELI SMITH

Was born in Belchertown, 17 Sept., 1759, and was the son of Joseph Smith.† His early life was spent on a farm, and

* Hist. Sermon, of Danville, Vt., by Rev. J. Dudley, pastor.

† His earliest American Ancestor was Joseph Smith; who removed from Hartford, Ct., to Hadley, 1680, and had four sons. The second son, John, b. 1686, settled in Hadley, and d. 1777, aged 91. He had five sons and five daughters: viz. John, Abner, (father of Rev. Abner, of Derby, Ct.;) Daniel, Joseph, and Elijah.

Joseph, just mentioned, was the father of Rev. Eli, above, also of Rev. Amasa, and Rev. John, D. D., of Bangor: (Licentiate No. 33.)

It may be added, that Elijah, the youngest son, had nine children. Among them were; 1. Asa, father of Rev. Asa, of Virginia, and of Rev. Theophilus, of New Canaan, Ct.; 2. Sarah, wife of Elijah Bardwell, of Goshen, and mother of Rev. Horatio B., of Oxford, and of Sarah, wife of Rev. Wm. Richards, of the India Mission: 3. Rev. Ethan, of Boylston; 4. Dea. Jacob, father of Elizabeth, wife of Rev. Wm. Hervey, of the India Mission, of Esther, wife of Rev. Mr. Dunbar, of the Pawnee Mission, of Martha, wife of Rev. O. G. Hubbard, of Leominster, and of Miranda, wife of Rev. P. Belden, of E. Amherst. — *Geneal. Register, Vol. I. p.* 183.

it was not until 1787, some time after the death of his first wife, at Sunderland, that he commenced his course of education. He graduated at Brown University, 1792, and A. M., at the age of thirty-three, and studied theology with Rev. Dr. Emmons. He was ordained as colleague pastor at Hollis, N. H., 27 Nov., 1793. He labored with fidelity and success for thirty-seven years, and was dismissed in 1831. After this date, he preached one year in Greenfield, N. H., one year in Montague, one year in Marshfield, and shorter periods in other places. He died 11 May, 1847, aged 87 years and 8 months.

Mr. Smith married, first, Miss Catharine Sheldon, of Northampton, by whom he had one son. His second wife, was Miss Ama Emerson, of Hollis, daughter of Dea. Daniel Emerson, and sister of Rev. Joseph Emerson, (Licentiate No. 40). By this marriage he had five children. His family were:

1. Eli. He formed the first church in Frankfort, Ky., of which he was pastor ten years. He was then ten years pastor of the church in Paris, Ky. He died at Frankfort, Ky.
2. Ama: m. Rev. Noah Emerson.
3. Luther, teacher in West Liberty, O.
4. Hannah C., m. Rev. Darwin Adams, now of Dunstable, Mass.
5. Joseph E., lives in Hollis, N. H.
6. John R., physician in Lexington, Ky.

Mr. Smith's ministry in Hollis was signally blessed. The first great revival among his people began in 1801, and continued over a year. It was preceded for three or four years, by an uncommon degree of religious feeling. As its fruits, one hundred and forty-two, mostly heads of families, united with the church. This was one of the first revivals of the present century. During his pastorate, between 400 and 500 were added to the church.

He was also an early and fast friend to missions, and once left his people, as a home missionary for a short time.

His prominent features of character, as gathered from his funeral sermon, by Rev. R. Emerson, Andover, were, an ardent temperament, and quick mental activity, which gave peculiar point and power to his extempore efforts; an invincible firmness, manifested in his boldness and distinctness in preaching the humbling truths of grace. He was a revival preacher, in the best sense of the term, plain, pungent, practical.

His late education prevented his being a learned theologian. Yet he was a diligent student, rising usually at four o'clock in the morning, and spending much of his time in secret devotions.

The system of christian doctrine taught by his revered preceptor, Dr. Emmons, he embraced in all its strictness, and with all his heart, and taught with all his power.

He published but two or three sermons. An ordination sermon, of Rev. Stephen Farley, and a Fast sermon, are known to exist.

30. REV. WILLIAM JACKSON, D. D.

Of his ancestry little is known, except that his paternal great grandfather lived and died in Norwalk, Ct.; and that piety distinguished his progenitors and their families for several generations.

His grandfather, Ebenezer Jackson, removed to Sharon, Ct. and was deacon in the church, and died in triumph, saying, 'Welcome, Welcome, I am ready.'

His father, Abraham Jackson, married Eleanor Bumpas, of Wareham, and settled in Cornwall, Ct., where the subject of this notice was born, 14 Dec., 1768.

Mr. Jackson was the youngest of five sons, and the tenth of

eleven children, all of whom lived to be married and become parents. When he was but three years of age, the father migrated with his numerous family, to Wallingford, Vt., in which town they were the first, and for several months the only settlers. Here amidst the severe toils, simple habits, and scanty means of culture, incident to a new settlement, his early life was spent. At sixteen he became a subject of grace.

He fitted for college at Norwich, Vt., and at Moore's charity school, Hanover, N. H., graduated at Dartmouth College, 1790, and A. M. He received a Doctorate from Middlebury College.

After graduation, he taught a female select school at Wethersfield, Ct., for a season, and then studied Theology for one year with Rev. Dr. Samuel Spring, of Newburyport, and completed his course with Rev. Dr. Emmons. He immediately commenced preaching, at Dorset, Vt., but declined an invitation to continue there, on account of his health, and journeyed south and preached, for a season, in New Jersey. After three years, he returned; and, on a renewal of their invitation, was settled over the church in Dorset and East Rupert, Vt., 27 Sept., 1796. He labored here until 1837, when his health, always feeble, induced him to accept a colleague. Rev. Ezra Jones, formerly of Greenfield, N. H., was settled in this relation, 12 Dec., 1838. He was dismissed, 28 Oct., 1841, and Mr. Jackson remained sole pastor of the church until his death, 15 Oct., 1842, in his 74th year, having been settled 46 years.

Dr. Jackson married, 3 Nov., 1796, Miss Susanna Cram, of Brentwood, N. H., who survived him. They had seven children; two of whom died young.

1. Samuel C., grad. Middlebury Col., 1821, settled at Andover. He is now Assistant Sec. of the Mass. Board of Education.

2. Margaret Graves, m. to Rev. John Maltby, Bangor, and died in 1851.

3. Susan, lives unmarried at Dorset.

4. Elizabeth Rogers, wife of Rev. Nathaniel Beach, of Milbury.

5. Henrietta Anna Lorain, m. to Rev. Cyrus Hamlin, Miss. at Constantinople. She died at Rhodes, 14 Nov., 1850.*

Dr. Jackson's bodily constitution was naturally frail, and subjected him to frequent and severe indisposition; yet he accomplished much as a builder in the temple of the Lord of Hosts. His most striking feature was that of deep solemnity when exhibiting the truths of God.

One intimately acquainted with him, says: "He had striking and uncommon powers in the pulpit. His sermons were solid and effective. His preaching, as a whole, was biblical, instructive. His manner was characterized by a natural dignity and an urgent, solemn earnestness. His whole appearance, in the pulpit, indicated a holy sincerity — that he spoke according to his own deep convictions."

His sermons were not usually fully written, but left with hints for amplification in the delivery. Said one of his aged parishioners: 'I never wish to hear any greater eloquence than comes from my minister, when he gets through his notes and shuts up his Bible.' It was then, that, having gained the convictions of his hearers, he pressed truth upon their consciences in fervid, forcible, and solemn appeals and expostulations, which often rose to the highest order of pulpit eloquence.

The solemnity which uniformly characterized him in the pulpit, is the more noticeable as he was rather distinguished for a keen and ready wit, and for shrewd, pointed, and laco-

---

* See Obit. in Miss. Herald, March, 1851.

nic sayings. But nothing of this ever found a place in his preaching. Through his whole public life he was never known to appear depressed, discouraged, or troubled.

He was a correct and thorough scholar in the ancient classics; and with some of them so familiar as to repeat large portions from memory. He was a warm friend to education, and one of the founders of Middlebury College, of which he was the first *elected* member corporate.

He originated and set in operation the first Education Society in the country for replenishing the ministry. This was in 1803, and was termed the Evangelical Society "to aid pious and needy young men in acquiring education for the work of the Gospel ministry." * He was its first president, and voluntarily undertook an agency for collecting its first funds; and was, throughout, its most efficient helper.

As a specimen of Dr. Jackson's unceasing earnestness in the work of the Gospel: after the settlement of his colleague, he became a teacher in the Sabbath School, as punctual and engaged as in the public ministry. Such devotedness received the blessing of frequent and powerful revivals of religion amongst his people.†

31. REV. KIAH BAYLEY

Was born in Brookfield, West Parish, 11 March, 1770, and was the son of Charles and Abigail (Safford) Bayley. He spent his early life at Haverhill, N. H., "Indians and

* The first meeting, for organization, was held at Pawlet, 6 March, 1804. The first regular meeting was held at Dorset, on the last Tuesday of June, 1804, at which Rev. Nathaniel Hall, of Granville, preached the opening sermon. Its plan was to aid suitable candidates for the ministry by loans, without interest, for not more than six years. The Evangelical Society continued, until superseded by the Am. Education Society and its Auxiliaries. More than fifty persons were, by it, helped into the ministry.

† Funeral Sermon by Rev. J. D. Winkham, of Burr Seminary.

old tories around, frequently running for dear life — mother, baby and all." *

He graduated at Dartmouth, 1793, and studied theology with Rev Dr. Emmons. He indulged a hope, during vacation, 1790, in his father's barn at Newbury, Vt. His first sermon was preached at West Taunton. He afterwards preached and received calls from Milford, and Ashby, and from Cornish, N. H. In 1796, he visited Maine, preached six months at Newcastle, Me., and was settled there in Oct., 1797.

The church at Newcastle was virtually extinct, — only *three* male members being alive on the list. There had been no preaching for ten or twelve years, and the forms of religion had nearly disappeared. The church was reëstablished by his labor, and the "foundations of many generations" were laid.

He was dismissed at his own request, Sept., 1823. He preached at Greensboro', Vt., the four years following. Thence he went to Thornton, N. H., 30 May, 1829, and staid three years. He commenced preaching at Hardwick, Vt., 29 June, 1833, where he also purchased a farm on which he still lives at the advanced age of 82, the *oldest living* licentiate of this association.

Mr. Bayley has published; a sermon, Salvation by Grace, Ashby, 1796; the Preciousness of Christ, 12mo.; eight or ten ordination and occasional sermons; and over three hundred articles on Anti-Masonry and Anti-Slavery. He was for three years, co-editor of the Christian Magazine, published in Maine.

Mr. Bayley, in company with some six other ministers of the Kennebec valley, most of whose names appear in this list, ardently labored together to plant the germs of Gospel institutions in the then District of Maine. He says — "they

* Letter of Rev. K. Bayley, East Hardwick, Vt.

were united, and tried to lay such foundations as would abide. They published a Christian Magazine — formed a Tract Society, a Missionary Society for Maine — an Education Society, and the Theological Institute at Bangor, — and were in the field as early as older churches. — How God blessed, results must show. — I claim the Academy at New Castle, and the Theol. School at Bangor, as my own children. Not that others did not help, — but on me the burden of laying plans and executing them without funds, for five or six years, rested."*

Mr. Bayley married, in 1794, Miss Abigial Goodhue, of Newburyport. She died 18 March, 1846, aged 90 yrs. She was a woman of uncommon excellence, and left the impress of her active piety upon the religious institutions of the State of Maine.† They have no living descendants.

32. REV. ABIJAH WINES,

The oldest child of Abijah and Deborah (Runnels) Wines, was born in Southold, L. I., 28 May, 1766.‡

At about fifteen years of age, he removed with his parents to Newport, N. H. He married at twenty years of age, and settled down with his wife and children to *live;* but the Lord had other work for him, and he was awakened and converted

---

* Bangor Seminary, to which Maine owes two thirds of her ministers, besides many in other states, originated in a female Cent Society proposed by the wife of Mr. Bayley. It is an interesting fact that its three Theological Professors — Smith, Wines, and Pond — were licentiates of Mendon Association and students of Rev. Dr. Emmons. Prof. B. Fowler was also a student of Dr. Emmons.

† See her Memoir by Mass. S. S. Society; also, Prof. Park's Memoir of Dr. Hopkins, in his Works, Vol. I, p. 95.

‡ His ancestry was Welsh, and settled on Long Island. His father removed to Newport, N. H., in 1780, with four children, — Abijah, Samuel, William, and Abigail.

to his Redeemer. He immediately set himself to the work of fitting for college under a neighboring clergyman, and entered Sophomore at Dartmouth College, 1792, and grad. in 1794, aged 28. He studied theology with Rev. Dr. Emmons, and was ordained, 5 Jan., 1796, at Newport, N. H., the place of his early residence.

After laboring 20 years, he was dismissed, with great reluctance on the part of his people, 4 Dec., 1816. He next went to Ohio, to found, if possible, a Theological School in that then newly-settled region. But failing in this desired project, — which had occupied his thoughts for many years,— he returned and accepted the professorship of Theology in the 'Maine Charity School,' just established in Hampden, Me. He filled this office but about a year, and resigned in 1819, with his colleague, Prof. Jehudi Ashmun, when the institution was removed to Bangor, and became the Theological Seminary now permanently established and endowed there.

After leaving the Seminary, Professor Wines supplied the pulpit of the Congregational Church on Deer Island, in Penobscot Bay. He labored here twelve years, earnestly devoted to his work, and especially to the cause of Temperance. With this some of his people were dissatisfied.

A morbid nervous affection, from which he had suffered in previous years, revisited him, induced by extreme exposure in the spring of 1832. He resorted to a farm; but the disease increased, and resulted in a deep melancholy and temporary insanity. In August, he was conveyed to the M'Lean Asylum at Charlestown, where he died, 11 Feb., 1833, in his 67th year. His remains were interred at Amesbury, by the side of his daughter.

Prof. Wines married, 27 April, 1786, Miss Ruth Giles, daughter of Hon. Benjamin Giles, of Newport, N. H.* She

* Benjamin Giles was born in Dublin, Ireland, and received a thorough English education in that city. When he was fourteen, his

survived him a few years, and died March, 1838. They had twelve children, — eight daughters and four sons. Three children died young. The adults are as follows: —

1. Abigail; married to Silas Buell, of Orwell, Vt. One of her daughters is the wife of Rev. Job Hall, of Orwell.

2. Sarah; married to Rev. Hosea Wheeler, pastor of the Baptist Church in Eastport, where he died, Dec., 1822. She died 25 Sept., 1847, leaving one son and three daughters. The son is Rev. Francis B. Wheeler, of Brandon, Vt.

3. Mima; married to Rev. Benjamin Sawyer of Salisbury. She died 8 Sept., 1817, leaving three children.*

4. Harriet; married to Rev. Weston B. Adams, of Lewiston Falls, Me. She died, Jan., 1841, leaving one daughter, the wife of Edward I. Little, Esq.; she died Sept., 1842.

5. Sophia; married to Peter Kimball, Esq., of Bloomfield, Me., and has three children.

6. Sophronia; married to Rev. Carlton Hurd, of Fryeburg, Me. Has three children living. Marion Lyle Hurd, who died 11 Feb., 1841, was their daughter.

7. Maria; married to Moses Kimball, of Bloomfield, Me. She died Feb., 1841, leaving one daughter.

Hiram, the eldest son, died in 1813, at the age of 20.

Edwards, the youngest, died Dec., 1840.†

"Prof. Wines was distinguished for personal accomplishments. He had a stature erect and high; a compact, well-

---

father migrated to Norwich, Ct. At the commencement of the Revolution, he removed to Newport, N. H., with his family, — a wife and two daughters. The daughters married brothers, Christopher and Isaac Newton.

Benjamin Giles married a second wife, Ruth Tracy, of Norwich, Ct., by whom he had one daughter, Ruth, married to Rev. Prof. Wines at the age of twenty.

* Obituary Notice, in the Panoplist, Jan., 1818, Vol. XIV. p. 21.

† Letter of Rev. C. Hurd, Fryeburg, Me.

proportioned frame; a piercing eye, a manly aspect, a comely visage.

"His feelings were chiefly of the tender and benevolent kind. He was seldom known to be angry.

"As a preacher, he was plain, pungent, and uncompromising, aiming to declare the whole counsel of God.

"As a theologian, he possessed uncommon talents. Here his great strength lay. A deep and discriminating force of mind enabled him to understand the system which he had adopted, to discern its foundations, to simplify its points, to explain its principles, and to defend its positions. His mind was accustomed to a critical and philosophical theology. He would have a *reason* for every article of his faith.

"He was not an orator. His manner was uncommonly plain and simple.

"He possessed a noble description of greatness. He detested every thought of what was mean, sordid, and covetous. His chief wish and aim were, that he might live for the moral benefit of mankind."*

His "Enquiry on the Taste Scheme," shows him to have been an acute thinker. His sermons were very thoroughly studied and carefully written. But when he came to the decision to preach no more, he committed all his manuscripts to the flames.

Prof. Wines excelled in conversation, and his company was always agreeable. He was remarkably hospitable, and welcomed everybody to his house. Clergymen felt at home under his roof.

REV. JOHN SMITH, D. D.

Was the son of Joseph Smith, and descendant of Joseph who removed from Hartford, Ct., to Hadley, 1680. He was

---

* See Funeral Sermon, by Rev. Stephen Farley.

the younger brother of Rev. Eli Smith, of Hollis, N. H., and of Rev. Amasa Smith.*

He was born in Belchertown, 5 March, 1766; graduated Dartmouth, 1794, A. M. and D. D.; studied theology with Rev. Dr. Emmons; and was ordained over the church in Salem, N. H., 2 Jan., 1797, as colleague with Rev. Abner Bayley. He was dismissed from Salem, 21 Nov., 1816; installed at Wenham the following year, 26 Nov., and left, 8 Sept., 1819, to take the chair of the theological professorship in Bangor Seminary, March, 1820. In this office he continued until his death, 14 April, 1831, at the age of 65.

"Dr. Smith possessed what is fitly termed a *reasoning* mind. He loved the naked truth; and, on subjects of a religious nature, few men could reason with greater ability.

"As a preacher, he dwelt much on the perfections of God, the great principles of the Divine government, and on all those truths which are adapted to make men feel their obligations to submit to God, and accept the salvation offered in the Gospel.

"As a theological professor, his constant aim was to imbue the minds of his pupils with clear, consistent, connected, systematic views of what he believed to be the doctrines of the Bible. He was greatly beloved and venerated by them all.

"His natural temper was marked by sympathy, kindness, good-will, and a great firmness of purpose. His piety was strongly marked with the character of *solidity*.

"A cold and slight affection of the lungs confined him to his house in February. He had some apprehensions, as his will was dated 5th March. On the 20th, the Sabbath, he sent a note requesting prayers, and asked his attendants to sing the 51st Psalm, "Show pity, Lord," etc. "That," said he, "meets my case, — just the language of my heart."

---

* See Biog. Sketch of Rev. Eli Smith, Licentiates, No. 29.

After this, there was a rally of strength, so that he conducted the family devotions. But, April 1, the disease returned, and in a few days he died.

"His close was peaceful. He could converse only in broken sentences. His closing words were, — "Perfectly willing — waiting — waiting — to be called — ready to depart, and be with Christ. Blessed Saviour — Eternity. It is near — but not too near — nor will it be too long." The Seminary was in his last thoughts, and his last prayer was for its success. "Thou wilt bless it, and keep it. I give it up to thee. I can do no more for it. Thou canst do all things." He died without a struggle."*

Rev. Dr. Smith married Miss Hannah Hardy, of Pelham, N. H. After his death, she was married to a Mr. Greely, of Portland; and again to Gen. Richardson of her native town, with whom she now lives.

Dr. Smith had no children.

34. REV. NATHANIEL OGDEN

Was born in 1768, near the village of Fairton, Cumberland Co., N. J. His parents, Joseph and Abigail Ogden, both died when he was about six years old, and he lived with a brother-in-law, engaged chiefly in farming, until about twenty years of age, but studying as he had opportunity. He then devoted himself to securing means for an education; for his patrimony was lost in the fluctuations and depreciation of the continental currency.

His studies were pursued with an intimate friend, afterwards Rev. John B. Preston, then a member of the University in Philadelphia. Mr. Ogden at length entered the same class, and graduated with Mr. Preston in 1793.

In the December following, he married Miss Ruth ———,

* Rev. Mr. Pomeroy's Funeral Sermon, Sp. Pilgrims, Vol. V., p. 125.

and commenced school-teaching in his native State, and reading theology at the same time. In 1794, he came to Massachusetts, and completed his theological studies with Rev. Dr. Emmons.

After approbation, he commenced preaching in Taunton, to the major part of the Cong. church, who, on the Rev. Mr. Judson's departure in 1790, had withdrawn from the first Society, and established worship in the western part of the town.

He preached here but *seven* Sabbaths, when he took cold from riding in a storm, and, in a severe fit of coughing, ruptured a blood vessel. He was sick about six months, and died of consumption 11 July, 1796, at the house of Mr. Peter Walker, in Taunton.

A month previous to his own death, his only child, a son eighteen months old, also died. Mrs. Ogden had left him in New Jersey, to attend upon her husband in his last illness. This fact will explain some allusions in the funeral sermon preached by Dr. Emmons upon the occasion.

Mr. Ogden was buried in Taunton, on the plain near the site of the old meeting house, and not far from the present residence of Rev. Mr. Cobb of West Taunton. His stone bears the following inscription;

IN MEMORY OF

MR. NATHANIEL OGDEN, A. B.

OF FAIRFIELD, N. J., PREACHER OF THE GOSPEL,

WHO DIED JULY 11, 1796.

Aged 28.

He had preached on seven Lord's days, when
our high expectations of his future usefulness
were suddenly blasted.*

---

* Rev. S. H. Emery, Taunton.

Mr. Ogden left no printed works to bear witness to his ability. A volume of his sermons was arranged by his intimate friend, Mr. Preston, to be published by subscription. But the project was never executed. His theological teacher entertained a high opinion of his talents, and prospects of usefulness. His congregation in Taunton regarded him as "sound in doctrine, clear in religious experience and forcible in argumentation." *

Nearly two thousand persons were present at his funeral. Says one who has examined the volume intended for the press; "From all that I can learn of Mr. O.: — from the expressions of those who knew him, from Dr. Emmons's remarks in his funeral sermon, and from the evidence of his manuscript sermons, I cannot doubt that he was a man of rich promise." †

The widow of Mr. Ogden, was married in Oct., 1813, to Rev. Abijah Davis of Millville, N. J. He died in 1817. She still lives a widow, in Fairton, N. J.‡

35. REV. JOHN BOWERS PRESTON

Was born in Fairfield, Cumberland Co., N. J., 3 Oct., 1770. His father was Col. Isaac Preston, who died in the service of his country, 5 March, 1777, aged 42. His mother, whose name was Hannah Bowers, died in 1782, at the age of 45, leaving him an orphan at 12 years of age.

His life in infancy was for a long time precarious, and he wholly lost the sight of one eye.

At ten, he was seriously awakened, and his pious mother had hope in his conversion. At fourteen he publicly professed religion, and turned his attention to the ministry.

---

* Rev. A. Cobb, Taunton.

† Rev. N. C. Burt, Springfield, O.

‡ Rev. B. B. Hotchkin, Brandywine Manor, Chester Co., Pa.

He graduated at William and Ann College, Philadelphia, 1793. He then taught school about two years, near his native place, when a protracted sickness compelled him to travel for health into New England. He providentially came to Franklin, May, 1795, and commenced the study of theology with Rev. Dr. Emmons.

He was ordained 8 Feb., 1798, at Rupert, Vt., and died on Sabbath morning, 21 Feb., 1813, aged 42 years, having been settled 15 years. Just before his sickness, he had watched with two sick children, both whose parents had been cut down by an epidemic fever, and buried in one day, of which disease he also soon after died. His last sermon was from Isaiah, 1 : 11.

Mr. Preston married, 6 Jan., 1799, Miss Polly Haven of Franklin, daughter of Asa Haven, and niece of the wife of Dea. James Metcalf, in whose family she resided. She was afterwards married to Dea. James Fisher, of Gouverneur, N. Y., where she died, 23 March, 1848, aged 71 years.*

Mr. Preston left five children :

1. Mary H.; married to Harvey D. Smith, Esq., of Poultney, Vt., now of Gouverneur, N. Y. They have no children.

2. John B.; grad. Middlebury Coll., 1827, Auburn, 1830, ordained over the Presb. church, in Attica, N. Y., 23 Oct., 1839; inst. at Byron, N. Y.; now at Berlin, Wis. He m. 1st., Mary Whedon, of Hebron, N. Y.; 2nd., Clarissa North, of Farmington, Ct.; Has 6 children.

3. Nathaniel O.; grad. Middlebury Coll., 1831; Rector of Epis. church of the Annunciation, at New Orleans; m. Charlotte Whedon, of Hebron, N. Y. Has no children.

---

* She was a woman of more than ordinary talents and piety, and found the promises of the widow's God richly fulfilled. Left poor, with five little children, she maintained them, carried two of them through college, and saw them all hopeful Christians. See *Obituary in N. Y. Evangelist, of* 1848*; also Geneal. of the Haven Family, Continuation, p.* 32, *Ed. of* 1849.

4. Julia R.; m. to Rev. Geo. S. Wilson, then pastor of the church in Windsor, Vt., afterwards of the Presb. church at Sackett's Harbor, N. Y. He d. 17 May, 1841. She then m. Rev. A. Cram, of Clinton, N. Y., where she now resides, a widow with two children.

5. Maria; m. to Rev. Stephen Johnson, of Griswold, Ct., and sailed as Missionary of the A. B. C. F. M., to Siam, returned and died at Philadelphia, 8 Jan., 1839.*

Mr. Preston left no printed works. His funeral sermon, printed, exhibits him as highly esteemed by his theological instructor, his ministerial brethren, and his people.

He was a man of noble spirit, of quick perceptions, and of a solid judgment. Solidity, system, energy, and perseverance were his peculiar characteristics. His discernment of characters, and especially of false merit, seemed as ready as instinct. His sensibility, both of favors and of injuries, was very acute; but was generally regulated by a pious heart, with dignity and propriety. He was singularly fervent and persevering in every duty; never resting till it was done, and well done. This fervor of spirit rendered him singularly punctual to all his engagements. He was an able instructor of students in theology.

He was one of the founders of the Evangelical Society of Western Vermont, — an Education Society, — and president of its board of Trustees at the time of his death.

In the extensive revival which visited Western Vermont, in 1802, one hundred and eleven were gathered into the church at Rupert, and his influence still bears fruit amongst that people, favored by his faithful ministry.†

His gravestone in Rupert, Vt., bears the following: —

---

* See Miss. Herald for Feb., 1839; also, Letter of H. D. Smith, Esq., Gouverneur, N. Y.

† Obit. notice by Rev. W. Jackson, D. D.

SACRED TO THE MEMORY OF

REV. JOHN B. PRESTON,

PASTOR OF THE CONGREGATION. CHURCH

In this town, who
Died Feb. 21, 1813,
AGED 42 YEARS.

As a friend, — greatly beloved ;
As a Christian, — alive and devoted ;
As a divine, — clear and penetrating ;
As a preacher, — eminently faithful,
Solid, plain, and pungent. Let
All who heard him, be prepared to
Meet him in the judgment of
The great day.

36. REV. JOSEPH ROWELL

Was the eldest of nine children, and was born in Rowley, in 1767. He graduated at Dartmouth, 1794, and A. M. He studied Theology with Rev. Dr. Emmons, and commenced preaching in Cornish, N. H., May, 1800, where he was ordained, 23 Sept., 1800. He was dismissed, 19 Feb., 1828, and was never resettled; but, in 1838, he removed to Claremont, N. H., where he died, Nov., 1842, aged 75. His death was occasioned by being thrown from his wagon, while on his return home from a meeting of his Association.

Mr. Rowell married Miss Hannah Chase, daughter of Daniel Chase, Esq., of Cornish. She now resides with her daughter, Mrs. C. Tracy, in New York city. Their family consisted of eleven children, viz. 1. Eliza, wife of Rev. Charles Shedd, pastor of the Cong. church in Campton, N. H.

2. Jonathan Edwards, a farmer in Claremont, N. H.

3. Maria C., wife of Mr. Calvin Tracy, for many years Principal of a Classical Institute in New York city, and author of a series of Mathematical works.

4. Daniel C., died while a member of the class of 1837, in Amherst College.

5. Martha L., wife of Edwin Locke. She spent, with him, six years in missionary labor, at the Sandwich Islands, where both now rest from their labors.

6. George Berkley, grad. Amherst, 1837, and is now Missionary at Sandwich Islands.

7. Timothy Dwight, has been merchant at Canandaigua, N. Y.; now resides in Orford, N. H.

8. Joseph, grad. Yale Coll., and is missionary at Panama. He m., 11 Oct., 1852, Miss Hannah, daughter of Rev. A. Cummings, D. D., of Portland, Me.

9. Samuel N., grad. Yale, is physician at New Haven.

10. Caroline E., wife of Doct. A. G. Skinner, Youngstown, N. Y.

11. Harriet L., wife of A. C. Stolz, recently merchant in New York city, but now embarked, together, for Australia.*

Mr. Rowell was blest with pious parents, and his early associations were connected with religion. His first reading was the writings of the Puritans, which he read and reread until he could almost repeat them. His mind became, consequently early and thoroughly indoctrinated with their principles.

His conversion was occasioned by the death of his father and grandfather — to him a severe affliction. But it was some years before he ventured to indulge a hope for himself. This gave a peculiar distrustfulness to the character of his subsequent experience, and mingled many doubts with his hopes. But the blessing of the Spirit evidently attended his labors, and he received the name of a devoted Christian and faithful minister.

He enjoyed three seasons of revival and an addition of 170 souls to the church in Cornish.

* Letter of Mrs. C. Tracy, New York city.

"Mr. Rowell possessed a mind of great strength and clearness. His sermons were logical in their arrangement, lucid in thought, and easily understood by the hearers. It was a common saying: '*Mr. Rowell's sermons would hold water.*' He dwelt much on the doctrines of the Bible. They were food to his soul.

"He was highly esteemed as a man. Upright, meek and kind in his deportment. He was a diligent student, a devoted pastor, and a very bold, fearless, and faithful preacher." *

None of his writings are published, save one or two funeral sermons.

37. REV. NATHAN HOLMAN.

[Members of Assoc., No. 26.]

38. REV. DRURY FAIRBANKS

Was born in Holliston, 13 Oct., 1772. He was the youngest of five sons of Drury and Deborah (Leland) Fairbanks.†

He graduated at Brown University, 1797, and A. M., and studied Theology with Rev. Dr. Emmons. He was ordained in Plymouth, N. H., 1800; and dismissed 18 March, 1818, in feeble health, induced by extra labor in the surrounding region, and by the additional care of teaching many youth.

He was next installed at Littleton, N. H., about 40 miles north of Plymouth, 3 May, 1820. He was dismissed in 1836, but still resides in the town, upon a farm, to which he has retired. In both Plymouth and Littleton, his labors have been blessed to the advancement of the cause of Christ. His publications have been confined to occasional sermons.

---

* Rev. A. Spaulding, Cornish, N. H.

† He is a descendant of John or Jason Fairbanks, brothers, of Roxbury, probably sons of John, Dedham, 1642.

Mr. Fairbanks married Miss Lucretia Rockwood, of Holliston. She died suddenly, March, 1818, having been married 17 years.* He afterwards married Miss Sarah Worcester, relative of the late S. Worcester, D. D., of Salem. He has had eight children, five of whom still survive, residing mostly in St. Johnsbury, Vt.

39. REV. LEONARD WORCESTER

Was the son of Noah Worcester, Esq., of Hollis, N. H., and was born 1 Jan., 1767.† His mother died when he was in his sixth year.

In some memoranda of his life, left for the use of his children, he says: "All my opportunity for obtaining an education was comprised in attending school, about three months annually, from my childhood until I had just entered my 18th year, in a common school, such as common schools then were

---

* See obituary notice, Panoplist, March, 1818.

† "His ancestry is traceable to Rev. William Worcester, from Salisbury, Eng., one of the 'reverend, learned, and holy divines,' mentioned by Cotton Mather. He settled in Salisbury, Ms., about 1638, and d. 28 Oct., 1662.

II. His oldest son, Samuel W., born in England, a farmer of Bradford. Returning home on foot from General Court, to which he was Representative, he froze to death on the road, 20 Feb., 1680.

III. Francis, b. 1662, and died 17 Dec., 1717.

IV. His son, Rev. Francis, b. 7 June, 1698. Blacksmith until 34 years old. Then studied Theology and was ordained over the 2d. church in Sandwich, 1735. Dis. 1745; removed to Exeter, N. H.; thence to Plaistow; and, in 1750, to Hollis, N. H. He was a Home Missionary until his death, 14 Oct., 1783.

V. Noah, was his youngest son; born 4 Oct., 1735, in Sandwich. He had, by two marriages, 16 children, of whom were Leonard, Samuel, D. D., of Salem, Rev. Noah, of Thornton, N. H., and Rev. Thomas, of Salisbury, N. H. His first wife was Lydia Taylor, of Hollis. She d. 6 July, 1772. — *Memoir of Samuel Worcester, D. D., by his Son, S. M. Worcester, Salem.*

in New England; in which, so far as my acquaintance then extended, the principal and indeed almost the only studies were, reading, orthography, writing, and common arithmetic. Beyond these, my own school-education never extended."

In Sept., 1784, he entered, as apprentice, the printing office of Isaiah Thomas, Esq., of Worcester, and became a member of his family. He continued in this business until 1 March, 1799. During several years of this time, he was editor, printer, and publisher of the Mass. Spy.

In 1786, he united with the First church of Worcester, of which Rev. Dr. S. Austin was then pastor. In 1795, while "still, I believe," he says, "the youngest male member," he was chosen one of the Deacons. By the advice of judicious friends, ministers and others, he left his profitable business of printer and became a preacher of the Gospel. Though without any previous preparatory study under the direction of a teacher, he was found so well versed in the doctrines of religion, as to receive the unanimous approbation of the Association, at a full meeting of fifteen members, at which Dr. Austin, his pastor, was present.

He was very soon requested to preach, as candidate, at Peacham, Vt., where two young men, former apprentices of his at Worcester, were then engaged in their business. He came, 21 June, 1799, and was ordained, as the first pastor of the church, 30 Oct. Dr. Austin preached the sermon. An aged female told him, 'he was the 80th person she had heard preach in Peacham.'

He continued as the active pastor nearly forty years, and nominally pastor till his death.

In 1837, he removed to Littleton, N. H., to reside with his son, pastor of the church; afterwards, to another son's in the ministry, at St. Johnsbury, Vt., where he died, 28 May, 1846, at the age of 79. He was buried at Peacham.

Mr. Worcester married, 1 Nov., 1793, Elizabeth, youngest daughter of Rev. Samuel Hopkins, D. D., of Hadley,* by whom he had fourteen children. Five died in infancy Four survived the father. Of his six adult sons, four entered thé ministry, and the father preached the ordination sermon of them all. The daughters all died unmarried.

His six sons were:

1. Samuel A.; grad. U. Vermont, 1819; Andover, 1823; Miss. to Cherokees, 1825; sentenced to Georgia Penitentiary, 1832; released, 1833; still Miss. of A. B. C. F. M. to the Cherokees. Hé m. Miss Ann Orr, of Bedford, N. H.

2. Leonard; grad. Dart. Coll., 1825; Principal of Female Academy at Newark, N. J. He died at Walpole, N. H., 24 Aug., 1835.

3. Evarts; grad. Dart. Col., 1830; ordained at Littleton, N. H., 17 March, 1836, and d. 21 Oct.; m. Ann, daughter of Rev. R. Shurtleff, D. D., Prof. in Dart. Coll.

4. Isaac R.; successor of his brother, as pastor at Littleton; now District Sec'y for Mass. of the A. B. C. F. M.

5. John Hopkins; grad. Dart. Coll., 1833; settled at St. Johnsbury; now at Burlington, Vt.

6. Ezra C.; M. D., physician at Thetford, Vt.

At Mr. Worcester's ordination, the church numbered 40 members, and the town 850 inhabitants. Two remarkable revivals of religion attended his ministry, in 1817–18 and 1831–2. As a fruit of the first, 225 were added to the church; and of the second, 154; the whole number of additions, during his active pastorate, 566; 484 by profession. But one religious society existed in the town till near the close of his labors, when the Methodists formed a small congregation. It is a true saying, that "much of the prosperity of Peacham is owing to Mr. Worcester."

Mr. Worcester, as the above particulars show, was an uncommon man. He possessed great energy, perseverance, and forethought, yet was very conciliatory and modest. "His per-

* See Note in Sketch of Dr. Emmons, Members, No. 12.

sonal appearance was commanding, tall, and of full proportions. A frame large, compact, strong, and capable of much endurance. With his commanding personal appearance, his voice and manner corresponded. Hence his sermons were remembered, and his works live after him." *

His course of intellectual training was peculiarly adapted to make him an independent thinker; and his sermons evince the work of an originating mind. Yet he is declared to have been a firm adherent to the Puritan doctrines — the more closely and confidently as he advanced in life. The subtle Socinian speculations of his brother, Rev. Noah W., of Brighton, caused but a temporary and superficial disturbance in his views.

He published several sermons and pamphlets, of which the chief are the following: 1. Letters and Remarks on a Sermon of Rev. Aaron Bancroft, on Election. (Published while a printer, and had much to do with his introduction to the ministry.) 2. Oration on the Death of Washington. 3. Fast Sermon. 4. Sermon on Isa. 35: 8. 5. Answer to Rev. Wm. Gibson's Rejoinder. 6. Sermon on 2 Sam. 7: 27. 7. Sermon — "Men sometimes their own worst Enemies." 8. Inquiries occasioned by, Address of the Gen. Assoc. of N. H., on the Trinity. 9. Funeral Sermon. 10. Sermon — Confession of Faith of the Peacham Church defended. 11. Appeal to the Conscience of Rev. Solomon Aiken, concerning his Appeal to the Churches. 12. Ord. Sermon of Rev. Elnathan Gridley and Rev. S. A. Worcester, as Missionaries. 13. Sermon on the Alton Outrage. 14. Sermon on the Close of his Ministry.

40. REV. JOSEPH EMERSON,

The son of Daniel and Ama (Fletcher) Emerson, was born in Hollis, N. H., 13 Oct., 1777.†

---

* Obit. notice, by Rev. D. Merrill.

† This family have been prolific in ministers. The first ascertained

He pursued his preparatory studies at New Ipswich, N. H., and entered Harvard Univ., whence he graduated, 1798, and A. M. While in college, he became the subject of Divine grace, and made a profession of religion in 1797. He took charge of the Framingham Academy, the first year after graduating, and then officiated as Tutor, at Cambridge, two years, meanwhile studying Theology with Rev. Dr. Emmons.*

In March, 1803, he commenced preaching in Beverly. In June, he received a call, and was ordained over the Third Cong. church in Beverly, 21 Sept., 1803. Dr. Emmons preached at his ordination. While here, his interest in Education prompted him to great exertions for its promotion. He was also occupied in preparing, and publishing his Memoir

---

ancestor was Rev. *Joseph* Emerson, the first minister of Mendon, ordained 1667. When the settlement was broken up by the Indians, he removed to Concord, and died there, 3 Jan., 1680. He m. Elizabeth, dau. of Rev. Peter Bulkley, of Concord. She afterwards married Capt. John Brown, of Reading, whose first wife was Elizabeth, dau. of Rev. John Fiske, first min. of Chelmsford.

2. *Peter* Emerson, s. of Rev. Joseph, m. Anna, dau. of Capt. Brown, and was father of Rev. *Daniel*, of Hollis, N. H. 3. Daniel was b. 20 May, 1716; converted under Whitefield; ord. first min. of Hollis, 1743; chaplain at Crown Point, 1755; pastor, over 50 years; and died, 1801. He m. Hannah, daughter of Rev. Joseph Emerson, of Malden, (who was son of Edward, and grandson of Rev. Joseph, of Mendon) and of his wife Mary, daughter of Rev. Samuel Moody, of York. 4. Dea. *Daniel*, son of Rev. Daniel, b. at Hollis, 26 Dec., 1746; m. Ama, daughter of Dea. Joseph and Elizabeth Fletcher, of Dunstable. He had 7 ch.: Daniel, Ama, Hannah, *Joseph*, Ralph, Samuel, and William. He d. 20 Oct., 1820.—*Farmer*. Other branches of this family are equally clerical.

* While in this office, he shewed the manuscript of Dr. Emmons's Sermon on 'Activity and Dependence,' (which the Dr. was then deliberating about printing) to Prest. Webber, for his opinion. After repeatedly answering his inquiries, by saying: 'I will read it again;' on the third or fourth interview, the President handed the Sermon back to Mr. E., with the exclamatory criticism: 'It 's a plaguy thing!'" —*Rev. T. Williams.*

of Miss Fanny Woodbury, and his Evangelical Primer. Under these additional labors his health failed, and he was seized, in 1811, with a species of paralysis,—first in his right wrist, and then in both wrists,— so that he was driven from his writing-desk. On a second attack, he was disabled in his ankles; and, being unable to stand, was compelled to sit and preach. He bore these painful attacks until serious inroads were made upon his general health, when he felt obliged to renounce his pastoral charge, to the deep regret of himself and his flock. He was dismissed, 21 Sept., 1816, after a settlement of just 13 years.

He immediately sailed to the South, to spend the winter. He stopped in Charleston, S. C., where, still laborious, he delivered and published a course of Lectures upon the Millennium. On his return to the North, he established an Academy at Byfield, and, in the winter following, gave a course of Astronomical Lectures in Boston. In 1821, he opened a school in Saugus, and supplied the pulpit at the same time; but he was compelled to seek a southern home, again, at Charleston, for the winter of 1823. Here he repeated his Historical Lectures, which had been given in Beverly. Again he returned to Saugus, but gave up his labors as a minister, in 1825, and removed to Wethersfield, Ct. At this place, he reëntered upon his favorite business of teaching. During his residence here, he visited Saugus, and gave familiar Lectures upon Pollok's Course of Time.

Such ceaseless activity cut short his days, and he died at Wethersfield, 13 May, 1833, at the age of 56.

Mr. Emerson married Miss Nancy Eaton of Framingham, daughter of Ebenezer and Rebekah Eaton, and one of his pupils in the Academy. She died 15 June, 1804, within seven months of her marriage, in her 26th year. He next married Miss Eleanor Read of Northbridge, daughter of Thomas and Martha Read, by whom he had one child, a daughter Nancy, still living. Mrs. E. died at Leicester on a journey for her health, 7 Nov., 1808. Her Memoir has been published.

Mr. Emerson married a third wife, Miss Rebecca Hazeltine of Bradford.

He had nine children in all, six of whom reached maturity.

1. Nancy; above mentioned.

2. Luther; grad. Amherst, 1831, went to Virginia, 1837, and now has charge of Sheremiah Church (O. S. Presb.) Augusta Co. He m. Miss Catharine Miner, Albemarle Co., Va.

3. Alfred; graduated at Yale and Andover; and ord. at South Reading, 1845. He m. Miss Martha E. Vose, Lancaster.

4. Ellen; Teacher in Scottsville, Va., where she died 1848.

5. Edwin; died 1841, at Matanzas, Cuba.

6. John; died 1851, at San Francisco, Cal., whither he went as Captain of a ship.

Mr. Emerson was, in personal appearance, tall and slender, with a dark complexion, and mild hazel eyes. His motions were quick but not strong. In the latter part of his life, he was much bowed down and emaciated by disease. He possessed an attractive vein of pleasantry, and, though he was sometimes reserved, yet generally, the natural enthusiasm of his character imparted a charm to his conversation and made him a most welcome guest and desirable companion.

As a student, he was diligent beyond the bounds of prudence. The rapidity with which he multiplied plans for the mental and moral improvement of mankind shows the activity of his mind.

As a Teacher of youth, he was original, practical and successful, and deeply interested in the moral culture of his pupils. His edition of Watts on the Mind has been and is extensively used, and invaluable in its influences.

As a man, he knew not how to dissemble or wear a mask.

As a Christian, he was characterized by the habitual fervor of his devotional feelings, an earnest love of truth, deep wrought humility, and a warm and expanded benevolence. His last earthly words were "Peace — more than peace."

41. REV. NATHAN WALDO, JR.

Was a native of Canterbury, Ct.. He was not a graduate of any college, but received the honorary degree of A. B. from Dartmouth college in 1805. He studied theology with Rev. Dr. Emmons, whose doctrinal system he adopted and ardently defended.

After preaching as a Licentiate about five years, he was ordained at Williamstown, Vt., 26 February, 1806. Rev. Dr. Parish, of Byfield, preached on the occasion. He was dismissed, 8 Sept., 1812, and soon after removed to Orange, N. H. His subsequent history is not known.

Mr. Waldo was never married.

'In person he was very singular, as well as in some of his habits. He was tall and slender. His joints seemed to be loose, and his spare, skeleton frame hardly to hold together. His gait was reeling, tottering, and apparently tending to fall. His health was generally good, and both body and mind were capable of much endurance. He was very abstemious of meats, and rich food he ate little. Of fruit he could never eat enough, although he was continually trying the experiment.

'As a writer, he united great purity of style with precision.

'As a man, he was modest, diffident, retiring. His piety was speculative and sedative.'*

His ordination sermon pays this high tribute to his character. "Having been acquainted with your pastor elect from early life; having known the high approbation and esteem

* Rev. J. P. Cleveland, D. D., Providence.

which he has enjoyed in many intelligent churches in our part of the country; knowing, also, his industry, his prudence, his respectable talents, natural and acquired, we cannot but consider it a token of the divine favor, an evidence of redeeming love, that he is this day to be set over you in the Lord."

42. REV. LEVI NELSON

Was born in Milford, 8 Aug., 1779. He was the son of Mr. Seth Nelson, and his wife Silence (Cheney) Nelson, both of Milford.*

He is the youngest, and with the exception of his brother Seth, — father of Rev. Henry Nelson, of Auburn, N. Y., — the only survivor of eleven children. Rev. Dr. Nelson, of Leicester, is his nephew.

His hopeful conversion took place in 1795, while preparing for college. He entered the sophomore class of Brown University, 1796; left the following June for Williams College, but was arrested by sickness, which induced feeble health for many years, and he was thereby prevented from graduating. But encouraged by Rev. Dr. Emmons, with whom he studied theology, he persisted in his intentions to preach the Gospel, and was finally approbated.

In 1803, he received a commission from the Mass. Miss. Society, to labor six months, in what is now the northern part of Oneida and Lewis counties, N. Y. Poor health prevented his preaching more than sixteen weeks. In Dec.

* The father, or grandfather of Seth Nelson, came to Milford from Rowley. He was probably a descendant of Thomas Nelson, who came from England, 1638, bringing two sons, Philip and Thomas, whom he left in the care of Richard Dummer, their great uncle, and returned to England, where he died. Aug., 1648. Philip grad. H. U., 1654, the only one of that year, and died 1691. He made some trouble in Rowley, by pretending to cure a deaf and dumb boy, by saying 'Ephphatha.' Thomas, Jr., died 1712, aged 77.—*Farmer.*

and Jan., he preached in Tewksbury. He first preached in Lisbon, Ct., 12 May, 1804, where he was ultimately ordained, 5 Dec., of the same year. Rev. D. Long of Milford preached from 1 Cor. 2: 2. In this connection he still remains.

Mr. Nelson married Miss Abigail Tyler, of Mendon. She died in Dec., 1806, within two years of her marriage, leaving a daughter, who was married Jan., 1826, and died in June following. He next married, Aug., 1809, Miss Mary Hale, of Franklin, Ct., daughter of Joseph Hale, of Coventry, Ct., who was brother to the late Rev. Enoch Hale, of West Hampton. She died childless, 2 May, 1851.

Mr. Nelson's publications are; 1. Sermon before For. Miss. Soc'y, of Norwich and vicinity, 1813; 2. Thanksgiving Sermon, 1830; 3. Annual Address, before the Norwich and Vicinity Temperance Soc'y; 4. Tract "On Attending Public Worship," 16 pp.; 5. A letter to the Theol. Professors, New Haven, 88 pp., 1848; 6. Letters to the Christian Public, pp. 128, 1851.

43. REV. JOSEPH CHENEY,

The son of Josiah and Lydia (Gleason) Cheney, was born in Holden, 16 Aug., 1775, graduated at Brown Univ., 1801, and studied theology with Rev. Dr. Emmons.

After Approbation, he preach in various places, until 1807, Sept. 15, when he received and accepted a call to settle in Milton, Vt., where he remained ten years. He was next settled in Salisbury, Vt., March, 1819, and dismissed in 1823. A short time before his dismission he was thrown from a horse. The fall greatly injured his nervous system, and put an end to his preaching, and finally to his life. He died, 6 June, 1833, at the residence of his daughter, Mrs. Avery, in Brandon, Vt., in the 58th year of his age, having spent nearly twenty years of active labor in the ministry.

Mr. Cheney married Miss Elizabeth Preston, of Northbridge. She died Sept., 1819, and he married Miss Hilpha

Nash, of New Haven, Vt., with whom he lived but a few years. Four children survived him, and still live;

1. Elizabeth C.; married Charles Flagg, Esq., of Holden, now Post-master of East Brookfield.

2. Lydia C.; the wife of Mr. Elijah Avery, of Brandon, Vt.

3. Joseph Preston, of New Braintree.

4. Willard, Rev.; pastor of the presb. church, in Springfield, Kentucky.*

The ministerial character of Mr. Cheney, is thus sketched by Rev. Mr. Ingraham, the minister of Brandon, at the time of his death.

"As it regards his knowledge of theology, he stood high among his brethren. As a preacher, he was clear, earnest, and faithful. Many, who were brought into the fold of Christ under his ministrations, will cherish with warm affections, the memory of one who was the instrument, in the hand of God, of leading them to the knowledge of the truth as it is in Jesus. During his last illness, which was of long continuance, his mind, until it became too much impaired, dwelt much on the revealed character and offices of God manifest in the flesh. He meditated much on the Epistle to the Hebrews, and derived great peace and joy from the views of Jesus, the Author and Finisher of our Faith. Such passages as Heb. 12 : 2, particularly confirmed his hope, strengthened his faith, increased his joy, and elevated his soul."

44. REV. SHERMAN JOHNSON

Was born in Southboro', 18 Aug., 1776. His parents were John and Persis (Sherman) Johnson.†

He graduated at Yale College, 1802, studied theology with

---

* Letter of Mrs. E. C. Flagg, E. Brookfield.

† His grand-parents were Isaac and Rachel Johnson, and Ephraim and —— Sherman.— *Rev. A. Rawson, Southboro'.*

Rev. Dr. Emmons, and was settled in Milford, Ct., in 1804; where he died, 1806, aged 30 years.

He married Miss Sally Daggett, of New Haven, and left one child, Sherman Johnson, Jr., now supposed to be a resident in Hartford, Ct.

The lack of information, prevents any exhibition of his character, or of his brief ministerial life.

45. REV. DAVID HOLMAN.

[See Sketches of Members, No. 33.]

46. REV. GAIUS CONANT

Was born in Bridgewater 6 September, 1776. His parents were Ezra and Mary Conant. His ancestral line upon both sides unites in Nathaniel Conant of Beverly.*

He graduated at Brown University, 1800; and studied theology with Rev. Dr. Emmons. He was ordained at Paxton, 17 February, 1808; and closed his ministry there, May, 1830. He was next installed over the second church in

---

* Ezra Conant, his father, was the son of Thomas, and grandson of Nathaniel, Jr., whose father Nathaniel, came from Beverly to South Bridgewater, before 1690. His mother, Mary, was daughter of David Conant, Jr., whose father David, was son of William Conant, brother of Nathaniel, Jr., just mentioned. This Nathaniel Conant, was probably son of Lot Conant, a son of Roger Conant, immigrant at Plymouth, 1623, and who built the first house in Salem, 1626.

Roger is supposed to be brother of Dr. John Conant, one of the Westminster Assembly of Divines. *History of Bridgewater*, p. 140. If so, he was the son of Richard and Agnes Conant, and born, April, 1591, at Budligh, Devonshire, Eng., and grandson of John Conant, "descended from ingenious parents of Gittisham, near Honiton, whose ancestors, for many generations, have been fixed there, but originally of French extraction." — *Gibbs, in Farmer.*

Plymouth, 24 April, 1834; and dismissed April, 1841, on account of the failure of his health. He then retired to Paxton, where he now resides.

Mr. Conant married Cassandra Whitman, daughter of Mr. Zechariah Whitman of Bridgewater. She died ——, and he married Mrs. Chloe Leonard, widow of Mr. Jonas Leonard, and daughter of Mr. Jesse Allen, all of Bridgewater.

He has had six children. Five sons and one daughter. The oldest, Cyrus Whitman, is amongst those approbated by this association. (See Licentiates, No. 86.)

47. REV. DANIEL THOMAS.

[See Sketches of Members, No. 41.]

48. REV. STEPHEN CHAPIN, D. D.

Was born in Milford, 1778, and was the son of Stephen Chapin and his wife, Rachel (Rawson) Chapin. She was a descendant in the fifth generation from secretary Edward Rawson.

Dr. Chapin graduated at Harvard, 1804, and S. T. D., Brown Univ. 1822, and studied theology with Rev. Dr. Emmons. He was ordained at Hillsboro', N. H., 19 June, 1805, and dismissed 12 May, 1808. Installed at Mt. Vernon, N. H., 15 Nov., 1809, and dismissed 18 Nov., 1818, on account of a change in his views respecting the mode of Baptism. He next preached at North Yarmouth, Me., and was afterwards, in 1822, elected professor of sacred theology, in Waterville College, which office he continued to fill until 1828. He was then called to the presidency of Columbian College, just established at Washington, D. C. This trust he fulfilled until his death, 1 Oct., 1845, at the age of 67.

In 1809, Dr. Chapin married Miss Sarah Mosher, of Hollis, N. H. She, with three sons and two daughters, survived him.*

Dr. Chapin possessed many admirable traits of character. "His mind was not brilliant, but close, discriminating, patient, and careful in investigation. He loved to study, yet he seemed to have but one object in view, — to make a sanctified use of all the knowledge he could acquire. He possessed an excellent literary taste, and his style of composition, for purity, precision, and a chaste and elegant simplicity, has rarely been excelled. His thoughts were always most carefully considered, and the utmost pains taken to present them in the clearest, most simple, and at the same time, most impressive manner. He lacked the graces of person and delivery, yet his performances were listened to with pleasure and profit. The Bible was his daily study and delight, especially towards the close of his life. Next to the Bible, he loved the works of the old English Divines." In sentiments he closely agreed with his theological instructor.

Though somewhat reserved in manners, and, to strangers, appearing rather distant, yet to his friends and family he was steadily and strongly attached.

"The crowning excellence of his character, was his consistent and devoted piety. He appeared, in a far more emphatic sense than is common, to regard himself as belonging to Christ, and to be only anxious to employ himself and all that he had in his service. His simple-hearted ingenuous, and underrating piety, made the strongest impression upon the minds of all who knew him."†

A list of his publications has not been collected. A sermon of his was published, delivered before the Trustees of

---

* Rev. W. B. Sprague, D. D., Albany.

† Rev. J. S. Bacon, D. D., Pres't of Columbian Coll., Washington, D. C.

Columbian College, with an obituary notice of its founder, Rev. Luther Rice. Sermon before the Me. Bap. Ed. Society, 1820. Also a sermon addressed to Mariners, North Yarmouth, Me., 1821.

49. REV. ELNATHAN WALKER

Was born in Taunton, 18 Feb., 1780, and was the son of Peter and Deborah Walker. He fitted for college at Bristol Academy, Taunton, under Rev. Simeon Doggett, and graduated at Brown Univ., 1803. He studied theology with Rev. Dr. Emmons, was settled over the Presb. church in Homer, N. Y., 25 Oct., 1809, and died there in the ministry, 4 ——, 1820, aged 40.

Mr. Walker married Miss Aurelia King, of Sharon, Ct., in 1809, and had three children, two sons and a daughter. James was lost at sea in the steamship "Home," 9 Oct., 1837. Elnathan G. is a merchant in W. New York.*

Mr. Walker was a slow, but patient and thorough scholar. In his youth he was sedate, amiable, and beloved by all in his native place. His mature character, is thus sketched in an obituary in the "Cortland Repository:"

"As a man, Mr. Walker possessed an assemblage of amiable qualities. As a Christian, he was diligent and exemplary. As a minister, he set an example of prudence, patience, and fidelity.

He was a firm advocate for the doctrines of grace. He preached them plainly and cheerfully, and decidedly bore testimony in their favor on his dying bed. He was a friend to revivals of religion by the efficacious influence of the Holy Spirit. No less than *three* general revivals were experienced in the congregation during his pastoral connection with them, and four hundred and sixty-eight members were added to the church.

---

* Letter of Rev. A. Cobb, Taunton.

It is related,* that several persons became at one time somewhat uneasy under Mr. Walker's ministry, and agitated the subject of his dismission. He promptly responded to the suggestion, and a council was invited to consider the question. An anxious people assembled to await the result. The Moderator opened the session with a prayer of peculiar fervor and earnestness, especially praying for the movers of so responsible a step as severing the pastoral relation. The spirit of the prayer awakened new thoughts and feelings in the assembly. At its close, one of the chief agitators requested a delay of the proceedings, and moved, before the church, a reconsideration of the matter to be presented to the council; which motion was unanimously carried.

The council, instead of dismissing the pastor, were invited to stay and assist him in gathering in the fruits of a most extensive and precious revival, of which God's answer to that prayer was the beginning. The question of his dismission was never afterwards agitated.

"Mr. Walker's funeral was attended by more than two thousand people, assembled to pay their last tribute of respect to departed worth. Eleven of the neighboring clergymen were present. The funeral sermon was preached by Rev. Mr. Lansing, from Heb. 11 : 27; "For he endured as seeing Him who is invisible."

50. MR. ALGERNON S. BAILEY

Was born in Berlin, 11 May, 1782. He was the son of Dea. Stephen and Sally (Crosby) Bailey. His mother was the daughter of Doct. Samuel and Azubah Crosby of Shrewsbury, afterwards of Winchendon.†

Mr. Bailey's attention was specially turned to personal re-

---

* Rev. S. Raymond, Bridgewater.

† Letter of Rev. H. Adams, Berlin.

ligion, by the labors of his room-mate, while he was preparing for college. He joined the church at Berlin, March, 1803, and entered Harvard University the same year. But he left Cambridge, and joined the Junior Class at Williams College; where he graduated in 1806. In March of this year, he was attacked severely with pleurisy, which developed his hereditary and final disease, Consumption.

After his approbation, Mr. Bailey commenced preaching in Douglas, but he preached only until Jan., 1807, when he was compelled to leave the pulpit on account of his failing health. He removed to Philadelphia, but the change resulted in no special benefit. The Winter of 1808, he spent in New York, still without visible improvement. He returned home to Berlin in the Spring, but his disease rapidly gained upon him, and he died 26 May, 1808, at the age of 26 years.

Mr. Bailey was neither ordained nor married.

His natural abilities and devoted spirit promised much usefulness. But his brief public life awakened high expectations only to disappoint them.

"He had a clear, discriminating mind, and promised to be a potent advocate of the distinguishing doctrines of revealed religion. His zeal was fervent, and rose superior to every discouragement. In his prayers, he was uncommonly devout, collected, humble; in his endeavors to do good, unwearied."*

Mr. Bailey is the author of "Letters on Fashionable Amusements," in the Missionary Magazine, Vol. II.; and also of "Letters to the Young," in Vol. IV. of the same work.

51. REV. SAMUEL W. COLBURN.

[See Members, No. 35.]

* Panoplist and Miss. Mag., Jan., 1809.

52. REV. NATHANIEL RAWSON

Was the son of Dea. Nathaniel and Elizabeth (Nelson) Rawson of Mendon, where he was born 26 Feb., 1780.*

He received a good academic education, but did not graduate, and studied Theology with Rev. Dr. Emmons. He was ordained in Hardwick, Vt., 13 Feb., 1811, and dismissed, 30 May, 1817. He then preached, until 1834, as a missionary, in Vermont, New Hampshire, New York, and Canada. Owing to bodily infirmity, he removed to Hampton, Ct., where he spent the rest of his life in cultivating a farm which belonged to his second wife. He was killed instantly, by lightning, while raking hay in his field, July, 1845, at the age of 65.

Mr. Rawson married, first, Miss Betsey Fitch, daughter of Rev. Elijah Fitch, of Hopkinton. His second wife was Miss Sarah Piper, of Hampton, Ct. He had six children; five of whom, with his wife, survived him.

"He was a large, stout man; kind, peaceable, retiring, and somewhat melancholy in his disposition. His mind was clear and strong, though far from showy. His theological views harmonized closely with those of his teacher, Dr. Emmons.

"He often expressed a preference for a death without any warning, like that from a stroke of lightning, — a wish which, in his case, was singularly granted. He not only died in a moment, but was *buried* in less than twenty-four hours from the time he entered his field in health."†

---

* Dea. N. Rawson was the son of Thomas and Anna (Waldron) Rawson, and grandson of Wilson and Margaret (Arthur, of Nantucket) Rawson, who was the son of Rev. Grindal Rawson, of Mendon, whose father was Edward, the well known Secretary of the Mass. Colony. — *Hist. and Geneal. Register.*

† Letter of Rev. W. Barnes, of Foxboro', formerly of Hampton, Ct.

53. MR. ISAAC PERKINS LOWE.

He is supposed to be still alive; but no information has been obtained of him or about him, other than that he is not a graduate of any college, and is not known to have ever been ordained.

54. REV. MARTIN MOORE

Was born in Sterling, 1790, and the son of Jonathan and Elizabeth (Richardson) Moore, whose ancestors appear amongst the original settlers of Sudbury.*

He graduated at Brown Univ., 1810, and A. M., and then took charge of Wrentham Academy four years; during which time he studied Theology with Rev. E. Fisk.

He was ordained in Natick, 16 Feb., 1814, and dismissed Aug., 1833. Installed at Cohasset, 4 Sept., 1833, and dismissed, Aug., 1841. In Jan., 1844, he became editor and proprietor oft he "Boston Recorder;" now united with the "New England Puritan," and issued as the "Puritan Recorder," with which paper he is jointly connected, as editor and proprietor.

Mr. Moore married Miss Sarah Fisk, of Natick, and has several children. His oldest son, Jonathan F., graduated at Middlebury, 1838, and is a Lawyer in Boston. His third son, Francis C., is of the well-known firm of Damrell & Moore, Printers, Boston.

Mr. Moore has published several volumes and pamphlets. Among them are: Memoir of Rev. John Elliot, 1822; 2d ed., 1842; History of Natick, 1817; Memoir of Sophronia Lawrence, Boston; Revival of 1842, with a History of Evangelical Religion in Boston; the "Old Way of the Pilgrims," 1835.

---

* John Moore was in Sudbury in 1643, and died, 6 June, 1674. He had a son Jacob, born 1645.—*Farmer*

55. REV. JOHN BURT WIGHT

Was born in Bristol, R. I., 7 May, 1790, and was the son of Rev. Henry Wight, D. D.* His mother was Alice Burrington.

He graduated, with the highest honors of his class, at Brown Univ., 1808, and A. M.; also A. M., at Harvard, 1816. He studied Theology with Dr. Emmons, and was ordained in Wayland, 25 Jan., 1815. He was dismissed in May, 1835. He was next settled over the First Congregational church in Castine, Me., from 1836 to 1839. Then over the two associated churches, in Milford and Amherst, N. H., from 1839 to 1841; and over the First Congregational church in North Dennis, from 1842 to 1846. Since this last date, he has resided in Wayland, where he was first settled.

Mr. Wight married Miss Sarah Grout, of Sudbury, by whom he has had four children: Martha, Henry, Sarah, and John.

Henry married Miss Isabella Mann, of Orford, Me., 28 May, 1848, and resides in Wayland.

Sarah was married, 14 Jan., 1852, to Mr. Edward P. Bond, of Boston. They reside in Kawai, one of the Sandwich Islands.

56. REV. JOSEPHUS WHEATON.

[See Sketches of Members, No. 38.]

---

* Rev. Dr. Wight, for over fifty years the pastor of the church in Bristol, R. I.; and, for many years, was one of the Fellows of Brown Univ. He was born in Medfield, 1752; Harv., 1782; ordained, 5 Jan., 1785; dis., 11 Nov., 1828; and died, Aug., 1837, aged 84.

The ancestral line is as follows:

1. Thomas Wight, immigrant from the Isle of Wight, England, 1637. 2. His son, Samuel Wight, of Dedham. 3. Jonathan Wight. 4. Jonathan Wight, Jr., of Medfield. 5. Rev. Henry Wight, D. D., of Bristol. 6. Rev. John B. Wight, of Sudbury.

57. REV. EMERSON PAINE

Was born in Foxboro', 5 Dec., 1786. He was the son of Abiel and Cynthia (Robinson) Paine.*

He obtained a liberal education through his own exertions, and graduated at Brown University, in 1813 ; studied divinity with Rev. Dr. Emmons ; and was ordained in Middleboro', 14 Feb., 1816. He was dismissed by a Council, called at his own request, 4 June, 1822. In Nov. 20, of the same year, he was installed at Little Compton, R. I., whence he was dismissed, on account of his health, 20 April, 1835. He preached again, a few months, in Middleboro', until invited to labor in Halifax, where he continued to preach until his death, which occurred 26 April, 1851, at the age of 65.

Mr. Paine married Miss Lydia Pendleton, of Dighton, who still resides in Halifax. They had five children, of whom four survive.

1. Joseph Emerson : m. Eliza Rebecca Glover, of Milton, and lives in New York.

2. Charles Henry; m. Mercy Bryant, of Halifax, and resides in that town.

3. Horatio Edwards ; m. and lives in Bridgewater.

4. Mary Niles ; m. to William Holmes, of Halifax, and lives there.

"Mr. Paine was an able vindicator of Dr. Emmons's Theology. He was a man of unblemished reputation, of a benevolent heart, of an humble, Christian walk, and of deep sympathy for his people; but a Boanerges to the sinner, 'in the hands of an angry God.' His great topic of conso-

---

* His father and grandfather, both named William, came from Malden. William Paine, Jr. m. Mary Bull, dau. of Jacob Bull, of Dorchester. He and his wife both migrated to Mansfield on the same day, at the ages of 15 and 13. — *Mrs. B. S. Paine.*

lation for all in affliction was, full, entire, absolute, and unconditional submission to the will of God; perfect trust in Him, as infinitely wise and good, and who doeth all things well. And in *this* frame of mind he gave up his spirit.

A volume of his Sermons has been printed, and they exhibit deep and energetic thought and true orthodoxy."*

He published a 4th of July Oration before the Students of Brown Univ., 1813; Farewell Sermons at Middleboro', 1822; Funeral Sermon of Mr. S. S. Sturtevant, Halifax, 1839; a volume of Sermons, 8vo, 1842.

58. REV. ENOCH POND, D. D.

Is a native of Wrentham, north parish, where he was born 29 July, 1791. His parents were Dea. Elijah and Mary (Smith) Pond.†

He graduated at Brown University in 1813, and A. M.; S. T. D., Dartmouth, 1835; studied Theology with Dr. Emmons, and was ordained at Ward, 1 March, 1815. He resigned his charge, 22 Oct., 1828, to take the editorial care of the "Spirit of the Pilgrims;" the first five volumes of which were published under his supervision. In the spring of 1832, while residing at Cambridge, he was elected Professor of systematic Theology in the Seminary at Bangor, Me.; and was inaugurated in the autumn following. He still occupies the Professor's chair in that institution,—a post filled from the beginning, and acceptably, by pupils of the celebrated Dr. Emmons.

Dr. Pond married, first, Miss Wealthy M. Hawes, daughter of William and Eunice Hawes of Wrentham. She died Sept., 1824, leaving three children: the youngest of whom was Rev. Enoch Pond, Jr., grad. Bowdoin, 1838, and at Bangor, and was settled at Georgetown, where he died, 17 Dec.,

* Puritan Recorder, 15 May, 1851.

† For paternal ancestry, see Note on Rev. Enoch Pond, Lic. No. 17.

1846, aet. 26. His second wife was Miss Julia Ann Maltby, daughter of John and Elizabeth Maltby of Northford, Ct., and sister of Rev. J. Maltby of Bangor. She died Sept., 1838, leaving five children. His present wife was Mrs. Anne M. Pearson of Bangor, formerly Miss Anne Mason of Dedham. Of his eight children, six survive and are all hopefully pious.

His eldest son living, Wm. C. Pond, grad. at Bowdoin, 1849; at Bangor, 1852. Was ordained as evangelist, and sailed, 13 Nov., 1852, as missionary for California. He married Miss Caroline A. Woodhull, daughter of Rev. R. Woodhull of Thomaston, Me.

His second son, Jeremiah E., is in Bowdoin Col., preparing for the ministry.

Dr. Pond is the author of several valuable contributions to the leading Quarterlies, and religious newspapers, and also has published some distinct volumes. Review of Swedenborgianism, of Millerism, etc.

59. REV. ALVAN COBB.

[See Sketches of Members, No. 37.]

60. REV. JONAS PERKINS

Was born in North Bridgewater in 1790, and is the son of Josiah, Jr. and Anna (Reynolds) Perkins.*

He graduated at Brown University, 1813, and A. M., and studied theology with Rev. Otis Thompson of Rehoboth. He was ordained pastor of the Union church of Weymouth and Braintree, 14 June, 1815. He still remains in the same field, one of the few pastors who, in these unquiet times, have the *strength* 'to sit still.'

---

* He descended from Mark Perkins, who came to Bridgewater from Ipswich, 1741. His eldest son, Josiah, was grandfather to Rev. Jonas Perkins.

Mr. Perkins married Miss Rhoda Keith, daughter of Mr. Simeon Keith of Bridgewater, and has two children.

61. REV. STETSON RAYMOND

Is a native of Middleboro', and the son of Samuel Raymond.*

He graduated at Brown University, 1814, and A. M., and studied theology with Rev. O. Thompson of Rehoboth. He was ordained, 9 April, 1817, at Chatham, and dismissed 24 June, 1829. He was next installed, 20 Sept., 1829, as the first minister at Assonet in Freetown, whence he took a dismission Nov., 1836. He was settled, 1 Jan'y, 1837, over the Trinitarian church in Bridgewater, Scotland parish, and was dismissed 1 April, 1851. He still resides in that place.

Mr. Raymond married Miss Deborah Loud, daughter of Mr. Elliot Loud of Weymouth. He has four children, two sons and two daughters.

1. Sophia Loud, m. to Mr. Otis Bullard of Boston.
2. Samuel Elliot, m. Lucretia Bryant of Bridgewater, and resides in New Bedford.
3. Francis Henry, in Boston, and 4. Ann Sarah, at home.

62. REV. LOT B. SULLIVAN

Was born in Wareham, 27 June, 1790. His Father was Lot Bumpas, a descendant of Edward Bumpas or Bonpasse, of Plymouth, 1623. The name of Sullivan was adopted by himself.

He fitted for College with Rev. Samuel Wood, D. D., of Boscawen, N. H., and grad. at Brown University, 1814.

---

* Samuel R. was the only son of Ebenezer Raymond, who married the daughter of Rev. Mr. Fuller, first minister of Middleboro'.

He studied theology with Rev. Otis Thompson of Rehoboth. After receiving approbation to preach the Gospel, he went into the missionary field of the Western Reserve, Ohio. He was ordained over the Congregational and Presbyterian church in Lyme, Huron Co., Ohio, 14 June, 1820. He labored here until 19 Feb., 1824, when he left and preached as a stated supply in Wellington, and Medina, Loraine Co., in 1824; and in Canfield, Trumbull Co., from 1 May, 1825, to 1 May, 1826. Thence he preached about a dozen years in Durhamville, Oneida Co., N. Y., and in other places in Western New York. His health, by this time, in a great measure failed him, and he returned to Massachusetts, in 1840, where he has since been able to labor in the Gospel occasionally. He is at this date, 1851, supplying the pulpit in West Tisbury, Martha's Vineyard.

Mr. Sullivan married Miss Lydia Stetson of Scituate, and has four children.

63. REV. MOSES PARTRIDGE

Was born in Medway, or Bellingham, the adjoining town. He graduated at Brown University, 1814, and studied Theology with Rev. Dr. Emmons. After his approbation, he engaged in the service of the Mass. Missionary Society.

In 1817, he preached some time in Freetown, and then removed to Penobscot Co., Me., where he preached, some years, under the same commission. On his return to Massachusetts, he received and accepted a call to settle over the church at Manomet Point, Plymouth. Within a short time after his ordination he died, 25 Sept., 1824, aged 36.

His early departure was universally lamented, as the loss of a devoted and faithful laborer, and one promising great usefulness amongst the people to whom a few months only had greatly endeared him. He was unmarried, and is not known to have left any printed publications.

64. MR. JOHN LUKE PARKHURST

Was born in Framingham, 7 Sept., 1789. He was the son of Ephraim and Betsey (Luke) Parkhurst, and descendant of George Parkhurst, one of the immigrant settlers of the town.*

At the age of 20, he began the business of school teaching, in East Sudbury, at the same time pursuing his studies; which method he pursued through his whole course. He entered Brown University one year in advance, and graduated in 1812. He taught school in Needham the remainder of the year; and, in 1814, had charge of Wrentham Academy. He studied Theology at Andover; and, after approbation by this Association, he commenced preaching at Plymouth.

The exercise of speaking in public affected him unpleasantly, and he resigned the idea of settling in the ministry, but devoted himself to his favorite employment of teaching, occupying the desk occasionally, as Providence called him.

He was, in succession, Preceptor of the Academies at Amherst, from 5 Dec., 1817 to the fall of 1819; of Plainfield, N. H., until May, 1821; and of Gilmanton, N. H., until 29 Apl., 1825. He then spent a year in a Monitorial School, at Wiscasset, Me., and returned to Gilmanton Academy, where he continued until Aug., 1832. In the mean time, he vigorously applied his pen to raising the standard of Common Schools, and also had the editorial care of the Christian Mirror, Portland, in 1826.

* The ancestral line of the family is as follows: Ephraim Parkhurst, b. 1765, was the son of Josiah and Elizabeth (Bigelow) P., b. 1737, who was the son of Josiah and Sarah (Carter) P., b. 1706, who was the son of John and Abigail (Morse) P., b. 1671, who was the son of John and Abigail ——, b. 1644, who was the son of George and Sara (Brown) P., b. about 1618, who was the son of George and Susanna P., immigrant ancestors. — *Hist. Framingham*, p. 352.

After leaving Gilmanton, in 1832, he opened a family-school for boys, in Portland, which continued two years. He then removed to Standish, Me., and taught a family boarding school, until May, 1843. His vigor now declined, and he withdrew to a small farm in Gorham, Me., where he closed his life, 20 May, 1850.

Four years before his death, he was deprived, by a paralytic stroke, of the use of his right hand. This led him to the study of Phonography, and to teaching it to his children. He finally died of consumption, in his conscious intervals rejoicing in the end of his laborious career. His grave-stone has this simple inscription: —

DIED, JOHN L. PARKHURST, MAY 50, 1850.
AGED 61.

Mr. Parkhurst married, 30 Aug., 1819, Persis Goodale, daughter of Dea. Abner and Mary Goodale, of Marlboro'. She died at Wiscasset, Me., 25 Jan., 1829, aged 34, leaving three sons. His second wife was Maria C., daughter of James and Sarah Harriman, of Wiscasset. She now lives, a widow, in Gardiner, Me. His children are as follows:

1. William Goodale; married, and is an assistant phonographic reporter, at Washington, D. C.

2. Henry Martyn; m., and has been phonographic reporter for the Senate four years.

3. Edward Warren; m., and is fancy painter at Gardiner, Me.

4. John Thurston; farmer, Gorham, Me.

5. Sarah Elizabeth; Assistant to her brother Henry M., as reporter.

6. Charles Stewart; resides in Bath, apprentice to a painter.

7. Leonard Woods; resided on a farm, in Gorham.

8. Alpheus Crosby; similarly employed in the same town.

9. Melville Cox; resides with his mother, in Gardiner.

Mr. Parkhurst published several school-books and treatises upon education; 1. A Systematic Introduction to English Grammar, 1820. 2. The Teachers' Guide and Parents' Assistant, 1821. 3. Elements of Moral Philosophy, 1832, which passed through two editions. 4. First Lessons in Reading and Spelling, two editions. 5. English Grammar for beginners, 1838. 6. First Lessons in Latin. He also compiled a little work, containing "Letters on Marriage, by Dr. Witherspoon."*

Mr. Parkhurst was of unexceptionable piety, and singly devoted to the good of his fellow beings.

As a preacher, though he was not popular, he was correct, logical, and very systematic in the exhibition of Divine truth. His Moral Philosophy, worthy of a reprint, exhibits his mental structure, — his exactness, and discrimination, and reverence for revealed truth.

His very precision and exactness, however, were so refined as to diminish much from his influence and usefulness. He could not conform to others, even in little things, nor touch men at points enough to make definite impressions. His metaphysical ideas were often too abstract for practical purposes, and gave such a fixedness to his manners and habits as allowed no deviation, even in things indifferent. He would carry a fish from the market to his house, borne horizontally in his two hands, as one would carry an infant, because this was its *natural* position in its native element. All things with him had their reason, sometimes many reasons. Such niceties probably interfered with his immediate usefulness, by making first impressions unfavorable, — yet his life was by no means unimpressive or useless. As a teacher of youth, he made impressions permanent as existence, and the happy influences of his care and instructions are still spoken of

* Mrs. M. C. Parkhurst, Gardiner, Me.

in the highest terms by parents who placed their children in his family school.*

65. REV. WILLARD HOLBROOK

Is a native of Uxbridge, but early removed to Sutton. His father was Stephen Holbrook,† a native of Bellingham. His mother, still living in Sutton, was Mary, daughter of Jesse Penniman, of Mendon.

He prepared for College, in part, at the Sutton Grammar School, under Mr. Hall, son of Dr. D. Hall, partly at Leicester, and finally with Rev. Mr. Goffe, of Millbury. He entered the second class in Brown University, and graduated, 1814, and A. M. He studied theology with Rev. Dr. Emmons, and at his suggestion, completed a regular course at Andover, 1817.

He engaged as missionary six months, at Nottingham West, N. H., now Hudson, where he declined an invitation to settle as pastor. He commenced preaching at Rowley, the first Sabbath in April, 1818, and was ordained there 22 July, 1818. He was honorably dismissed, 12 May, 1840, and installed over the church at Millville, in Mendon, now Blackstone, 18 Aug., 1841, where he was dismissed, 19 Feb., 1850. In April following, he removed to his own house, in Rowley, where he still lives. Since March, 1851, he has supplied the pulpit of the West parish, in Ipswich, (Linebrook).

Mr. Holbrook married Miss Margaret Crocker, daughter of Mr. John Crocker, and his wife Margaret (Choate) Crocker, aunt of Hon. Rufus Choate. She and her parents were natives of Ipswich, but early removed to Derry, N. H.

---

* Letters of Rev. Drs. Pond, of Bangor, and Cummings, of Portland.

† Stephen Holbrook was son of Stephen, who was a son of Simeon, a descendant of Dea. Peter Holbrook, one of the first settlers of Mendon.

They have had six children, of whom the three youngest, daughters, died in infancy.

Amory, the eldest, grad. Bowdoin Coll., 1841, studied law with Hon. Rufus Choate, and Judge Perkins, of Salem, and has been for over two years, District Attorney for Oregon.

2. John Crocker; died in 1829, at 7 years of age.

3. Willard R.; is merchant in New York.

Mr. Holbrook has issued no publications.

66. REV. ABEL MANNING

Was born in Sterling, March, 1788, but pursued his studies in the adjoining town of Holden, and he is mentioned as an inhabitant of Holden in the history of Holden by Rev. S. C. Damon.

He graduated at Brown University, 1817, and immediately commenced the study of theology with Rev. Dr. Emmons.

He commenced preaching in Candia, N. H., thence went to Pittsfield, and afterwards to Goffstown, in the same State, where his labors of several months were blessed with an interesting revival and the hopeful conversion of nearly a hundred souls. He left Goffstown for Plymouth, Vt., as a missionary to a small and feeble church, which had never enjoyed a settled ministry. An extensive revival prepared the way for his settlement, and he was ordained at Plymouth, 8 Nov., 1820: where he continued until dismissed, May, 1824, by an ecclesiastical council, for want of support.

After laboring two years in Goshen and vicinity, as a missionary of the N. H. Miss. Society, he was employed nearly five years, by the Presbyterian church at Chester, now Auburn. But as they were feeble and he was "no Presbyterian," he was not installed. He next preached three years in Epsom, and again three years in Ossipee; all in N. H., and excepting Chester, missionary ground.

In 1838, Mr. Manning came to Dartmouth in this State, and labored there a year, as the successor of Rev. T. T. Richmond. In 1839, he preached for a season in Barrington, R. I., and then returned again to his former fields of labor in N. Hampshire, where he preached until 1844. Since this last date he has preached but occasionally. He now resides in Pembroke, N. H.

His wife was Miss Mary Little of Goffstown, N. H. They have had no children.

67. REV. WILLIAM TYLER

Is the oldest son of Ebenezer Tyler, Esq., late of Pawtucket,* and was born in Attleboro', 7 Jan., 1789.

He graduated at Brown Univ., 1809, and studied theology with Rev. Dr. Emmons. He was settled over the second church in Weymouth, 24 Feb'y, 1819, dismissed 17 Oct., 1831; Installed at South Hadley Falls, 10 Aug., 1832, and dismissed in 1839, by the same council which ordained his successor, Rev. W. W. Thayer. He afterwards preached in Pelham, New Salem, Erving and Shutesbury. For some time he resided in Northampton, but is now at Pawtucket. Mr. Tyler married Betsey, daughter of Jacob Balcom, Esq., of Attleboro'. She died at Weymouth, 9 June, 1822, aged 32, leaving one son, William Ebenezer; who graduated at Amherst Coll., Oct., 1844, and is now a teacher in Jasper, Steuben Co., N. Y. His second and present wife is Nancy W., daughter of Mr. Ebenezer Newell of Natick, who has six children, four sons and two daughters. Elizabeth, resides at home. The second daughter, Annie N., is a teacher at Fairmount, near Cincinnati, O. Henry E. is clerk with a dis-

*The immigrant ancestor of Mr. Tyler was Job Tyler, b. 1619; came to N. E., 1639, and was one of the original proprietors of Andover. He afterwards settled in Mendon. His grandson, Ebenezer, removed from Mendon to Attleboro', 1709, and was great grandfather to Rev. William Tyler.

pensing apothecary in Providence, R. I. The Junior members of his family are, Evarts C., clerk in a drug house, N. Y. city. Edmund W., bookbinder. Francis M. W., at home.

Mr. Tyler has issued no publications.

68. REV. JONATHAN LONGLEY,

The son of James and Polly Longley, was born in Boylston, 1790.

In 1811, he entered Harvard University; but straitened pecuniary circumstances did not permit him to graduate. Endowed, however, with great perseverance, he pressed onwards, and commenced the study of Theology with Dr. Emmons.

After approbation, in 1819, he preached, for different periods of time, in various places. He was never married, and never settled in the pastoral office. Much of his time, he was engaged collecting facts and statistics relating to the interests of religion and the church of Christ. He died in Northbridge, 20 Jan., 1850, aged 60 years.

'Mr. Longley was assiduous in cultivating his mental abilities; and, assisted by a remarkably tenacious memory, his treasure of knowledge, particularly of facts and dates, was large and always available. His sermons, although systematic and cohering, were unadorned, and, to *popular* taste, unattractive. He was not a popular preacher. He lacked the allurements of an attractive delivery. His "neglect of the cultivation of a polished manner," and consequent "want of the amenities of refined life," coupled with his characteristic modesty, probably alone prevented him from being a most effective preacher.

His intimate acquaintance with the Bible was unusual. He was equally at home in all its parts, and could give the exact phrase and locality of particular passages, to a surprising extent. His friendships were few, but the few were mutually prized and cherished. Singularly conscientious in his piety, he cautiously lived and peacefully died, lamented by his brethren and friends, but welcomed by his Redeemer in a better world.*

69. REV. DAVID BRIGHAM

Is the son of Mr. David and Lucy H. Brigham, of Westboro', where he was born, 3 Sept., 1794.†

He graduated at Union Coll., N. Y., 1818, and studied Theology with Rev. Dr. Emmons and Rev. J. Ide, D. D., of Medway.

He was ordained over the church in East Randolph, 29 Dec., 1819, and was dismissed, 15 Nov., 1836, to take pastoral charge of the church in Framingham, where he was installed, 29 Dec., 1836. He was dismissed, 14 May, 1844, and was settled in Bridgewater, 23 April, 1845, where he now labors.

His wife was Eliza H. Durfee, daughter of Charles and Welthe Durfee, of Fall River.

Mr. Brigham has published a Funeral Sermon of Miss Mehitable Torrey, 1847.

70. REV. ZOLVA WHITMORE

Is a native of Rutland, Vt.

He graduated at Union College, 1818, and studied Theology with Rev. Dr. Emmons. He was ordained and settled at North Guilford, Ct., 5 Sept., 1821. He was dismissed

* Congregationalist, Feb., 1850.

† Mr. Brigham's ancestral line is: his father, David, who was the son of Jonas, the son of David, the son of Thomas, the son of Thomas Brigham, immigrant ancestor from the south of Scotland, 1634, and original settler in Sudbury. Thomas Brigham married 'Mercie Hurd.' — *Rev. D. Brigham.*

thence, 31 August, 1846, after a pastorate of 25 years. He next labored, as stated supply, in Heath, from Nov., 1848 to June, 1851, when he was installed pastor of the church in Becket, 18 Feb., 1852, and there now resides.

71. REV. SEWALL HARDING.

[See Sketches of Members, No. 61.]

72. REV. SILAS SHORES

Was the son of Mr. Benjamin and Jemima Shores, of West Taunton, and was born there, 1 Sept., 1784.

He studied the Classics with Rev. A. Cobb, of Taunton; but did not graduate at any college. He pursued the study of theology with Rev. Mr. Cobb, and Rev. Otis Thomson of Rehoboth. After approbation, he was settled, 31 July, 1822, at Falmouth, Second church, and was dismissed, June, 1828. After laboring in various places, he was engaged, as stated supply in Shutesbury, in 1834, where he continued to preach occasionally until his death, 10 Feb., 1844, aged 60.

Mr. Shores married Miss Abigail Stacy, of West Taunton, 11 Dec., 1822, and left three children, a son and two daughters, now residents of Shutesbury.

"Mr. Shores was a man of good judgment and of remarkably exemplary piety; gifted in conversation, and never weary in trying to persuade people to love the doctrines of the Gospel. He seemed to be so absorbed in this, as to forget there was anything temporal to care for. So the Lord took him home."*

73. REV. JOHN M. PUTNAM

Is a native of Sutton, and the son of Dea. Reuben and

* Rev. J. Tisdale, Shutesbury.

Elizabeth (Mason) Putnam. His parents were both of the orthodox faith, and strictly pious.

He served an apprenticeship as painter at Worcester, and indulged a hope at 16 years of age. On his majority, he commenced study at Kimball Union Acad., Plainfield, N. H., and after two years, entered Brown University, but was obliged to leave from ill health. After partial restoration, he studied theology with Rev. Dr. Ide.

He commenced preaching at Ashby, June 1820, the week after being approbated, and was ordained 13 Dec., 1820, over the church and Society newly seceded from the town.

In 1822, this church was visited by a precious revival, and received over fifty members. After five years' labors, Mr. Putnam's voice failed, and he was dismissed, 13 December, 1825, to the mutual regret of pastor and people.

Supposing his ministerial labor done, he removed to Keene, N. H., and established a religious newspaper, called the "New England Observer," which, after six months, was united with the "N. H. Repository," under the title of "Repository and Observer." A year's respite so far restored his voice that he transferred the paper to other hands * and commenced preaching at Epsom, N. H., where he was installed, 1 Nov., 1827.

This was a feeble church, and though the connection was harmonious, he was obliged to leave, 12 May, 1830, for want of support.

The next sabbath, he preached at Dunbarton, N. H., where he was installed, 8 July, 1830, by the same council which dismissed his predecessor, Rev. Dr. Harris. In 1837, he requested dismission on account of his health, but the request was declined by the church. After a few weeks, he

---

* Tobias H. Miller removed the office to Portsmouth. In 1835, it was published at Concord, and the name changed to "Christian Panoply," which it bore until 1840.

returned to his labors, which he has since been able to perform to this date, with only three sabbaths' interruption.

Mr. Putman married Arethusa, daughter of David and Lucy (Harrington) Brigham, of Westboro', and sister of Rev. D. Brigham, of Bridgewater. Of their eight children, two only survive; a son, George Augustus, now at Plainfield Academy, and looking to the ministry; and a daughter, elder, Antoinette B., one of the first class of teachers who went to the West under the Nat. Popular Ed. Soc'y. She has lately returned to Dunbarton.

Mr. Putnam's publications have been; 1. Ordination Sermon of R. A. Putnam, Fitchburg, 4 Feb., 1824. 2. S. S. Address, Dunbarton, 4 July, 1831. 3. Thanksgiving Sermon, 1832. 4. Sermon on Divine Sovereignty and Man's Free Agency, 1833. 5. Address before Concord Female Anti-Slavery Soc., 1835. 6. Dedication Sermon, Dunbarton, 1836. 7. Sermon on "Communion with Extortioners," 1838. 8. Do. on "Christian Courage," 1839. 9. A Sermon on the Death of Rev. W. Harris, D. D., 1844. 10. Sermon on Future Punishment, 1845. 11. Historical Sermon, Dunbarton, 1845. 12. Sermon on Civil Government, 1851. Also, "English Grammar," with an Improved Syntax, 1825; 4 Editions Comprehensive Grammar, and Analysis; in which he was co-editor with Rev. H. D. Hodge, 1848, two editions.

74. REV. GEORGE FISHER

Was born in Wrentham, and is the son of Luther and Betsey Fisher, grandson of James, and the great grandson of Ebenezer Fisher, all of Wrentham.

He graduated at Brown University, 1819, and A. M. in course: studied theology with Rev. Dr. Ide, and was ordained over the second church in Harvard, 12 Sept., 1821, where he still continues in office.

Mr. Fisher married Miss Mary Hall Fisk, eldest daughter of Rev. Elisha Fisk, of Wrentham, by whom he has had five children.

1. George Elisha; grad. Amherst, 1846, and Andover, 1849; and settled at Rutland, Feb., 1850. He married Miss Harriet B. Holt, of Amherst. Mr. Fisher is now settled at North Amherst.

2. Mary Robinson: married to Mr. Andrew Farwell, of Harvard.

3. Elizabeth Smith, 4, Harriet Fiske, 5, Henry Martyn, reside at home.

Mrs. Fisher died, 29 April, 1852.

Mr. Fisher has published: 1. Funeral Sermon of Rev. James Howe, Senior Pastor at Pepperell, 21 July, 1840.

75. REV. JOHN FERGUSON.

[See Sketches of Members, No. 42.]

76. REV. MOSES THATCHER.

[See Sketches of Members, No. 43.]

77. REV. AUGUSTUS B. REED

Was a native of Rehoboth, and born 19 Nov., 1798.*

He became a subject of renewing grace when he was 18 years old, and made a public profession of religion the following summer, 4 May, 1817. Hereupon he turned his purposes from the profession of law to preparing for the Gospel ministry, and entered Brown University, whence he graduated, 1821, and A. M., in course, with the reputation of being "a diligent, accurate and punctual scholar." He studied theology with Rev. Otis Thompson of Rehoboth, and was

* His father, Dea. E. A. Reed and his maternal grandfather, Deacon Brown, were deacons in the Cong. church at Rehoboth. His paternal grandfather was deacon in the Cong. church in Dighton.

ordained the first pastor of the first Cong. church in Fall River, 2 July, 1823. He was dismissed 2 April, 1825.

In 1826, July 19, he was installed in Ware. His health became gradually impaired, — with intervals of returning strength, — but he felt himself sinking under his labors, and finally asked a dismission. The pastoral relation was severed 5 June, 1838. Soon after, he died in Ware, 30 Sept., 1838, aged 39 years.

Mr. Reed left a wife and five children to mourn his early departure. Her name was Melinda Boyden, daughter of the late William Boyden, Esq., of Fall River.* She is now the wife of Mr. Nathaniel Eddy, of Middleboro'.

Mr. Reed's children were,

1. Theodora C.; resides in Middleboro' with her mother.

2. Delight Brown; died at Fall River, 29 Oct., 1849, aet. 21 years.

3. William Augustus; in mercantile business, in Westfield.

4. John Richard; book-keeper in Fall River.

5. Theophilus; died at Westfield, 23 Aug., 1843, aged 7 years.

Two children died previous to his own death.

Mr. Reed's ministry was too short to bear much fruit; yet the first year of his labors in Ware was blest with an extensive revival, and the addition of about seventy members to the church.

"As a scholar, Mr. Reed was diligent, accurate, punctual. His standing in his class was above mediocrity. He loved the sound doctrines of the Gospel, and he loved them unto the end. He preached them with plainness and perspicuity; dwelling upon the truths most displeasing to the carnal mind with the more distinctness and frequency. He was a better writer than speaker."†

* The first Cong. church in Fall River was formed at the house of Mrs. Reed's grandfather, Dea. Richard Durfee.

† See Funeral Sermon, by Rev. L. Packard, Spencer.

In temperament he was ardent, earnest and sympathizing. None of his sermons have appeared in print.

78. REV. LEVI PACKARD

Was born in North Bridgewater in 1793. He is the son of Levi and Ruth P., and is the sixth in direct descent from Samuel Packard, who came from Windham, near Hingham, England, in the "Diligent," and settled in Hingham, 1638.*

Mr. Packard graduated at Brown University, 1821, and A. M.; studied theology with Rev. Dr. Ide of Medway, and was ordained at Spencer, 14 June, 1826. He still "dwells among his own people."

Mr. Packard married Clarissa Sanford, the daughter of Mr. Philo Sanford, of Medway, and sister of Rev. David Sanford, of Medway Village.

His oldest living son, Levi Sewell, is now an undergraduate of Amherst College.

79. REV. JAMES O. BARNEY.

[See Sketches of Members, No. 44.]

80. REV. HENRY HARRISON FAYETTE SWEET

Was born in Attleboro', 1 Nov., 1796, and was the only son of Henry and Lucinda Sweet.

He was converted, and joined the church, under Rev. N. Holman, in 1816; graduated at Brown University, 1822, and studied theology with Rev. Dr. Ide.

He was ordained at Palmer, 9 Nov., 1825. He died, 28 Feb., 1827, in his 31st year. The last sermon he preached was upon the anniversary of his ordination.

---

* The ancestral line is: 1. Samuel Packer or Packard, of England. 2. Zacheus, m. Sarah Howard. 3. David, b. 1687, m. Hannah Ames. 4. Abiah, b. 1727, m. Phebe Paine. 5. Levi, b. 1761, m. Ruth Snow of Eastham. 6. Rev. Levi, of Spencer.—*Mitchell's Bridgewater.*

He left only a widow, formerly Miss Elizabeth Henshaw, of Roxbury, now the wife of Mr. Cyrus Merrick, of Sturbridge.

As a man, Mr. Sweet was gentle, unassuming, and kind in his manners and intercourse with others. His mind, though not brilliant, was above the ordinary level, — patient, logical, fully grasping, and thoroughly understanding its themes of thought.

As a preacher, he was interesting and impressive.

He was thoroughly Calvinistic in his doctrinal views.

As a pastor he was solemn, deliberate, wise. He particularly excelled in the conference meeting, and in his interest in the lambs of the flock.*

81. REV. TYLER THACHER.

[See Sketches of Members, No. 64.]

82. REV. JAMES TISDALE

Was born in West Taunton, 7 Nov., 1799. He is the son of James Tisdale, Esq. and of his wife Abigail (Freeman) Tisdale. His mother was from Norton.†

He graduated at Brown University, 1821; and then taught an academy, during the two years following, at Darlington

* Funeral Sermon by Rev. Dr. Nelson, Leicester.

† Mr. Tisdale descended from John Tisdale, of Taunton, by the following line: his father, James Tisdale (1740—1811) was the son of Job, who died, 19 May, 1755, aet. 47. His father was Capt. Joseph, Jr., (1682—1739) the son of Joseph, who died about 1722. Joseph was the son of John Tisdale, of Duxbury, 1636; afterwards of Taunton, 1653. In 1655, he was constable, and afterwards selectman and deputy to Plymouth Court. He was killed by the Indians, at Taunton (now Raynham), 27 June, 1675.

In the Plymouth Court Records is the following item: — "1638. John Tisdale, upon the good report made of him and of his good carryage, is allowed to keepe house and plant for himself, provided that he shall continue his carryage still." — *Mr. E. H. Reed, Taunton.*

Court House, South Carolina. While there, he became converted, and returned and commenced the study of theology, with Rev. A. Cobb, of West Taunton.

He was ordained, 29 Sept., 1830, over the churches in Guildhall and Granby, Vt. He was dismissed, 4 May, 1836, and next supplied the pulpit, four years, at Dublin, and seven years at Gilsum, N. H. He now officiates at Shutesbury, where he has acted as stated supply since Oct., 1851.

Mr. Tisdale married, 5 Oct., 1831, Miss Margaretta Caroline Tubbs, of West Taunton, and has three children.

He has, for years, declined a resettlement in the pastoral office, on account of the precarious state of his health.

83. REV. LUCIUS WATSON CLARKE

Was born in Mansfield, now Chaplin, Ct., and is the son of Mr. James and Jerusha Clarke, and the youngest of eleven children. His parents were both hopefully pious, and trained their household in the ways of wisdom.

He graduated at Brown Univ., 1825, and studied theology with Rev. Dr. Ide, of Medway. He was ordained over the church in South Wilbraham, 9 Dec., 1829, and dismissed, 18 Sept., 1832. Afterwards he engaged, as stated supply, to the Fifth church in Plymouth, where he labored four or five years. He was next installed pastor of the church in West Amesbury, Oct., 1838, and continued there over five years.

He now resides at Middlebury, Vt., and preaches, occasionally, in the vicinity.

Mr. Clarke married Miss Lucy Beard, daughter of Rev. Daniel and Lucy Tomlinson, of Oakham, and has two children, Lucy Maria and Lucius Watson. Both children are hopefully pious, and the son is in Middlebury College, preparing for the Ministry.*

---

* Letter of Rev. L. W. Clarke.

84. MR. SYLVESTER GRAHAM

Was the son of Rev. John Graham, of West Suffield, Ct., where he was born. He prepared for college at Amherst Academy, but did not enter any institution; studied theology under the general direction of Rev. Emerson Paine, then of Little Compton. He requested ordination as Evangelist, by Mendon Association, 28 Oct., 1828; and, after considerable delay and examination, was ordained at Rehoboth, 18 Nov., 1828. He afterwards preached a short time in New Jersey, to a Presbyterian church; but soon after resigned the duties and titles of the ministry, and became known simply as a Lecturer upon Diet and Regimen. The subsequent part of his life was spent at Northampton, when not lecturing abroad. As a writer upon Dietetics, he became extensively known. He died at Northampton, 17 Sept., 1851, at the age of 50, leaving a widow and two children: a daughter, the wife of Mr. John Musgrave, of Leedsville, Northampton; and a son, now resident of Boston.

85. REV. CHARLES JARVIS WARREN.

[See Sketches of Members, No. 47.]

86. REV. CYRUS WHITMAN CONANT,

The son of Rev. Gaius Conant, was born in Bridgewater, where his father was then settled, 27 Nov., 1803.*

He graduated at Union College, Schenectady, 1824; studied theology with Rev. Dr. Ide; and, after approbation, preached in several places in Worcester county.

On account of ill health, he went to the Southern States, in the autumn of 1829, and there preached to a society of

* See his ancestry, under Rev. G. Conant, Licentiates, No. 46.

colored people, in Savannah, Georgia. Soon after his return, he entered on a Tract Agency, in the State of Indiana. He spent a year in this mission; and then applied to the Presbytery for a renewed license to preach the Gospel. But he was refused, on account of his religious sentiments. He was a thorough and consistent advocate of Dr. Emmons's views in theology!

He next engaged as a school teacher, and finally settled down as a farmer, in Greene county, Indiana. Here he has established a Sabbath school, where they were destitute of regular preaching; and here he still resides, planting and watching over the seeds of future Gospel institutions.

87. REV. WILLIAM HARLOW

Is the son of Dea. John and Betsey (Torrey) Harlow, and was born in Plymouth, 27 Oct., 1805.*

He graduated at Yale College, 1826, and studied theology with Rev. Dr. Ide. He was ordained as Evangelist, by the Mendon Association, at Wrentham, 28 Oct., 1828, and preached, as stated supply, in Canton, during the years 1829 and '30. He next supplied at Waterford, until 1832. He afterwards preached, for different periods, in vacant pulpits, in the vicinity of Wrentham, in which town he has resided since 1830.

Mr. Harlow married, 19 March, 1829, Miss Caroline Porter, daughter of Lebbeus and Mary (Brastow) Porter, of Wrentham, and has had two children, daughters; the youngest, Caroline F., is living.

* Mr. Harlow descended from William Harlow, who came in the *second* ship to Plymouth. His line, as far as furnished, begins with Jonathan Harlow, b. in Plymouth, 1712. His son, Jonathan, Jr., b. in Plymouth, 1742, m. Betsey Blackmer, of Plymouth, and removed to Middleboro'. His son John, b. in Plymouth, 1779, m. Betsey Torrey, of Plymouth, and still lives in Plymouth. He is the father of Rev. William, above.

Mr. Harlow published a tract on the Divinity of Christ, 1828; and a sermon on "False Standards in Religion," 1828.

88. REV. ELAM SMALLEY, D. D.

[See Sketches of Members, No. 49.]

89. REV. GILBERT FAY

Was the son of Otis and Mary (Morse) Fay, and was born in Westboro', May, 1803.

He graduated at Brown University, 1826, and studied theology with Rev. Dr. Ide. After two years labor in various places, he was ordained as Evangelist, at Westboro', 6 Oct., 1830, and went under a commission of the A. H. M. S., into the Western Reserve, and engaged in missionary labors in that important, but then destitute region.

He labored as stated supply at Wardsworth, Medina Co., O., until his death, 27 Oct., 1835, at the early age of 32. He was not unable to preach a single sabbath, until his final sickness.

"He was much loved and lamented by his church and his brethren in the ministry."

Mr. Fay married 11 Sept., 1831, Miss Clarissa Walker, daughter of Comfort and Tamar Walker, of Medway. They had two children: one of whom, a daughter, died before him. The other child, Gilbert Otis Fay, lives with his mother, who has returned to Medway.

Mr. Fay's labors were too brief to develop his full abilities. They were, however, signally blessed. The little church of eleven members at the commencement, numbered seventy at his death.

90. REV. JOHN FORBUSH

Is the son of Dea. Samuel Forbush, of Upton, and was born in that town, 4 Sept., 1800. His mother's maiden name was Lydia Gibson, of Hopkinton. Both parents are living in Upton.

He made public profession of religion, in Sept., 1815, and in 1823, began his literary studies with Rev. Samuel Wood, D. D., of Boscawen, N. H. He graduated at Amherst College, 1828, and studied theology with Rev. Dr. Ide. He preached his first sermon at Milford, Jan'y, 1830. Then supplied Dr. Ide's pulpit, during his illness, until May, when he went to Mendon, where he preached three months. He was ordained 6 Oct., 1830, as an Evangelist, at Westboro', by the Harmony Association, and went to the West, under a commission from the Am. Home Miss. Society.

In this great "place," he labored for many years, amongst the feeble churches and new communities, with encouraging success. He was one year at Burlington, Lawrence Co., O. A new meeting-house was built, and several additions to the church. Two and a half years, he officiated as *pastor* of the Mt. Leigh church, Adams Co. There were over sixty additions. From Dec., 1834, he labored six years at Brush Creek, — in a moral waste, — the first year without a church and sanctuary. He left a church of fifty members, and two meeting-houses, seven miles apart. One year at Homer, Licking Co. A year and a half at Bremen, Fairfield Co. Two years pastor at Lexington, Perry Co. Forty were added and a new church of thirty members was formed in the field, — Unity Church, — with a new meeting-house. Over four years at New Plymouth, now Vinton Co.

Besides these multiplied missionary and pastoral labors, Mr. Forbush spent much time as agent of the Am. Sunday

School Union. Nearly fifty Sabbath Schools were organized by him, many of which are still in successful operation.

In May, 1850, he returned with impaired health, to the place of his nativity, — where he now resides, — preaching recently to a small congregation in the South West corner of Hopkinton.

On the evening of his ordination, Mr. Forbush married Miss Sarah Lesure, of Upton. He has two children, both of whom are alive to bless his household.*

91. REV. VARNUM NOYES,

The son of Josiah and Mehitable (White) Noyes,† was born in Acton, but, at four years of age, removed with his parents to Westmoreland, N. H.

He made profession of religion, in Nov., 1821, and commenced fitting for the ministry, at the academies of Chesterfield, N. H., and of Amherst, Ms., and entered Dartmouth College, 1824. In his second year, his course was arrested by a severe and protracted disease. On his recovery, he taught school for a while, and then studied theology with Rev. Dr. Ide.

He was ordained as Evangelist for the West, by Mendon Association, at Medway, 25 Aug., 1831, and commenced preaching in Guilford, O., 2 Oct., 1831. Half of the time, for a few years, was spent in other neighboring places. In 1836, Sept. 21, he was regularly installed as pastor, in which relation he continued until 8 May, 1849, when it was dissolved at his own request.

The reason of the step was found in the prevalent impression, among a portion of the people, that, as he had been with

---

* Letter of Rev. J. Forbush, Upton.

† Son of Thomas Noyes, of Acton, and brother of the late Rev. Thomas Noyes, of Needham.

them a long time, a change of labors might be beneficial. The pastor was willing the experiment should be tried. But after a trial of about three years, he was invited to return, which he did, March, 1852. In the interval, he was the stated supply of the church in Wayne. His ministerial connection is with the Wooster (O. S.) Presbytery.

Mr. Noyes married, 17 June, 1833, Miss Lois Walker, daughter of the late Comfort Walker, of Medway, and sister of Mrs. Gilbert Fay. They have eight children, and one has fallen asleep.

92. REV. ISAAC ERWIN HEATON

Is a native of Franklin, and the oldest son of Mr. Nathan Heaton. His mother was Sarah Boon, of Upton.*

At twenty years of age, he experienced the power of the Gospel, and joined the church, under the care of Rev. Dr. Emmons. He entered Brown University, two years in advance, and grad. in 1832. Studied theology with Rev. Dr. Ide, and was ordained as an Evangelist, by Mendon Association, at North Wrentham, 25 April, 1837. He then engaged in the service of the Home Missionary Society, and in May, removed to Wisconsin.

In this State he was, with the exception of Rev. C. Marsh, foreign missionary to the Indians, the *pioneer* herald of the cross. For more than a year he was the only *congregational* minister in Wisconsin. Rev. C. Caldwell, the *second* minister, resided more than a hundred miles from him; and they were strangers for two years.

Mr. Heaton spent the first six months in Elk Grove, where is now a flourishing church, and meeting-house. The present active and useful deacon, was then an avowed atheist, and seen at meeting but once during Mr. H's abode there.

---

* His father and grandfather were Isaac, and were descended from the original settlers in Wrentham, Nathaniel and Mary Heaton.

He next spent three years at Belmont, where the legislature first met, before the capital was located at Madison. The place declined as a settlement, and he removed to Mt. Zion, in Rock Co., — a pleasant eminence, so named in sport, by an irreligious settler. His present place of labor is at Waterloo, where he has been for six years. It was swayed by a strong Universalist influence, now on the wane.

The church at first consisted of five members, all, excepting one female, unmarried. It now numbers 24. The place has grown rapidly since the Gospel was established there. Ten years ago, only one or two white persons could be found within a radius of ten miles, where now a funeral procession has been seen one hundred and twenty rods in length.*

Mr. Heaton married Miss Miranda N. Metcalf, daughter of Samuel and Mary Metcalf, of Franklin. They have had three children, daughters. The eldest died in infancy.

93. REV. THOMAS EDWARDS

Is a native of London, England, and the son of Miles and Ann (Debenham) Edwards.

He became interested in the Gospel of Christ, under the ministry of Rev. John Clayton, Sen., of London, and pursued classical studies under a private tutor.

After arriving in this country, he reviewed the usual course of theology with Rev. Dr. Ide, and was ordained and settled over the Evangelical church, Mendon, 28 Dec., 1836, and dismissed 4 Feb., 1840.

He next preached in Ackworth, N. H., and after several months' delay on account of health, was installed, 19 Aug., 1841. Dismissed, 13 Feb., 1843. He has since preached in Salem and various other places. His present residence is Charlestown.

Mr. Edwards married Miss Amelia Spear, daughter of Gershom and Elizabeth Spear, of Boston. She died in 1851,

* Letter of Rev. I. E. Heaton, Waterloo, Wisconsin.

leaving two children to survive her. His second wife was Miss Caroline ——, of Charlestown.

94. REV. ELI THURSTON

Was born in Brighton; removed thence, at an early age, to Jamaica Plains, and to Westboro'; and was converted to God while learning the trade of gunsmith in Millbury. He immediately turned his thoughts to an education for the Gospel ministry.

He pursued his preparatory studies at Day's Academy, Wrentham; graduated at Amherst College, 1834, and studied theology at Andover, and with Dr. Ide, of Medway.

He was ordained over the Congregational church in Hallowell, Me., 3 Jan., 1838, and dismissed July, 1848.

On the 21 of March, 1849, he was installed over the Central Cong. church in Fall River, where he still continues.

Mr. Thurston married M. Caroline, daughter of Mr. Philo Sanford, of Wrentham, now of Boston; who is a brother of Rev. David Sanford of Medway Village, and grandson of Rev. David Sanford of West Medway.

95. REV. CHARLES TURNER TORREY

Was born in Scituate, 21 Nov., 1813. He was the son of Charles and Hannah Tolman Torrey.

His father died in 1815, and his mother in 1817; and he was left, at little over three years of age, to the care of his grandparents, who, as often happens, did not guide and restrain their young and impulsive charge with a *parent's* anxious care and fidelity. When but five or six years old, he attended the town-meetings, sat with his grandfather, Hon. Charles Turner, who was generally moderator, watched every movement and counted every vote. Thus he acquired, perhaps, his strong penchant for political affairs, so fully developed in his subsequent life.

In 1828 he entered Phillips Academy, at Exeter, N. H., where he prepared for college. He entered Yale, as Sophomore, at 17, and graduated, 1833. It was during his first year that he became a subject of Divine grace.

After graduation, he took charge of the Female Seminary, West Brookfield; but the school-room was not his field of action, and he resigned, after keeping about four months. He next spent the academic year 1835–6 at Andover Theol. Seminary. On account of his health and pecuniary circumstances, he left, tried a pedestrian journey, for the former, with success, and resumed his studies, with Rev. L. A. Spofford, then of Scituate. In the summer following, June, 1836, he repaired to Rev. Dr. Ide, and completed his preparation for the ministry. In March, 1837, he was ordained over the Richmond St. Cong. church, Providence, R. I.; and was dismissed, at his own request, in October. Soon after, he simultaneously received calls to resettle, one from Randolph, the other from the Howard St. church, Salem, over which Rev. Dr. Cheever, now of New York city, had been settled. This latter call he accepted, and was installed, Jan., 1838. Here his earnest entering into the Anti-Slavery cause, and his calls abroad to labor for its advancement, rendered necessary a yielding either of his pastoral connection, or of his services in the Abolition field. He considered the latter more important, and accordingly was dismissed from his charge at Salem, and engaged as a public lecturer by the Mass. Abolition Society.

The exciting theme of American Slavery furnished ample material to inflame his zeal and employ his energies and time. His labors in this field are detailed in his published Memoir. He travelled, lectured, wrote, and published, in furtherance of the cause of Emancipation.

While he was at Washington, as a correspondent for several newspapers, a slaveholders' convention was holden, 12 Jan., 1842, at Annapolis, Maryland, to further the interests of the 'peculiar institution.' Mr. Torrey determined to attend and gather up the developments, and report for the press. He took his seat with other reporters; but, by a series of manœuvres, he was ejected, from the *floor* into the lobby, and thence into jail; on what definite charge, even his accusers could not find to say. After vexatious legal quibbles, he was released and bound over to 'keep the peace,' until April. Thus began his practical acquaintance of slavery and slave-prisons, — an acquaintance to end, not yet.

In 1842, he went to Albany and edited and finally published the "Tocsin of Liberty," afterwards "Albany Patriot." But his warm and readily-awakened sympathy for them in bonds, would not suffer him to operate in their behalf at this distance. He repaired to Delaware, and became, as was suspected, the *active* coadjutor of slaves escaping from servitude.

He was arrested, 24 June, 1844, at Baltimore, on complaint of Bushrod Taylor, of Winchester, Va., for aiding, as affirmed, certain slaves of his to escape from Virginia. Immediately upon this, William Heckroth brought a similar suit for aiding the escape of slaves from Maryland. This latter case took precedence, and he was committed to jail for trial. That event at length took place, 29 Nov., 1844; and, on the 3d of December, terminated in a verdict of guilty, upon every indictment; and he was condemned to six years' hard labor, in the State Penitentiary. Sentence was suspended nearly a month.

During part of this time, Mr. Torrey wrote his little volume, "Home, or the Pilgrims' Faith revived."

On the 30th day of December, 1844, he was removed to prison. His treatment was as humane as the rules would allow; but the seeds of disease, sown in previous labors, germinated in the solitudes and silence of the cell, and speedily ripened for the reaper, Death. Every rational effort for his deliverance was made by his friends, but without avail. But a deliverer was coming whom no prison walls could exclude, and no Executive could prevent accomplishing his work. Consumption opened his way beyond the reach of man.

Mr. Torrey died 9 May, 1846, aged 33 years. Three days before his death, the sacrament of the Lord's Supper was administered to him by Rev. Dr. Smalley, of Worcester. The occasion was solemn; and, to him, seemed a foretaste of that communion above, which he was speedily to enter. His remains rest in Mt. Auburn Cemetery, marked by a monument, raised by his friends, to his memory.

Mr. Torrey married Mary, the second daughter of Rev. Dr. Ide, of Medway. He left two children, still living.

Mr. Torrey was of pale visage, slender form, and nervous temperament. As a scholar, he was marked by a ready intuition and grasp of subjects, and by versatile talents; but he lacked concentrativeness and perseverance. It is no common man that could write, in the circumstances and the manner he did, such a book as "Home," of 255 pages, in twelve days, on the eve of an incarceration of six long years! As a preacher, his marked characteristics were obviously impressed upon his every performance. His pastoral labors were too brief to leave any very permanent impressions.

It is as an earnest laborer in the cause of Abolition, that he will be known hereafter. The part he acted, has been the subject of general speculation. It will come up again, in future review, and with truer conclusions, when the dark system of oppression which cut short his days, with all its perverting influences, will have passed away.

As to his *legal* guiltiness, on the specific charges made against him, we have nothing to say. But assuming the fact of his actual agency in aiding fugitives escaping from slavery, as to his *moral* guilt, we may use his own language to a friend, while in prison: "If I am a guilty man, I am a very guilty one; for I have aided nearly *four hundred* slaves to escape to freedom; the greater part of whom would, probably, but for my exertions, have died in slavery."

96. REV. ELNATHAN DAVIS

Is the 3d son of Ethan and Sarah Davis, late of Holden. He graduated at Williams College, 1834, and at East Windsor, Ct., 1836; ordained as Evangelist, at Holden, 9 Nov., 1836. An engagement with the A. B. C. F. M., was resigned on account of opinions upon Infant Baptism. A Chaplaincy from the Am. Seamen's Friends' Society, was arrested by the commercial pressure of 1837.

He supplied vacant pulpits: among them, that of the Lunatic Asylum, Worcester. In 1839, went to Indiana, and returned in 1845, on account of his wife's health. He was also engaged in the cause of peace, as delegate of which, he attended the Peace Congress of 1839, at Paris.

He was installed in Ashburnham, 16 Sept., 1846; and dismissed, May, 1851, to take charge of the Trinitarian Cong. Church, Fitchburg; where he was installed, 23 June, 1851.

Mr. Davis married Mary Avery, daughter of Mr. Aaron White, of Boylston, and granddaughter of Rev. Joseph Avery, former pastor of the church in Holden.

97. REV. JOHN DWIGHT

Was born in Shirley, and is the son of Mr. Francis and Maria Dwight.

He prepared for college at Woburn Academy, graduated at Amherst, 1835, and studied theology with Rev. Dr. Ide.

He was ordained over the South Church in North Bridgewater, 12 April, 1837, and dismissed in feeble health, March, 1839. He was installed over the Manomet Church, Plymouth, 28 July, 1841, and dismissed at his request, March, 1846. He is at present employed as stated supply, at North Wrentham.

Mr. Dwight married Miss Sally Hastings, daughter of Mr. Benjamin Hastings, late of Boston, and has six children.

Mr. Dwight has published two Farewell Sermons, delivered to his people, at Plymouth.

98. REV. MORTIMER BLAKE.

[See Sketches of Members, No. 56.]

99. REV. EDMUND DOWSE

Is the son of Benjamin and Thankful (Chamberlain) Dowse, of Sherborn.

He fitted for college at Day's Academy, Wrentham, and graduated at Amherst College, 1836, and studied theology with Rev. Dr. Ide.

He was ordained, 10 Oct., 1838, over the church in his native town, where he still remains.

Mr. Dowse married Elizabeth R., daughter of Dea. Daniel Leland, of Sherborn. She died 16 June, 1842, leaving a daughter. His present wife was Elizabeth Bowditch, daughter of Galen and Sally (Davenport) Bowditch, of Sherborn.

100. REV. CHARLES CHAMBERLAIN.

[See Sketches of Members, No. 74.]

101. REV. SAMUEL HUNT.

[See Sketches of Members, No. 75.]

102. REV. DANIEL J. POOR.

[See Sketches of Members, No. 55.]

103. REV. WILLIAM PHIPPS, JR.

Is a native of Franklin, and the son of William and Fanny (Morton) Phipps.

He graduated at Amherst College, 1837, and A. M.; studied

theology with Rev. Dr. Ide, and was ordained at Paxton, 11 Nov., 1840.

Mr. Phipps married Miss Mary Partridge, daughter of Mr. Eleazer Partridge, of Franklin, and has several children.

Mr. Phipps has published a Funeral Sermon of Mrs. E. T. Smith, wife of Rev. John C. Smith, missionary to Ceylon, 1842.

104. REV. JONATHAN GROUT

Was born in Westboro', in 1811.

He studied at Amherst Academy, and graduated at Yale College, 1836. He followed teaching about *two* years, in North Carolina, and then returned, and studied theology with Rev. Dr. Ide. He preached a few months in Millville, South Mendon, when he withdrew from the ministry, and settled upon the paternal farm.

Upon the death of his wife, — Mrs. Florella Mills Grout, daughter of Rev. David Holman, of Douglas, — he resolved to preach again.

He was ordained as an Evangelist, at Westboro', Oct., 1845, and went to Southeastern Ohio, in Meigs and Athens Cos. His health began to be impaired, and he left the pulpit for the school room. He taught school for three years in Coolville, Athens Co., Ohio.

In this latter place, he now resides, engaged in business, as partner in a mercantile firm, and occasionally preaching in destitute places. He is ministerially connected with the Marietta Consociation.

105. REV. JOSEPH HOLMES BAILEY

Was born in West Newbury, 15 Sept., 1808.

He indulged hope at the age of 21, and, though feeble in body, bent his steps towards the ministry. After many struggles, he graduated at Amherst Coll., 1838. He then taught school some two years, at Edgartown, M. V., studied theology with Rev. Dr. Ide, and also attended lectures at Andover.

He commenced preaching in 1843, at Dighton, where he was ordained, 31 Jan'y, 1844. Rev. Dr. Ide preached the Sermon. In the Autumn of the same year, he was seized with the prevailing typhoid fever ; recovered partially, and went prematurely, to his parents, in West Newbury, where he relapsed and died in a few days, at the age of 36.*

Mr. Bailey secured a strong hold upon the affections of his people in his brief ministry, and awakened promising hopes of usefulness to the church and the world. But his sudden end destroyed their fruition, and left his page a blank.

106. REV. PRESTON POND, JR.

[See Members, No. 72.]

107. MR. RICHARD CECIL SPOFFORD

Was born at East Bradford, now Groveland, 22 Dec., 1817. He was the son of Rev. Luke A. Spofford and his wife Grata (Rand) Spofford, the daughter of Col. Daniel and Susan Rand, of Rindge, N. H., and was grandson of Dea. Eleazer and Mary (Flint) Spofford, of Jaffrey, N. H.

He fitted for college at Groveland Academy, where he was converted, 1831, and graduated at Amherst Coll., 1839. He then engaged a year, or more, in teaching, in which occupation he was highly efficient. He studied theology with Rev. J. Ide, D. D. From November to March, after his approbation, he preached in Barre. His labors were too exhausting for an already diseased frame, and he retired to the

* Rev. A. Cobb, W. Taunton.

family of his father, on Martha's Vineyard, to recruit. But weeks passed, and consumption indicated its grasp so decidedly and powerfully, that he resigned the hopes of recovery. He lingered through the winter, and died at Chilmark, 25 May, 1843, in his 26th year.

In Mr. Spofford's early death, many high hopes for this world were forever blasted.

In college, he sustained a high reputation for accurate scholarship, and purity and elegance of literary taste. His style as a writer was pure and classical, and his descriptions peculiarly chaste and graphic.

He wrote many poetical effusions, evincing an ability, which, one who knew him well has said, might, with life and favoring circumstances, equal a Thompson or a Cowper.

The ministry was to him the highest and holiest calling; and when he entered upon it, it engrossed his supreme regard, and enlisted his undivided labors. His season of preparation for the sacred office was marked by earnest labors for the salvation of men, and the fidelity of his public and private exhortations at Medway are still remembered.

While there he prepared the copious Index to Dr. Emmons's works, then in process of publication by his instructor, Dr. Ide.

The Gospel, which had been the theme of his deep and prayerful study, was his sure foundation in his closing sickness and death.

108. REV. HORACE DEAN WALKER

Is the son of Mr. Dean and Rebecca (Wright) Walker, of East Medway.*

* His ancestry first appears among the early settlers of Rehoboth. Comfort Walker, son of Caleb, Jr., removed from Rehoboth to Killingly, Ct. His son, the father of Deane Walker, migrated thence to Medway, where the latter was born. Rev. Augustus Walker, of the Syrian Mission, and approbated by Mendon Association, Jan., 1852, is brother of Rev. Horace, above.

He prepared for college mostly at Franklin Academy, and entered Western Reserve College at Hudson, O., in 1837. He then removed to Yale College, where he graduated, 1841. He studied theology with Rev. Dr. Ide one year, and completed his course at Bangor Seminary, in 1843. He was ordained over the third church in Abington, 15 Feb., 1844, where he remains.

Mr. Walker married Mercy A. Mason, daughter of Horatio and Julia (Adams) Mason, of Medway. Her mother was sister to Rev. Jasper Adams, D. D., Prest. of Geneva Coll., N. Y., of Charleston Coll., Charleston, S. C., and Prof. of Moral Philosophy at West Point Academy.

109. REV. ABRAHAM JENKINS, JR.

Is the son of Abraham Jenkins, of Barre.

He graduated at Amherst College, 1838. After graduation, he assisted Prest. Hitchcock in his chemical lectures, and in his geological survey of the State, until the summer of 1839, when he taught school, for more than two years, at Troy and Keene, N. H.; also, part of the year 1842, at Edgartown, M. V. He entered upon the study of theology with Rev. Dr. Ide, and received approbation to preach.

A bronchial affection soon disenabled him from occupying the pulpit, except occasionally; which he did, in 1843, at Hardwick; in the autumn of 1844, at River Head, Long Island, and in 1845 at Halifax, Vt. Here he declined a call, as he did also from the church of River Head, on account of a fresh attack of bleeding at the lungs. Subsequently, he labored a few months at South Woodstock, Ct., at Gorham, Me., at Winchendon and Royalston. In 1847, he preached some months at South Brookfield and Tisbury, M. V.

In October, he was invited to Fitzwilliam, N. H., where he was ordained and settled, 16 Feb., 1848. He is now pleasantly situated, and able to preach most of the time; although with anticipations on his part, that 'he can hardly hope to preach much more.'

110. REV. EDWARD PRATT

Is a native of Marblehead, and the son of Jonathan and Sarah (Beckford) Pratt, natives of Salem.*

He commenced studies with reference to a collegiate education, but was compelled, by his health, to relinquish them. After engaging some ten years in business, his returning health encouraged the former idea of entering the ministry. As his age seemed to forbid the usual complete course of study, he entered Gilmanton Theol. Seminary, and graduated, 1844. He was Resident Licentiate at Andover, until Feb., 1845.

In April, he commenced preaching at Abington, Ct.; was ordained Evangelist, by Mendon Association and others, at Wrentham, 13 Aug., 1845. He left Abington, April, 1849, and engaged as exploring agent of the Norfolk Co. Bible Society. In May, 1851, he entered the service of the N. Y. City Tract Society, as their missionary in the III. and V. Wards, and is now in the same employ.

Mr. Pratt married Miss Sarah Blake, daughter of Mr. Robert Blake, of Wrentham, who was lost in the steamer Lexington, on Long Island Sound.

---

* Mr. Pratt's paternal grandfather, — born Salem, 1745, and died Orford, N. H., 1831, — was captain of the famous privateer, "Grand Turk," during the revolutionary war. After the close of the war, he retired to Orford, N. H., and became one of the parishioners of the late Rev. Jotham Sewall.

His maternal ancestor was Benjamin Beckford, Salem, 1640. Benjamin Beckford, the patriarch of Congregationalism in Illinois, and who recently died at Griggsville, Ill., aged 87, was his descendant, and uncle to Mr. Pratt.

Rev. Horace Pratt, lately at Seekonk, is brother of Rev. Edward, above.—*Rev. E. Pratt.*

111. REV. MALACHI BULLARD,

The son of Malachi Bullard, was born in West Medway, 1817.

He pursued his preparatory studies at Franklin Academy, and entered Amherst College, 1837; but left, the second year, for Dartmouth College, where he graduated, 1840. He studied theology with Dr. Ide.

He was engaged, more or less for some years, in teaching school. In 1842, he had the preceptorship of Atkinson Academy, N. H. He continued in this employment, and occasionally supplied vacant pulpits, preaching several months in Dighton, — among other places, — until 1846; when he was ordained over the church in Winchendon, 19 Nov., 1846. But his work on earth was speedily finished. After a sickness of several months, he died, 10 May, 1849, aged 32.

His wife was Sabrina, the daughter of Mr. Nathan Bullard, of W. Medway.

As a scholar, Mr. Bullard was laborious and persevering. If his progress was slow, it was sure. He left no ground unsurveyed, no student's duty unperformed.

"He was a man of few words, but those were spoken with discretion; of few promises, but they could be relied upon with entire confidence.

He was a faithful and useful Minister of the Gospel, industrious, methodical, kind, prudent, and devoted to his duties.

The people of his charge, and the association of ministers to which he belonged, regarded him with respect, confidence, and affection. During his entire sickness, he was calm, happy, and hopeful, and manifested entire acquiescence in the Divine Will." *

The only published production of his pen, an occasional

* Obituary-notice in Puritan Recorder.

sermon on "Sinful Amusements," shows him to be a clear thinker, and an unshrinking reprover of what he considered wrong, even amongst his own people.

112. REV. ALLEN LINCOLN

Is the son of Mr. Thomas and Nancy N. (Norcross) Lincoln, of Cohasset, where he was born, 24 November, 1813.

He first learned the house and ship joiner's trade in Boston, but afterwards fitted for college at Woburn Academy, and grad. at Dartmouth, 1839.

He had charge of Austin st. Academy, Cambridgeport, four years, and then studied theology with Rev. Dr. Ide.

He was ordained at Gray, Cumberland Co., Me., 5 Nov., 1845, where he now is.

Mr. Lincoln, m. Lucy Richardson, only daughter of Dea. Stephen Richardson of Woburn. She died 25 July, 1846. His present wife was Julia A. Holmes, d. of Asa Holmes, Esq., of North Auburn, Me.

113. REV. WILLIAM M. THAYER

Is the son of Maj. Davis and Betsey (Makepeace) Thayer of Franklin.

He fitted for college at Franklin Academy, and grad. at Brown University, 1843. After graduation, he engaged for awhile in teaching, at Attleboro', Franklin, and South Braintree. He studied theology with Rev. Dr. Ide of Medway, and Rev. M. Blake of Mansfield.

He preached in Edgartown, M. V., for a year, and declined a call for settlement. He was employed for a season in North Chelsea, and in other places, and finally was ordained over the church in Ashland, 20 June, 1849, and there he continues.

He married Miss Rebecca Richards, of Dover, and has one child.

Mr. Thayer has published, a Review of Rev. Mr. Lovejoy's sermon on Prohibitory Law, 1851. The Price of Gold, a funeral sermon on a young member of his congregation who died in California, 1852. The Worth of the Soul, and Happy New Year: a juvenile series, 1852.

114. REV. JAMES M. BACON

Is the son of Joseph and Beulah (Fuller) Bacon of Newton.

He fitted for college at Phillips Academy, Andover, but did not graduate, on account of ill health. After an irregular study of over six years, he became the theological pupil of Rev. Dr. Ide, with whom he attended the usual course.

He was ordained in Littleton, 8 Oct., 1846, and dismissed, on account of ill health, 13 Nov., 1849. He was installed over the Union Evangelical church of Amesbury and Salisbury, 25 June, 1851, where he now is.

Mr. Bacon m. Miss Maria Woodward, daughter of Dea. Elijah F. and Anna Woodward of Newton.*

115. REV. JOSIAH LYMAN ARMES

Was born in New Salem, but early became a resident of Randolph.†

He spent some time in Hamilton Coll., N. Y., and entered

* The Deaconship of the Newton church seems to be an heirloom in this family. Six of them, in direct lineal descent, have held the office, and have also lived and died in the same house; which is now occupied by the seventh generation of their line. — *Rev. J. M. Bacon.*

† His father bore the same name as himself. His mother was a Trask, of New Salem. He is a descendant, in the fifth generation, from William Armes, who came from the Island of Jersey, and settled in Hadley, about 1700.

Amherst College, 1836; but was compelled to leave, as many others, for want of funds. He engaged in teaching, in the Academy at South Dennis, and the Classical School in Belchertown. In 1841, he took charge of the Mansfield Academy, where he continued until 1845. During his connection with this school, he prosecuted his theological studies, under the direction of Rev. M. Blake, of Mansfield.

He was ordained pastor of the Manomet church, Plymouth, 25 June, 1846; and was dismissed, 31 July, 1850. He was again settled, 30 Oct., 1850, in Mason, N. H., as colleague with Rev. Ebenezer Hill, where he now is.

He married Marcia K., daughter of Mr. Arza Keith, of N. Bridgewater, and has five children, daughters.

116. REV. EZRA NEWTON, JR.

Was born in Princeton, 30 Sept., 1818.

He studied at Monson Academy, 1838–9, graduated at Dartmouth, 1843, and studied theology with Rev. S. Harding, then of East Medway. He preached in Dighton one year, from 1 July, 1846, where he declined a settlement. He was ordained in Shutesbury, 1 March, 1848; and was dismissed, on account of his health, 10 Sept., 1850. The following summer, he acted as Agent of the N. Hamp. Bible Society, and preached, part of the time, in Raymond, N. H.

Mr. Newton married Miss Clark, of E. Medway, and now resides at Kingston, N. H. He is unable to preach.

117. MR. HIRAM C. DANIELS

Is a native of E. Medway, and the son of Amos and Sally Daniels. His father died recently, and his mother married a Bullard, and resides in Sherborn.

He graduated at Dartmouth College, 1845, and studied theology in private.

He has preached in various places, supplying the pulpit in Kennebunk, Me., for a considerable time; but is now compelled, by a bronchial difficulty, to forego the labor of public speaking.

He is employed as travelling Agent of the American and Foreign Christian Union.

Mr. Daniels married Miss Susan Cressy, of Rowley.

118. REV. JOHN W. HARDING

Is the oldest child of Rev. Sewall Harding of Boston, and was born in Waltham.* He fitted for college at Phillips Academy, Andover; graduated at Yale College, 1845; and at Andover. He is at Longmeadow, where he was ordained, 1 Jan., 1850.

Mr. Harding married, 29 Dec., 1852, Mehitable P. Lane, daughter of Jenkins Lane, Esq., of East Abington.

119. REV. FREDERIC A. FISK

Is the youngest son of Rev. Elisha and Margaret (Shepherd) Fisk, of Wrentham.†

He prepared for College at Day's Academy, Wrentham; and graduated at Amherst Coll., 1836, and A. M. After his graduation, he followed school-teaching for *ten* years, both in Connecticut and Massachusetts. After the death of his wife, he resided awhile at New Haven, and prosecuted the study of divinity there, in 1850.

After approbation, he supplied the pulpit in Norton and in Ashburnham, at which latter place he received a call, and was settled, 30 Dec., 1851.

---

* See Rev. S. Harding, Members, No. 61.

† See Rev. E. Fisk, Members, No. 29.

Mr. Fisk married Anne A. Nelson, daughter of Rev. Stephen S. and Emilia (Robbins, of Suffield, Ct.) Nelson, late pastor of the West church in Amherst. She died, 7 May, 1848, leaving one child — a son. Mr. Fisk's present wife was Rebecca J. Robbins, daughter of Dea. Josiah Robbins, of Plymouth.

120. REV. HENRY LOBDELL

Was born in Danbury, Ct., 25 Jan., 1827, and is the son of Henry C. and Almina Lobdell. His life, from ten to sixteen, was spent in the family of Mr. John Covill, of Reading, Ct., engaged in labor upon a farm. In the course of preparation for College, he taught school, one year, in the city of New London, Ct.

Previous to entering college, he studied medicine three years with Dr. Hanford of North Bennet, Bethel, Ct. In 1849, he was graduated at Amherst College, and received the degree of M. D., from New Haven, March, 1850. He studied theology, at New Haven, at Andover, and while teaching a boarding school, in Danbury, Ct.

At the time of his approbation, he was under a prospective appointment to the Foreign Mission Field, by the American Board, expecting to occupy the post in Syria, made vacant by the death of Doct. A. Smith.

He was ordained as an Evangelist to Koordistan, 5 Oct., 1851, at the Broadway Tabernacle, New York, and has since sailed to his destined field of labor.

121. MR. JOHN EDWIN COREY

Is the connecting link of the lists of candidates of the past and present centuries.

He was born in Mansfield, and is the son of Mr. Leonard

and Adah (Skinner) Corey. He fitted for college at Mansfield Academy, graduated at Amherst, 1850, and studied theology with Rev. M. Blake, of Mansfield.

He was immediately employed, as stated supply, at Edgartown, Martha's Vineyard, where he preached until Oct., 1852. He is now supplying at Dighton.

Mr. Corey married Fanny M., the daughter of Mr. Daniel and Lavina (Clark) Williams, Jr., of Mansfield.

COMPARATIVE TABLES.

I. Of Members.

N. B. Periods are reckoned up to the close of the century, Nov., 1851.

Names.	Alma Mater.	First Pastorate.		Pastoral Life.		Active Ministry.		Age.		Remarks.
		y.	m.	y.	m.	y.	m.	y.	m.	
J. Dorr,	H. U.	52		52		52		79		
N. Webb,	H. U.	41	1	41	1	41	1	97		
A. Frost,	H. U.	48	3	48	3	48	3	71	5	
E. Fish,	H. U.	44	2	44	2	44	2	76		
D. Thurston,	N. J.	16	8	16	8	16	8	50		Left preaching 8 y. 8 m. before death.
D. Hall,	H. U.	59	6	59	6	59	9	84	9	
A. Hutchinson,	Y. C.	22	5	22	5	50	3	76	6	
C. Barnum,	N. J.	7	9	14		16	2	39	2	
E. Chaplin,	Y. C.	27	4	27	4	27	4	89	3	Left preaching 30 y. before death.
I. Stone,	H. U.	34		34		54		88	11	
D. Sanford,	Y. C.	34		34		34		72	4	
N. Emmons,	Y. C.	54	1	54	1	54	1	95	4	Resigned 13 y. 4 m. before death.
E. Fitch,	Y. C.	16	11	16	11	16	11	42	6	
J. Spalding,	Y. C.	5	1	39	2	40	8	72	4	
J. Crane,	H. U.	48	9	48	9	52	2	80	5	
D. Avery,	Y. C.	4	1	15	1	46	3	71	6	

C. Alexander,	Y. C.	1	4	18		47	2	72	8	
T. Dickinson,	D. C.	24	5	24	5	24	5	52		
E. Mills,	Y. C.	35	5	35	5	35	5	73		
J. Robinson,	Y. C.	18	9	18	9	43	4	72		Preached seldom for 25 yrs.
N. Howe,	H. U.	45	4	45	4	45	2	72	4	
S. Judson,	Y. C.	40		40		40		65		
J. Wilder,	D. C.	32	10	32	10	46		77	11	
B. Wood,	D. C.	52	11	52	11	52	11	76	7	
J. Cleaveland,	——	9		25	8	29	4	65		
N. Holman,	B. U.	20	7	20	7	44		75	5	
O. Thompson,	B. U.	32	1	41	1	49		Living		Retired.
D. Long,	D. C.	43		43		43		78	1	
E. Fisk,	B. U.	51	6	51	6	51	6	81	4	
S. Austin,	Y. C.	3	2	32		39		70	2	
W. Warren,	D. C.	13		13		13		Unknown		Left the ministry.
P. Smith,	B. U.	16	6	33	1	44	8	75	2	
D. Holman,	B. U.	33	10	33	10	43	1			Still preaches.
E. Rockwood,	D. C.	26	4	41	4	41	4			Now settled.
S. W. Colburn,	D. C.	3	3	19	7	42	3			Still preaches.
J. Ide,	B. U.	37		37		37				Still settled.
A. Cobb,	B. U.	36	7	36	7	36	7			do.
J. Wheaton,	B. U.	9	2	9	2	9	2	36	11	
T. Williams,	Y. C.	4	11	4	11	44	11			Still preaches.
C. Park,	B. U.	14		14		30		72	4	
D. Thomas,	B. U.	39	7	39	7	39	7	67	6	

Names.	Alma Mater.	First Pastorate.		Pastoral Life.		Active Ministry.		Age.		Remarks.
		y.	m.	y.	m.	y.	m.	y.	m.	
J. Ferguson,	——	13	1	17	4	29	9			Still preaches.
M. Thacher,	B. U.	9	2	20		28	3			Now settled.
J. O. Barney,	B. U.	26	3	26	3	27	9			Still preaches.
W. Pierce,	B. U.	14	11	25		25	6			Retired.
C. Fitch,	W. C.	4		10	4	30				Still preaches.
C. J. Warren,	B. U.	2	4	7	10	23	9			do.
P. Cummings,	B. U.	1	6	17	3	23	10			do.
E. Smalley,	B. U.	9	1	22	3	22	5			Now settled.
A. A. Phelps,	Y. C.	1	6	8	8	16	10	42	8	
H. G. Park,	B. U.	5		10		21	11			Still preaches.
A. Bigelow,	H. U.	20	9	22	3	23	7			Now settled.
D. Sanford,	B. U.	2		23	3	23	6			do.
T. D. Southworth,	H. C.	4	1	15	4	17	5			Still preaches.
D. J. Poor,	A. C.	7	2	7	2	7	2			School-teaching.
M. Blake,	A. C.	12		12		12				Still settled.
M. G. Grosvenor.	D. C.	1		11		25				Still preaches.
T. T. Richmond,	——	4	9	13	9	19	4			Now settled.
T. D. P. Stone,	A. C.	6		6		7				Principal Ct. Normal School.
S. Harding,	U. C.	16	9	30	10	30	10			Sec. Am. Doct. Tr. and Bk. Soc.
D. R. Barnes,	——	——		——		Unknown				
A. H. Reed,	A. C.	3		7		17				Still preaches.
H. James,	Y. C.	8		8		8				Still settled.*
T. Thacher,	B. U.	8	8	8	8	23	11			Still preaches.

S. B. Goodenow,	B. C.	1	2	4	8	8	3	Still preaches.
C. Simmons,	——	5	10	5	10	18	11	do.
C. White,	B. S.	1	9	5	7	22	1	do.
O. W. Cooley,	B. S.	2		2		3	6*	Still preaches.
H. L. Bullen,	D. C.	——		——		1	6	Prof. Iowa Coll.
W. Barnes,	Y. C.	5		9		9		Still preaches.
J. T. Tucker,	Y. C.	6		10	7	14	11	Now settled.
P. Pond, Jr.,	B. C.	1	6	3	3	8	1	do.
G. H. Newhall,	A. C.	1	2	1	2	1	2	Still settled.
C. Chamberlain,	B. U.	2		2	4	9	4	Now settled.
S. Hunt,	A. C.	10	10	11	7	12	4	do.
J. Haskell,	B. C.	——		——		——		Just settled.
A. Hixon,	B. U.	3	2	3	2	3	2	Disabled.

II. Graduates.

Harvard University,	9	Dartmouth College,	9	Hamilton College,	1
Yale College,	17	Bowdoin College,	3	Union College,	1
New Jersey College,	2	Williams College,	1	Not graduated,	7
Brown University,	21	Amherst College,	6		——
					77

* Dismissed 19 Jan., 1853, to become the pastor of the Old South Church, Worcester.

III. Averages.

Of the 77 Members, 35 are dead, 42 are living.

Of the 42 living, 6 have retired or entered other employments, and 16 are in the pastoral office; of whom, 6 continue in their *first* pastorate.

Of the 35 deceased members: —

The average of their first pastorate is 28 yrs. 3 m.
" " " whole pastoral life, 32 yrs. 2 m.
" " " " ministerial life, 38 yrs. 2 m.
" " " " natural life, 68+yrs.

Of the survivors: —

The average first pastorate of 39 is 10 yrs. 1 m.
" " whole pastoral life of 39, 12 yrs. 8 m.
" " ministerial life of 40, 20 yrs. 10 m.
" " pastorate of 5 still undismissed, 18 yrs. 11 m.

Of the deceased members, Rev. Dr. Emmons of Franklin attained to the greatest age; viz. 95 yrs. 4 m. Rev. Dr. Hall of Sutton was the longest settled over the same people; viz. 59 yrs. 6 mos.

Rev. O. Thompson of N. Abington, is the oldest minister who has belonged to the Association; being now in his 77th year.

Rev. Dr. Ide, of the living members, has been the longest settled in the same place; being now in the 39th y. of his pastorate at W. Medway.

Five members have been settled over fifty yrs., in one parish, Seven have been settled over forty years, and Nine over thirty years.

II. OF LICENTIATES.

N. B. Candidates who afterwards became *members*, and those who never entered the ministry, or have not been ordained, are omitted in this table. Dates are computed up to Nov., 1851.

Names.	Alma Mater.	First Pastorate.		Pastoral Life.		Active Ministry.		Age.		Remarks.
		y.	m.	y.	m.	y.	m.	y.	m.	
M. Taft,	H. U.	39	2	39	2	39	2	69	3	
C. Jones,	H. U.	5		5		Unknown		Unknown		
N. Potter,	N. J.	3	7	3	7	"		"		
A. Rice,	H. U.	50	5	50	5	54		83		
B. Caryl,	H. U.	49		49		49		79		
E. Emerson,	N. J.	41		41		45		80	9	
S. Bigelow,	H. U.	2	1	2	1	2	1	30	1	
A. Thayer,	N. J.	11	8	11	8	11	8	63	8	Retired 25 yrs. before his death.
E. Fish, Jr.,	H. U.	7	1	19	11	21	9	51		
M. Warren,	H. U.	40	6	40	6	40	6	70	3	
J. Cram,	D. C.	2	10	2	10	Unknown		71	2	
S. Aiken,	D. C.	24		24		30		75		Retired 15 yrs. before his death.
E. Pond,	B. U.	18		18		18		51	3	
W. Harris,	D. C.	40	11	40	11	40	11	82	6	Retired 13 yrs. before his death.
R. Page,	D. C.	24	10	24	10	24	10	51	11	
E. Dudley,	D. C.	7	11	7	11	7	11	46	5	Retired 9 yrs. before his death.

Names.	Alma Mater.	First Pastorate.		Pastoral Life.		Active Ministry.		Age.		Remarks.
		y.	m.	y.	m.	y.	m.	y.	m.	
H. Daggett,	B. U.	4		11	6	40		66	7	
R. Tyler,	D. C.	24	10	30	10	32		56		
H. Fish,	D. C.	31		31		31		62		
J. Morse,	B. U.	23		35		50		80	1	
N. Hall,	D. C.	22	10	22	10	22	10	56	3	
J. Fitch,	B. U.	23		23		25		57		
E. Smith,	B. U.	37		37		52		87	8	
W. Jackson,	D. C.	45	11	45	11	45	11	73	10	
K. Bailey,	D. C.	25	11	25	11	54				Retired.
A. Wines,	D. C.	20	11	20	11	36		66	9	
J. Smith,	D. C.	19		20	10	34	3	65	1	
J. B. Preston,	P. U.	15		15		15		42	4	
J. Rowell,	D. C.	27	5	27	5	42	1	75		
D. Fairbanks,	B. U.	18		34		36				Retired.
L. Worcester,	——	38		38		38		79	4	
J. Emerson,	H. U.	13		13		22		55	7	
N. Waldo,	——	6	7	Unknown		Unknown		Unknown		
L. Nelson,	——	47		47		47				Still settled.
J. Cheney,	B. U.	10		14		14		57	10	
S. Johnson,	Y. C.	2		2		2		30		
G. Conant,	B. U.	22	3	29	3	33	2			Retired.
S. Chapin,	H. U.	2	11	2	11	40	3	67		
E. Walker,	B. U.	11		11		11		40		

N. Rawson,	——	6	3	6	3	23		65	5	Retired 11 yrs. before his death.
M. Moore,	B. U.	19	6	27	5	30				Editor for past 8 years.
J. B. Wight,	B. U.	20	3	29	3	31				Retired for past 5 years.
E. Paine,	B. U.	6	4	18	9	35	2	64	4	
E. Pond,	B. U.	13	8	13	8	36	9			Prof. at Bangor.
J. Perkins,	B. U.	36	5	36	5	36	5			Still settled.
S. Raymond,	B. U.	12	2	33	7	34				Retired.
L. B. Sullivan,	B. U.	3	8	3	8	31	5			Still preaches.
M. Partridge,	B. U.		6		6	——		36		Preached 8 yrs. as Home missionary.
W. Holbrook,	B. U.	21	10	30	4	33	4			Still preaches.
A. Manning,	B. U.	3	6	3	6	24				Retired.
W. Tyler,	B. U.	12	8	19	8	32	9			Still preaches.
D. Brigham,	U. C.	16	11	30	11	31	11			Now settled.
Z. Whitmore,	U. C.	25		25	5	30	2			Now settled.
S. Shores,	——	6		6		21	6	59	6	
J. M. Putnam,	——	5		28	10	30	11			Now settled.
G. Fisher,	B. U.	30	2	30	2	30	2			Still settled.
A. B. Reed,	B. U.	1	9	13	8	14	11	39	10	
L. Packard,	B. U.	25	5	25	5	25	5			Still settled.
H. H. F. Sweet,	B. U.	1	3	1	3	1	3	30	4	
J. Tisdale,	B. U.	5	7	5	7	21	2			Still preaches.
L. W. Clark,	B. U.	2	9	8		21	11			Still preaches.
W. Harlow,	Y. C.	——		——		4				Retired the past 9 years.
G. Fay,	B. U.	——		——		5		32	5	
J. Forbush,	A. C.	2	6	2	6	21	1			Still preaches.

Names.	Alma Mater.	First Pastorate.		Pastoral Life.		Active Ministry.		Age.		Remarks.
		y.	m.	y.	m.	y.	m.	y.	m.	
V. Noyes,	D. C.	12	8	12	8	20	3			Still preaches.
I. E. Heaton,	B. U.	——		——		14	7			do.
T. Edwards,	——	3	10	5	4	14	11			do.
E. Thurston,	A. C.	10	6	13	2	13	10			Now settled.
C. T. Torrey,	Y. C.		7	1	7	2		32	6	
E. Davis,	W. C.	4	8	5	1	15				Now settled.
J. Dwight,	A. C.	1	11	6	7	14	7			Still preaches.
E. Dowse,	A. C.	13	1	13	1	13	1			Still settled.
W. Phipps, Jr.,	A. C.	11		11		11				do.
J. Grout,	Y. C.	——		——		7				Retired.
J. H. Bailey,	A. C.		10		10		10	36		
H. D. Walker,	Y. C.	7	9	7	9	7	9			Still settled.
A. Jenkins, Jr.,	A. C.	3	9	3	9	3	9			do.
E. Pratt,	——	——		——		6	3			Still preaches.
M. Bullard, Jr.	D. C.	2	6	2	6	2	6	32		
A. Lincoln,	D. C.	6		6		6				Still settled.
W. M. Thayer,	B. U.	2	5	2	5	2	5			do.
J. M. Bacon,	——	3	1	3	6	5	1			Now settled.
J. L. Armes,	——	4	1	5	2	5	5			do.
E. Newton,	D. C.	2	6	2	6	3	8			Preaches occasionally.
J. W. Harding,	Y. C.	1	10	1	10	1	10			Still settled.
F. A. Fisk,	A. C.	——		——		——				Lately settled.
H. Lobdell,	A. C.	——		——			1			Foreign missionary.

Graduates.

Harv. Univ.	11	Penn. Univ.	2
Yale Coll.	6	Union Coll.	3
N. J. Coll.	3	Not grad.	13
Brown Univ.	32		—
Dart. Coll	17		100
Wms. Coll.	2		
Amh. Coll.	11	Members.	21

Averages.

Of the 121 Licentiates, 21 became members of the Association, 5 never entered the ministry, and 8 have not been ordained. They are omitted in the preceding list. Of the remaining 87, 6 have been ordained, but not settled as pastors; 45 are dead, and 42 are still living. Of the latter, 10 have entered other avocations, or retired from active labors, and 19 are now pastors; of whom, 12 are still in their first pastorate.

Of the deceased members: —

The average first pastorate of 44 is 17 yrs. 9 m.
" " pastoral life of 43, 19 yrs. 4 m.
" " ministerial life of 40, 26 yrs. 1 m.
" " natural life of 42, 58 yrs. 4 m.

Of the survivors: —

The average first pastorate of 36 is 12 yrs. 9 m.
" " pastoral life of 36, 16 yrs. 4 m.
" " ministerial life of 40, 21 yrs.
" " pastorate of 11, still undismissed, 16 yrs. 9 m.

Rev. Asaph Rice of Westminster, was the longest settled in one place; viz. 50 yrs. 5 m. Rev. Eli Smith of Hollis, N. Hampshire, reached the most advanced age; viz. 87 yrs. 8 m.

Rev. Kiah Bayley of Hardwick, Vt., is the oldest of living Licentiates, being nearly 83. Rev. Levi Nelson of Lisbon, Ct., has been the longest settled over one charge; viz. 48 years.

III. OF MEMBERS AND LICENTIATES.

Graduates.

Harv. Univ.	20	Wms. Coll.	3
Yale Coll.	23	Amh. Coll.	17
N. J. Coll.	5	Hamilton Coll.	1
Brown Univ.	53	Union Coll.	4
Dart. Coll.	26	Penn. Univ.	2
Bowd. Coll.	3	Not grad.	20
Total			177

Averages.

Of the 164 Members and Licentiates contained in the preceding tables, 80 are dead, and 84 are living; of whom, 68 still exercise the functions of the ministry.

Of the deceased: —

The average first pastorate of 79, is 22 yrs. 5 m.
" " pastoral life of 78, 25 yrs. 1 m.
" " ministerial life of 75, 31 yrs. 10 m.
" " natural life of 77, 62 yrs. 9 m.

Of the living: —

The average first pastorate of 75 is 11 yrs. 4 m.
" " pastoral life of 75, 15 yrs. 9 m.
" " ministerial life of 80, 21 yrs. 2 m.
" " pastorate of 16 still undismissed, 17 yrs. 6 m.

GENERAL INDEX.

BIOGRAPHICAL INDEX.

www.ingramcontent.com/pod-product-compliance
Lightning Source LLC
LaVergne TN
LVHW010201110826
845151LV00002B/573